CLUG

COMMUNITY LAND USE GAME

Player's Manual

with selected readings

by Allan G. Feldt

with

Anthony B. Dotson
Margaret Warne Monroe
David S. Sawicki

 *the free press, new york*
collier-macmillan limited, london

To
Barbara, Diane, Deborah, and John

Contents

TEAR-OUT SHEETS

Player's Information Form (2 copies)

Shopping Contracts and Land Purchase Offers (5 copies)

CLUG Tax Records (2 copies)

CLUG Community Financial Status (2 copies)

Summary of Changes for Urban Politics Experiment

Summary of Changes for Rural-Urban Interdependence Experiment —
Stage I

Summary of Changes for Rural-Urban Interdependence Experiment —
Stage II

Summary of Changes for Transportation and Technology Experiment —
Stage I

Summary of Changes for Transportation and Technology Experiment —
Stage II

Summary of Changes for Transportation and Technology Experiment —
Stage III

Summary of Changes for Municipal Finance Experiment

Summary of Changes for Environmental Pollution Experiment

LIST OF READINGS

LIST OF FIGURES

LIST OF TABLES

Environmental Pollution

Preface

This manual, together with its companion *Instructor's Manual*, is intended to present a new and promising dimension to the teaching of urban studies. The idea behind these materials is to provide an opportunity to create a "laboratory experience" for students of urban and regional problems, by giving them a "city" to play with and experiment upon.

The *Player's Manual* provides background information on operational gaming followed by a simple description of the rules of play of the basic game model. This introduction not only acquaints the player with the nature of the laboratory equipment he is expected to use in conducting the later experiments, but also teaches some fundamental concepts of urban and regional studies. Following this introductory section is a series of experiments that illustrate and provide experience with some important problems of urban growth and development. Accompanying each experiment is a brief reading from the literature to assist in interpreting experiences in the game in terms of social science concepts.

The *Instructor's Manual* is designed to supplement the *Player's Manual* and provides more detail on operating the basic game model and particular experiments. This manual, together with the forms provided in the *Player's Manual*, provides all the equipment needed for running the game, except for dice and pencils. Thus the two volumes are intended to be used in conjunction: one *Player's Manual* for each participant in the game and one *Instructor's Manual* for each game being run.

Normally between five and twenty players can be accommodated in a single game run, although some of the experiments call for a few more or less players for specific purposes. When more than twenty play a single game, there may be a problem of control and access to the playing materials rather than any inherent problem in the game itself. We generally recommend that approximately fifteen players be accommodated in a single game in order to insure full participation and involvement by all concerned.

Someone who has studied both the *Player's* and the *Instructor's Manual* must lead at first, but the students themselves can take over and manage the game once they have learned the basic mechanics of play. If the game can be considered a form of laboratory equipment such as might be used in chemistry or physics courses, the manuals seek to show how the equipment can best be employed. Although the equipment provided is in the form of various paper playing pieces, the instructor should realize that repeated use of these materials will probably result in deterioration and the need to replace them with either an equivalent set of paper pieces (available in another copy of the *Instructor's Manual* from The Free Press) or a more durable "game kit." Several suggestions for constructing more durable materials are offered in the *Instructor's Manual*, as well as addresses of suppliers who sell standard packages of CLUG materials in commercial form.

CLUG has already established itself as one of the older and more generally useful of a variety of operational games intended for teaching purposes in courses dealing with urban problems and urban theory. It has been used in a wide variety of fields, including sociology, history, geography, law, city planning, architecture, economics, and regional planning. It has also been found to be effective for a surprisingly wide range of educational purposes—from junior-high through graduate-level courses, and extramural or extension courses intended for professionals and interested citizens. Since its first development in 1963, over a thousand CLUG games have been run in this country; it is estimated that between twenty and thirty thousand persons have played CLUG in one form or another. Modifications for special purpose applications have also been developed by many users, including several from foreign countries of somewhat different development patterns and policies. In almost every reported use of the game, the instructors have indicated remarkable levels of involvement and motivation on the part of participants, and a great interest in developing improvements and modifications of the basic model. The accepted power of the game, together with the carefully chosen modifications and reading materials presented here, will, we believe, provide an even stronger and more widely-used set of applications of the model.

This is the fifth version of CLUG, although it is the first version to be published. The authors are indebted to many persons and institutions for support and encouragement during the gradual evolution of CLUG as a teaching device. Of particular significance are Richard Meier, Burnham Kelly, and John Reps who were sympathetic during the early years when operational gaming was still considered a suspicious and frivolous form of academic entertainment. During the same period a great number of Cornell students in City and Regional Planning played the game, helped to run early versions, and offered innumerable suggestions for improvements and modifications of the model. The many contributors to the growth of CLUG both at Cornell and at other universities are too numerous to be mentioned individually, but to all of them we wish to express our appreciation for their efforts and imaginative contributions. The remaining flaws and deficiencies in the model must, nonetheless, remain the responsibility of the current authors.

Financial support during various stages of the development of CLUG has been provided by the Cornell College of Architecture, the Cornell Social Sciences Research Council, and the Ford Foundation. We are indebted to them not only for the funds provided but for their willingness to provide support for unorthodox lines of research and development such as these. We hope their early faith has been fully justified. Early contact with Richard Duke (now at the University of Michigan) and his staff was also helpful in providing both moral support for our efforts and stimulating and rewarding colleagues with whom we could freely exchange ideas.

The principal author wishes to express particular appreciation for the efforts of his associates—Anthony Dotson, Margaret Monroe, and David Sawicki. Their contribution to the development of CLUG and to the preparation of this volume is much greater than the title of associate author implies. Jean Withiam also deserves special thanks for her patience and skill in preparing the manuscript.

Finally, the families of each of us deserve our special thanks for their patience and understanding during the many nights and weekends that had to be devoted to the preparation of the manuscript.

Ithaca, N. Y.

Allan G. Feldt
Anthony B. Dotson
Margaret Warne Monroe
David S. Sawicki

Operational Games as Educational Devices

The use of games as teaching tools has a substantial history extending over several centuries in a limited number of areas. For example, in recent decades the game technique has been adopted by many business firms and schools of business administration. These management games are designed to provide students with some first-hand experience in making complex decisions under a fairly realistic and rapidly changing set of conditions similar to those found in business firms. Games of this type are often called "operational games" and represent a form of simulation, whether they are played with computer assistance or not. Some adaptations of operational gaming techniques to more traditional academic fields were attempted during the late 1950s and early 1960s with reasonable success. Most notable among these applications are games now used in the fields of international relations, animal ecology, social psychology, economics, and city planning. Some understanding of the general properties of operational games is desirable before proceeding to the specific properties of CLUG.

An operational game may be most simply defined as an analogue to some pattern of exchanges and interactions that occur in the real world. In terms of presenting theoretical concepts, a game, as an analogue, can be considered an alternative to the more common techniques of providing verbal or mathematical description and expressions of real-world patterns of behavior. The advantages of gaming models over verbal and mathematical models are that a game provides relatively specific designation of concepts and at the same time avoids the semantic problems inherent in most verbal models. Furthermore, the degree of precision required in defining a concept and its relationship to other components of the model is much less than that required in most mathematical models. Thus the game model builder may deal with relationships and components which are not easily quantifiable.

An operational game may be classed as a form of simulation model. This term is often reserved for mathematical expressions of time-sequential real-world conditions whose outcome or solution is most readily attainable by running the conditions over a progressive number of repetitions on a computer. Nevertheless, an operational game is a true simulation. It is a simulation in which all or most of the decisions as to outcomes of the events being represented are left in the hands of human players, with relatively minor decisions and accounting problems handled either by human operators or by computers.

The most simple example of an operational game is the case of elementary school children playing store. In this case the usual educational purpose is to teach children how to count money and to handle coins and bills of various denominations. The mechanics and rules of this game are simple, involving the selection of differently priced items for purchase, tallying up their total costs, paying out play money to a storekeeper, and receiving the correct amount of change. It would be possible to design more elaborate versions of such a game to teach children how to recognize different cuts of meat, how to evaluate the quality of fresh produce, how to protect them-selves against deceptive packaging, how to plan a proper diet, and any one of the multiplicity of skills that are involved in present day shopping practices.

Between the simple form of playing store and the relatively advanced operational games useful in education and research at the university and professional level lies a broad spectrum of games. Chess, Monopoly, Go, and other popular games of this type present highly stylized representations of a real world situation that make no pretense of providing a true analogue of any actual patterns of interaction and exchange in today's world. These games are not truly operational games in that the attempt to model reality is no longer obvious in their construction or their use.

Yet the fact that a game is entertaining and commercially available as a parlor game does not exclude it from consideration as an operational game. An excellent example of commercially available operational games is the family of war games produced by Avalon Hill of which Gettysburg is one of the better known. In this game two opposing players are provided with playing pieces corresponding to the characteristics and strengths of the opposing armies and are allowed to deploy them upon a terrain subject to the topographic and time constraints which existed in the real world. The outcome of the battle is indeterminate and rests largely upon the strategies chosen by the players and partially upon chance. External factors are controlled in that changes in weather conditions, weapons technology, and so on are not allowed. Although Gettysburg is a reasonably accurate simulation of real-world events, the combination of chance and the strategies chosen by particular players often results in the South winning the battle. This outcome suggests that operational games and other simulations may model reality quite closely without necessarily producing the same results as occur in the real world.

Basic Characteristics of Operational Games

A substantial amount of experience in the use and development of the Community Land Use Game (CLUG), together with observation of the use and characteristics of a number of other games in urban studies and allied fields, has convinced a number of persons of the importance of this new set of techniques in fields dealing with urban and regional problems. Given the lack of exposure of many persons to these devices, it is worth noting their basic characteristics:

1. The operational games in general use appear to lie along a continuum between games which may be termed "role-playing games" and those which may be called "systemic games." The former involve games in which particular positions in the real world and the relationships among these positions are presented as the basic components of the game. Players are then assigned to the various roles and are given a specified set of tasks to perform in the operation of their game role. Thus, players might be assigned the role of politician, planner, state legislator, secretary of state, and so on depending upon the particular requirements and purposes of the game. The critical factor in the development of such a game is the specification of the

relationships between roles. Too often, however, more attention is given to the specification of the roles themselves, and the relationships among roles are left to one or two simple exchanges and interdependencies.

Systemic games, on the other hand, generally define a system of inter-relationships and interdependencies among components of an economic, political, or social system and then let the players themselves evolve their own role behaviors through the particular positions into which the play of the game thrusts them. In this case, the major focus of attention in game construction is upon the relationships. Less attention is given to the specification of the particular tasks to which a player should address himself as he establishes a role position for himself. Most games lie somewhere between these two extremes and some valuable properties are to be found in both approaches.

2. Most operational games may be classed as non-zero sum games. That is they are not fully competitive in that the "winnings" of one player need not derive from the "losses" of another player. In role-playing games different goals are often provided for players occupying different roles. All players may win or lose in each of their positions with the outcome of each position dependent to some extent upon the actions, though not the outcomes, of players in other positions. In systemic games the overall standings of all players may increase or decline, so that a player may be said to win if his own level of increase is greater than that of his fellow players. Multi-valued standings are common in such games, however, and there cannot be generally said to be any clearly defined criteria for winning the game. In a word, everyone can win in most operational games unless they are representative of real-world situations where there are well-defined positions of victors and vanquished, e.g., a war game. Even in this case it is seldom clear as to who has "won" after the outcome of a particular battle or war has been decided. Criteria for winning are of great concern to players at the start of an operational game, but they are generally ignored by the time the game has been under play for some period of time.

3. Most operational games are not dependent upon mathematical models or equations for understanding or operation (aside from the relatively simple arithmetic required for bookkeeping purposes). Thus the relationship between operational gaming and those sets of mathematical techniques known as "game theory" is tenuous. The level of precision required in operational gaming is relatively low, while the level of complexity which may be represented is relatively high. The converse appears to be true of game theory models. Although mathematical sophistication is not a basic requirement of operational games, it is possible to represent mathematical interrelationships in non-mathematical terms, i.e., use games as analogues of mathematical simulation models.

4. With almost all operational games it is difficult to appraise their potential adequately. Most games tend to be either deceptively simple while actually representing a very complex construction, or else appear to be very complex while actually being very simple in their basic construction. This problem is related to their recent acceptance in many fields and the lack of experience of users in evaluating their potentialities. Too many games are

accepted after a superficial overview of their operation (and too many are rejected on the same basis). It seems fair to argue that an adequate evaluation of any game requires careful weighing and judging of its structure, which is usually best accomplished by playing the game itself.

5. It appears that in the better operational games a high proportion of decision-making tasks rest on strategy and a relatively small proportion are based upon chance. Elements of both appear to be important, however. The strategies employed may be either against other players or against the "nature" represented by the game rules themselves. Games that rely too heavily upon chance to determine the outcome are both unrealistic and boring.

6. Most players leave a game wishing that some particular aspect of reality with which they are especially concerned had been more adequately represented. Hence modifications to existing games are commonplace. Such innovations are very desirable, because they lead to more sophisticated games or games of wider applicability. Yet innovations and modifications must be weighed carefully for their effect upon the overall game structure and their basic validity. For example, to introduce a well-defined role in a game which is basically systemic in orientation is unwise; to introduce strategic economic or political interrelationships into a role-oriented game can cause chaos. Also, superficial modifications, which are thrown together in an afternoon or over a weekend, are seldom worth the trouble of playing and should be treated with suspicion.

7. Finally, the most important property of all games is their ability to collapse time and space for the players involved. Every game is constructed at some level of abstraction. Many real world decisions are reduced to background noise to be handled as random factors or ignored by the players.

At any given level of abstraction and time scale, certain decisions and characteristics take on great importance to the players and others quickly become irrelevant. The decision problems appropriate to the scale at which the game is being played must be identified by both the game builder and the players, and the applications of the game must be restricted to this level.

Conclusion

After participating in one or more runs of the Basic CLUG model and playing through several of the experiments which have been provided, you should stop to reflect upon what you have learned and the manner in which you learned it. It is always difficult to evaluate the learning experience generated in an operational game because the kind of information conveyed is often significantly different from that conveyed in normal classroom experience.

The process of living through a series of decisions such as those generated in this game and of seeing the results of those decisions (both in the short run and the long run) will provide you an opportunity to view the urban growth process in a fashion generally available only to a small group of decision makers. You will have learned something about a process and the operation of a moderately complex system rather than about the facts and events that have occurred at a particular time and place.

The task then remaining for you is to learn to use this greater understanding generated in better evaluating the real world in which you live. The processes in CLUG are real but they operate beyond the scale with which one normally views the world. Take note of the patterns of residential development which actually occur in communities and their relationship to places of work. Notice the kinds of commercial centers which exist and the extent to which different kinds of stores are more or less sensitive to the location of their potential customers. Follow the arguments about tax rates, community assessed value, bond issues, and debt limits in some communities to see how these issues relate to the level of community services provided and the rate of expansion of capital plant and equipment. Many of the elements found in CLUG are surprisingly real when they are used as a basis for learning more about everyday activities. They provide a carefully constructed and consistent perspective with which to view some aspects of the world and with which to better understand it.

A final caution to all CLUG players is necessary. Although realistic, the model does not represent all of reality. Many important aspects of community processes are omitted from the game and the scale of the game is appropriate only to those aspects of reality which operate at the same scale. Social class, race, and demographic processes are not represented at all in CLUG. Only minimal attention to problems of housing construction and quality has been given and no provision for a realistic mortgage finance mechanism has been provided. The model does not in any way represent processes at the "micro-community" level and many important local effects in urban structure are missing from consideration. Care must be taken not to misuse the concepts conveyed here. Consequently, the structure of urban growth and the operation of the urban system in terms of CLUG operations must be seen and understood for what they are and they must be employed in perspective.

The Basic Community Land Use Game

Basic CLUG: A Theoretical Summary

Urban theorists in fields such as geography, sociology and economics have long understood the importance of certain basic principles of organization of cities and regions. Using and transmitting this understanding to others has been difficult due to the problems inherent in adequately using verbal descriptive methods to portray the dynamic and fluctuating process involved in an economic system and its associated patterns of land use. In recent years, many theorists have turned to mathematics and simulation models to attempt to better express these basic processes; this step has excluded many persons from utilizing their work, since not all theorists are as yet well skilled in basic mathematical techniques.

A straightforward mathematical description of the basic elements of urban growth and change by Brian Berry summarizes the basic elements that CLUG seeks to convey:*

The Spatial Structure of Land Uses Within Cities

One way of stating the argument lying behind recent studies of the internal structure of cities is as follows: Cities are supported by "basic" activities, whose locations are determined exogenously to the city by comparative advantage in regional, national, and international economic systems. Such basic activities universally include a central business district, the focus not only of the city, but also of its tributary region. Various specialized activities will also be present, such as steelmaking [sic] in Chicago, aircraft production in Seattle, or meat packing in Omaha. Locations of the basic activities, plus a transport system, provide the skeletal features of the urban pattern.

This pattern is filled out in part by the residences of workers in the basic activities, and is given a dynamic quality by the daily ebb and flow of commuters and, from beyond the city's limits, of goods and customers to and from the sites of the basic activities. There will, of course, also be modifications based upon the qualities of [terrain] upon which the city spreads.

Further patterning is provided by the orientation of business services to the basic activities and by tertiary activities to the consuming workers and their families. Shopping trips create yet another ebb and flow. Then appear all the "second-round" effects: locations of the residences of workers in the "nonbasic" activities, additional commuting, more demands for tertiary activities, and so forth, in an increasingly complex chain of multiplier effects.

*Brian Berry, "On Research Frontiers in Urban Geography," paper prepared for the Committee on Urbanization of the Social Science Research Council, Spring 1961. Printed with the author's permission.

We can state the argument symbolically:

Definitions:

A = a locational pattern of basic activities
B = a transport system
C = a set of urban sites
D = employees in A
E = the residential pattern of D
F = a basic commuting pattern
G = a system of business services
H = a system of tertiary activities
I = all "second-round" effects

Then, given A:

$$D = f(A)$$
$$E = f(A,D \text{ subject to } B,C)$$
$$F = f(A,E \text{ subject to } B)$$
$$G = f(A)$$
$$H = f(E,D \text{ subject to } B)$$
$$I = f(G,H)$$

Specification of the precise form of these functional relationships has been the objective of the work dealing with the internal structure of cities. . . .

CLUG takes these technical and static statements and brings them to life in a situation that is more realistic, dynamic, and fraught with many of the unforeseen complications and events experienced in urban growth and change. In operation, CLUG becomes a form of simulation model using human beings as the principal decision-makers; it allows these same human beings, as players, to witness the process of growth and decay of a city by participating in the process. Although highly limited in terms of what elements of urban growth the game attempts to include, and seemingly very simple in its structure, the game soon generates a complex and largely unpredictable pattern of development which is fairly representative of at least some of the components of growth and their interrelationships as described by Berry, particularly with reference to American cities.

The playing board provides a variety of possible urban sites (C) separated into a matrix of equal area land parcels by a grid coordinate system. Superimposed upon this field of possible sites and land use parcels are a transport system (B) in the form of secondary and primary roads and a terminal, which provides the major locational determinant for basic industries (A).

These basic activities are represented by partial and full industries which may be "constructed" and operated by players. The economics of their operation in light of the transport system provided make their locations tend to cluster as close to the terminal as possible. Employees for these industries (D) are provided by residential units constructed by other players in the game. The costs of commuting to and from work (F), along with the players' attempts to minimize these costs, result in a pattern of residential locations that tend to focus around the industries subject to the availability and price of land and the transport system [E = f (A,D subject to B,C)]. The number of residential units developed is dependent upon the number and types of industries provided [D = f (A)].

A system of business services is represented by a building type called office (G). The profitability of this type of construction depends upon the number of potential customers available, made up primarily of the industries [G = f (A)]. Tertiary activities are represented by Local and Central Stores (H) which depend upon the residential units for customers. The number and location of these stores is dependent upon the number and location of the previously established residential units within the constraints and opportunities provided by the available transport system [H = f (E,D subject to B)].

Following the location of the business and tertiary units, new locational opportunities arise which are called "second-round" effects by Berry (I). These involve the construction of additional residential units to work in the stores and businesses and their subsequent location as near as possible to their places of work [I = f (G,H)]. These additional residences might then create some possibilities for additional tertiary services in the same or subsequent rounds. These second round effects continue until the system is relatively well balanced at any particular point in time.

The evolution of the city in CLUG follows this basic round of events, and in addition the later construction of additional industries with the corresponding impetus to further cycles of growth and development. Further on in the game, processes of decay of older structures, coupled with possible dislocations due to natural or economic disasters or changes in the transport system, result in continuous modifications and readjustments to these processes.

Basic CLUG: A Procedural Summary

CLUG has been designed to provide a basic understanding of some of the more important underlying factors affecting the growth of an urban region. The game emphasizes certain aspects of an urban economy: the relationships between basic industry and employment, housing, and transportation costs; the development of commercial facilities; the financing and provision of municipal services; and the location and interdependence of all these activities in an urban region.

As a CLUG participant, you will have an opportunity to invest in land, construct buildings of various types, and seek ways to fit these investments into the evolving local economy to make a return on your investment (when investments are well-planned). Although competition with fellow participants for a place in this system is expected, there are of course limits to competition. The individual's well-being is, to a large degree, dependent upon the well-being of all players. Although competing, players must learn to cooperate with each other for some purposes if the community is to grow and prosper.

An instructor manages the game by explaining and interpreting the rules. He also represents the economy outside the local community by purchasing manufactured products and selling commercial services to players who are not able to obtain them at a suitable price within the community. The instructor may announce a series of unexpected catastrophes which may damage the community's stability through the loss of some of its investments. He does not interfere directly with game play except to order events or enforce rules. Within the limits of human frailty, he operates objectively and dispassionately towards the players and the community. As someone more skilled with the game than beginning players, the instructor may occasionally offer advice on investments and decisions taking place. His advice should be carefully considered, but even the most skilled individual has great difficulty in anticipating all the events which may occur in the game. The instructor is not omnipotent—he does not control the direction or evolution of the community. This is entirely within the hands of the players as constrained by the rules given below.

Once in a while, an especially interesting event may occur within the game that has important implications for some similar real-world phenomenon or theory. At such times, the instructor may interrupt play to illuminate the details of what has occurred and to show how it relates to real-world events. Although such interruptions may slow the progress of growth in the community, they provide important opportunities to learn more about the way the urban system operates, both in the game and in the real world.

The instructor is usually assisted by an Accountant who keeps records of property ownership, the assessed values of buildings and land, the age of buildings, and the financial status of the community including taxes due. His accounts represent public records and are open for inspection by players at any time during the game. Learning to understand the meaning and significance of the public records, however, will require some experience.

The rules which follow provide the basic framework for game play in its simplest form. Although they may appear difficult to comprehend at first, almost all new players learn them quite well during the course of the initial two hours of play. The same series of steps occurs in every round. After several rounds, these steps become familiar and the numbers and quantities employed become well known to all players. Because of unfamiliarity with the operation of the game, only a round or two is usually covered during the first two hours of play. After this initial period, however, play usually progresses at the rate of thirty minutes or less per round.

The speed with which the game can cycle is in large part determined by how efficiently players arrive at decisions, both within individual teams and as a total community. The game contains so many decisions, based upon so much information, that players must choose relevant information and thus gain practice as urban decision-makers. They must learn to distinguish important decisions from trivial ones and how to evaluate whatever information is available to them quickly and then to make their choice, always anticipating the complimentary choices which may be made by other players. Full rationality is almost impossible even in this simple game and players must learn to live in a world where the pressures of time and lack of information force them to settle for only partially rational or "satisficing" behavior.

CLUG is played most effectively with three to five teams of one to three persons each. More teams or more persons per team are possible but the accounting procedures become more complex. Moreover, getting a team to arrive at a decision when more than three people are involved is difficult unless the team is well organized internally. Clear lines of authority within each team can be helpful in arriving at decisions quickly and smoothly. Players are encouraged to select team leaders to be the spokesman and voting representative of each team.

The basic CLUG game described in the following rules is sufficiently complex to satisfy most players for five or ten rounds of play. Extensions beyond this are possible but beyond Round 15 additional learning appears to drop off unless some additional rules and modifications are introduced.

Following the Basic Rules is a set of experiments designed to allow you to explore systematically the effects of certain kinds of urban phenomena. After learning to play the basic game, most players are in a good position to undertake their own runs for experimental purposes, choosing one of their fellow players to be instructor, one to be Accountant and others to fill roles required by particular experiments. A quick review of the appropriate sections of the *Instructor's Manual*, which may be borrowed from the instructor, will fill in a few of the missing details in game operation which might still arise.

The experiments are intended to highlight each of a number of particular questions and problems in urban growth. Each experiment is coupled with readings carefully selected to help relate game phenomena to real-world phenomena. Combinations of two or more experiments are possible, although very quickly the total structure of the game can become almost too complicated to fully comprehend. Considerable care is advised in attempting to develop combinations of experiments and adequate time for testing and revising them should be allowed. Designing a new modification for the game can be very instructive and efforts in this direction are encouraged. I would be happy to know of such modifications. However, modification of a system even as simple as CLUG is a very sensitive task. Seemingly very simple changes in the rules often produce profound and disruptive effects in the operation of the game. Discovering these effects and learning their implications can be a very worthwhile experience.

In reading the following rules, do not expect to understand their full meaning and the significance of each of the items indicated. Read them initially for a general knowledge of the flow of the game and the kinds of factors which will effect play. Particular numbers and quantities given in the rules will always be available for reference during play, so you need only gain a general understanding of the tables employed and their general content.

Basic CLUG: Detailed Rules

A single reading of these rules is generally sufficient to provide a player with a sound basis for beginning play. The specific meaning and purpose of many of the rules will become clearer to you as play progresses. As with all games, the best way to understand CLUG is to play it rather than read about it. Although seemingly difficult, the rules are repetitious, so that full understanding of them is surprisingly easy.

CLUG Money

At the beginning of the basic game, each team is provided with $100,000 in cash. This money can be spent on land purchases, building construction, payments of taxes, and making payments to other players as necessary. Additional money enters the game each round when the instructor makes payments to owners of industries. A portion of this money then circulates to other players in the form of payrolls to employees, and payments to Stores and Offices for various services. Money leaves the game when players make payments for Transportation Costs, purchase goods from the outside economy, pay for municipal services through taxes and make payments for construction or renovation of buildings. In the basic game no borrowing of money from the instructor is allowed, although the community as a whole may incur debts up to its debt limit. Loans between teams are allowed as long as their bargaining for terms does not interrupt play. Prudent players may expect to receive approximately a ten per cent return for good investments made in the community, although substantially higher and lower rates of return occur for particularly good or bad investments and management.

Land Use Types

CLUG provides for three basic types of land use: industrial, commercial, and residential.

There are two densities of industrial buildings: Full Industry (FI) and Partial Industry (PI). At the Construction Step of any round a Partial Industry may be upgraded to a Full Industry by paying the difference in their initial Construction Costs and exchanging the two building forms on the board. The building designation of these land use types together with their initial Construction Costs is illustrated in Figure 1.

Commercial land uses consist of three basic types of buildings: Local Store (LS), Central Store (CS), and Office (O), also illustrated in Figure 1. A Local Store provides frequently used goods and services such as groceries, drugs, gasoline, household products, and simple medical treatment. Every residential unit on the board must buy a standard market basket of LS goods each round from one of the Local Stores on the board or from the instructor. The Central Store offers a range of more specialized and less frequently consumed goods and services such as jewelry, furniture, auto-

Figure 1. CLUG Playing Pieces

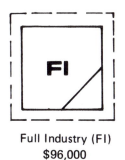

Full Industry (FI)
$96,000

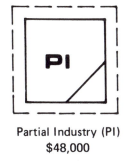

Partial Industry (PI)
$48,000

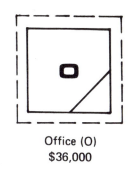

Office (O)
$36,000

Local Store (LS)
$24,000

Central Store (CS)
$24,000

Single Residence (R1)
$12,000

Double Residence (R2)
$30,000

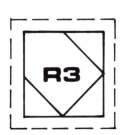

Triple Residence (R3)
$48,000

Quadruple Residence (R4)
$72,000

mobiles, and brain surgery. Every residential unit on the board must purchase a standard market basket of CS goods and services each round as well, from either a Central Store on the board or from the instructor. Finally, the Office provides a variety of clerical, accounting, and administrative services to industries and stores. Every industry and store (PI, FI, CS and LS) must buy a standard market basket of these services each round from an Office on the board or from the instructor. No conversion from one type of commercial land use to another is allowed unless the original building is completely demolished and the new commercial use built in its place.

Residential land uses consist of housing units which may be built at any of four density levels: R1, R2, R3, or R4 (illustrated in Figure 1). Each housing unit contains one employee unit and its families, who must purchase standard market baskets from both a Local and a Central Store each round. A high density, R4, residential unit thus provides four employee units and four potential sets of customers for a Local Store and a Central Store. The density of a residential land use may be increased at the Construction step of play of any round by paying the difference between the costs of the two building types and exchanging the building forms accordingly. Construction Cost per unit for Residences is somewhat greater at higher densities than at lower densities, exclusive of site and utility costs. This reflects, in part, the fact that the basic game assumes all residents to be of the same socio-economic class living in the same basic kinds of housing units.

Employment

Each industrial and commercial land use on the board must employ residential units in order to make money. A Full Industry can employ up to four residential units at full capacity; a Partial Industry can employ up to two residential units; the Local and Central Stores and the Office can each employ one residential unit when in operation. All salary levels are fixed in the basic game. An owner of a residential unit employed in an industrial or commercial property receives a payroll of $6,000 for each such employee on the Pay Employees step of each round. This money is received from the team owning and operating the employer land use. Employment contracts are negotiated between the two teams owning the employer and employee land uses, and are indicated by placing matching coded markers on both buildings. All employment agreements are binding upon the placement of the coded markers and remain in effect until the next round divisible by five (fifth, tenth, fifteenth, etc.). At that time, on the Designate Employment Step, new contracts may be negotiated by mutual agreement of employer and employee.

Shopping

As mentioned above, each commercial land use offers a standard market basket of goods and services to their potential customers on the board. Land users who must purchase these goods and services may agree to buy them from those vendors offering the most advantageous prices and location. Once agreements to shop at particular Local Stores, Central Stores, and Offices are reached for each residential building independently, however, these agreements and prices must be maintained until the next round divisible by five.

The Price set for each kind of standard market basket is at the discretion of the owner of each Local Store, Central Store or Office, who is constrained by three basic factors. The first is that these goods and services are available to players from the outside world, i.e., from the instructor. The instructor sells these same market baskets of goods at a fixed price to any player wishing to buy from him: $2,000 for the Local Store basket; $1,000 for the Central Store basket; and $4,000, $2,000, and $1,000 for the Office basket, depending upon whether sales are to Full Industry, Partial Industry, or Stores, respectively. The second constraint is the cost to customers of a shopping trip each round. The instructor offers his market baskets at prices that include delivery to the location of the customer; thus the player pays no additional Transportation Costs. Each Store or Office owner should, however, consider the Transportation Costs of his potential customers in travelling to and from his store before setting his price. Thus his price is always lower than that of the outside world in order to compensate for transportation costs. The third constraint on pricing is that only one price may be set by each Local Store, Central Store, or Office. This single price will apply to all customers uniformly and must be kept until the next round divisible by five. Thus the commercial developer, in arriving at a price, must consider both present and future development and its probable location relative to the commercial unit.

The quantities and numbers used in the preceding three sections are summarized in Table 1.

Table 1. Summary of Unit Characteristics

	Construction Costs	Max. Round Income	Max. No. Employees	Max. Payroll	Max. LS Price	Max. CS Price	Max. O Price
FI Full Industry	$96,000	$48,000	4	$24,000	—	—	$4,000
PI Partial Industry	48,000	22,000	2	12,000	—	—	2,000
LS Local Store	24,000	*	1	6,000	—	—	1,000
CS Central Store	24,000	*	1	6,000	—	—	1,000
O Office	36,000	*	1	6,000	—	—	—
R1 Single Residence	12,000	6,000	—	—	$2,000	$1,000	—
R2 Double Residence	30,000	12,000	—	—	4,000	2,000	—
R3 Triple Residence	48,000	18,000	—	—	6,000	3,000	—
R4 Quadruple Residence	72,000	24,000	—	—	8,000	4,000	—

*Incomes for LS, CS, and O depend upon the number of customers obtained and the price charged. A gross income of $10,000–$15,000 should be anticipated before one of these units is opened.

The Playing Board

The CLUG Playing Board is made up of a "12 × 12" matrix of 144 squares, each of which represents a single land parcel of several square miles. In Basic CLUG the thinner black lines represent Secondary Roads, while the heavier black lines represent Primary Roads. The coordinate system is designed such that even numbers designate each column or row of squares and the intervening odd numbers designate the vertical or horizontal lines separating the squares. Thus a pair of even numbered coordinates such as 8-66 indicates a particular parcel of land while a pair of odd numbered coordinates such as 7-67 indicates a particular corner of that same parcel as described by the intersection of the two grid lines. Similarly, a combination of odd and even numbered coordinates such as 9-66 indicates a line segment along one particular edge of the parcel, in this case the horizontal lower edge of parcel 8-66.

Although any simple topographic configuration can be introduced on the playing board, Figure 2 provides an elementary setup which is useful for most basic games. This provides a Primary Road pattern horizontally along line 7 from 51 to 75 and vertically along line 63 from 3 to 25. Also indicated are several other parameters important to the basic game. A lake or ocean harbor is shown in squares 2-62, 2-64, and 2-66. Included too in Figure 2 is a Terminal at 3-63 and a Utility Plant at 3-67. The Terminal provides shipping facilities to the outside world and is the point to which all industrial products must be shipped for sale. The Utility Plant is the point from which all Utility Lines must originate. This plant provides a broad range of municipal services which flow along the Utility Lines constructed during the game. Although thought of primarily as water and sewer services, this plant and its associated lines are intended to represent a broad range of municipal services such as police and fire protection, power and heat, solid waste disposal, libraries, education, and so on. Utility Lines are placed along grid lines by majority vote of the teams. A land parcel is considered to be serviced and ready for development when one of its sides has a Utility Line running along its length.

Transportation

One important factor in many decisions in the game is the Transportation Cost required for the operation of certain land uses; these costs are one of the major determinants of location for land uses in the game. Transportation Costs are represented through payments made by players to the instructor. Costs are paid by Full and Partial Industries for shipping products to the Terminal, by Residences for journeys to work and to shop in Local and Central Stores, and by industries and stores for moving information and materials to and from the Offices. Costs increase with the distance between two associated land uses and are less when movement is along a Primary Road than along a Secondary Road. For the basic game, the relative efficiency (Mode Weights) of the Primary Road to Secondary Roads is set at 1:2. Costs are added up over the number of unit distances traveled on either

Figure 2. The CLUG Playing Board

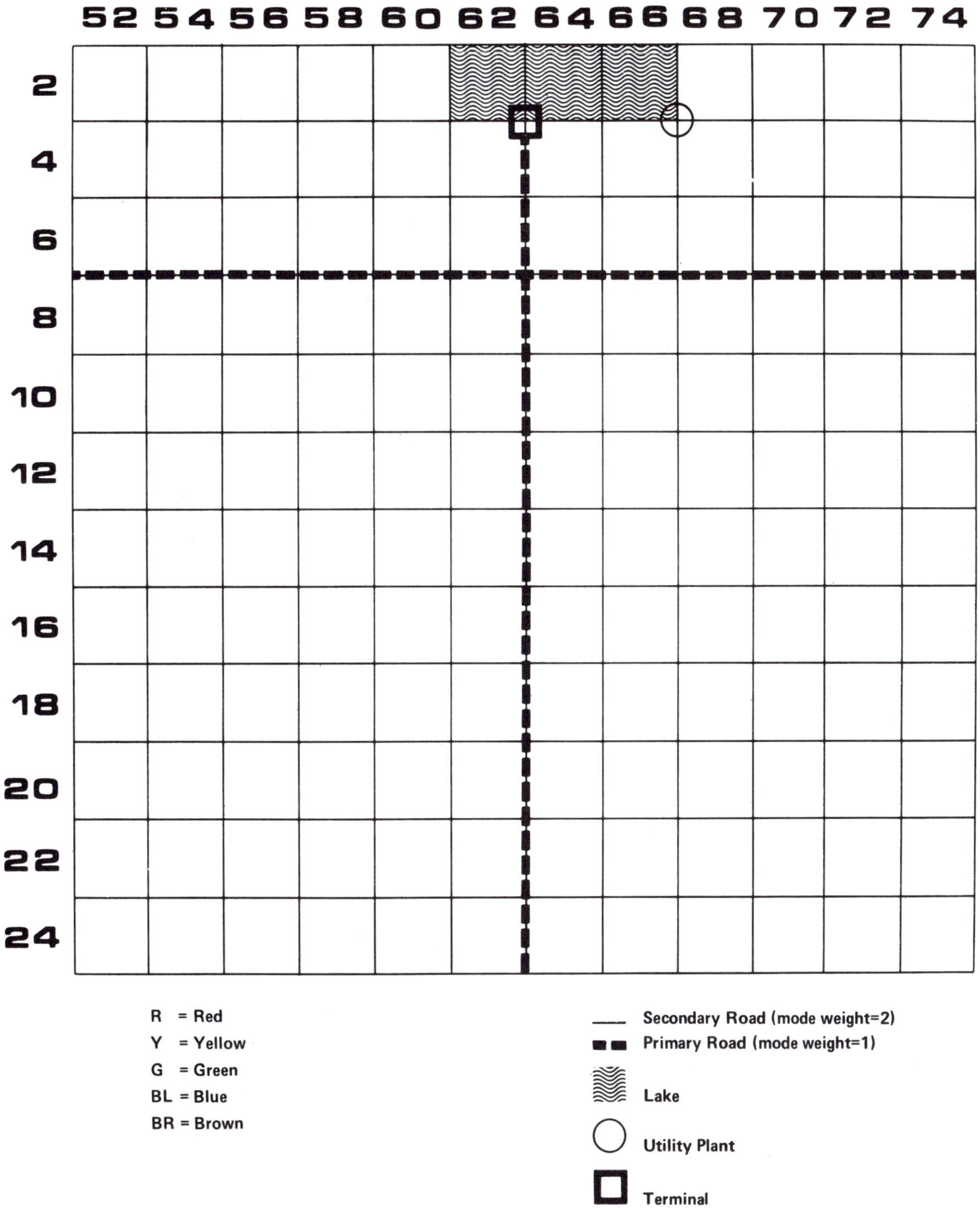

R = Red
Y = Yellow
G = Green
BL = Blue
BR = Brown

——— Secondary Road (mode weight=2)
■ ■ Primary Road (mode weight=1)
〰 Lake
○ Utility Plant
□ Terminal

Primary or Secondary Roads. (A unit distance is one side of a parcel of land.) All movement must be in straight lines along the edges of parcels and is counted from the nearest corner of the origin square to the nearest corner of the destination square. Thus the distance traveled between two touching parcels is zero and the Transportation Cost is zero.

The unit cost of a trip depends on the frequency and volume of a particular kind of trip in the real world. Volume is very high for shipment of manufactured products and relatively low for journeys to shop and to work. This weighting factor for a particular kind of trip is called the Association Weight and is given in Table 2. The Association Weight is summed up over the number of squares traveled, multiplied by a Mode Weight of 1 or 2 according to whether or not travel is along a Primary or Secondary Road, respectively. Thus, for a journey to work for a Residence (R1) to his employer involving travel over two units of Secondary Roads and two units of Primary Road the following calculation is made: Given an Association Weight of $300 for Residence to work, the cost would be two times $300 for each unit of Secondary Road traveled plus one times $300 for each unit of Primary Road traveled, or $1,800 per residential unit at that location. The resulting Transportation Costs are paid to the instructor each round by the team owning each operating land use. Reductions in cost are only possible by decreasing the distance traveled, or, in some experiments, by providing improved transportation facilities.

Table 2. Association Weights for Required Trips

Travelling from	Travelling to				
	Terminal	Office	Employment	Shopping (LS)	Shopping (CS)
Full Industry (FI)	$4,000	$400	—	—	—
Partial Industry (PI)	2,000	200	—	—	—
Central or Local Store (CS or LS)	—	100	—	—	—
Residences, per unit (R1)*	—	—	$300	$200	$100

*For R2, R3, or R4 multiply by 2, 3, or 4, respectively.

Taxation and Community Finance

Community-wide costs paid from taxes will be incurred each round according to the number of Utility Lines constructed and the number of residential units which exist on the board. A construction cost of $2,000 is made initially for each new Utility Line segment. The continuing operation and maintenance of each line, after its construction, costs the community $1,000 per round. Utility Line construction and location is determined by majority vote of the teams playing. No building may be built on any land that is not serviced along one edge by a Utility Line. One section of a Utility Line is a unit along the edge of one parcel; all costs are computed on a per unit basis. All Utility Lines must, of course, feed into a system connected ultimately with the Utility Plant. In addition to Utility Costs, a charge for social services is made at the rate of $1,000 per round for each residential unit on the board. This cost, together with the Utility construction and maintenance Costs, must be paid for by the community out of taxes it levies on itself.

In the basic game, a simple property tax (on land and buildings) system is used. A Tax Rate is set by majority vote of the teams. This rate, multiplied by the Assessed Value of an individual team's property holdings, determines the amount to be paid in Taxes in the following round. In successive rounds, the rate may be lowered or increased according to the financial needs of the community and its plans for growth.

The community is allowed to run a Surplus or Deficit in financing its costs in any given round and this Surplus or Deficit accumulates over successive rounds. However, the Deficit may not exceed ten per cent of the Total Assessed Value of the entire community at any time. A basic interest rate of ten per cent will be charged the entire community on any existing Deficit. No interest is paid on accumulated Surplus. If the ten per cent Debt Limit is exceeded, no new Utility Construction will be allowed until all previous Deficits have been paid by the community, i.e., until the community's entire debt is reduced to zero. The accounts on Assessed Value, Taxes, Surplus or Deficit, and outstanding debt will be kept by the Accountant for the community. The players' major tasks will be to set Tax Rates, pay their Taxes, and take care not to accumulate so large a Deficit that it will destroy the community's financial flexibility and credit standing.

Depreciation

Each building depreciates in value at a rate of five per cent per round of its initial Construction Cost. Every five rounds the owners of each building will be informed of the age and state of depreciation of each of their buildings and asked whether or not they wish to renovate any or all of their buildings. Renovation is accomplished by paying the instructor the accumulated five per cent Depreciation Costs, thereby renewing the building and effectively decreasing its age. Renovation payments may be made in any five per cent increment—the equivalent to one round's depreciation. A building may then be fully brought back to "age zero," or partially renewed a round or two, depending upon the value and usefulness of the structure and land.

After making the decision whether or not to renovate a particular building, each team must then roll a pair of dice for each building. The odds of losing the use of a building are proportional to its state of depreciation. Once a building is "lost," in effect it is condemned and may not be used for another five rounds. After five rounds have elapsed a building is again eligible for Renovation and must be rolled for again. However, the building is now five rounds older, with accordingly higher probabilities of loss. At this point the building may be renovated in order to reduce the chance of losing it again.

Every building has at least a minimum five per cent probability of loss, even if fully renovated in the current round. Higher probabilities result from adding an additional five per cent for each additional round of age to this basic level. Any building, including one which has been condemned, may be demolished at a cost of twenty-five per cent of its current Assessed Value during the Construction Step of any round. The employee and employer relations tied to condemned or demolished buildings are automatically terminated, with renegotiation of employment and shopping contracts allowed in that round. Table 3 provides the probabilities of loss of buildings at various ages, together with the losing numbers on a pair of dice which correspond to these probabilities and the per-round costs of renovation for each type of building. Reassessment of all land and buildings is begun by the Accountant at the end of rounds divisible by five.

Table 3. Probabilities of Building Loss and Depreciation Costs by Type of Building

Age of Building (Current Round Number Minus Round Built or Renovated)	Probability of Losing Building	Equivalent Losing Numbers on One Pair of Six-Sided Dice
0	.056	3
1	.111	5
2	.167	7
3	.195	2,7
4	.250	2,7,11
5	.306	2,7,9
6	.362	3,7,8
7	.417	5,7,8
8	.445	6,7,8
9	.500	3,6,7,8
10	.556	5,6,7,8
11	.612	3,5,6,7,8
12	.667	5,6,7,8,9
13	.695	2,5,6,7,8,9
14	.750	4,5,6,7,8,9
15	.806	3,4,5,6,7,8,9
16	.861	2,4,5,6,7,8,9,10
17	.889	3,4,5,6,7,8,9,10
18	.944	3,4,5,6,7,8,9,10,11
19	1.000	2,3,4,5,6,7,8,9,10,11,12
20	1.000	2,3,4,5,6,7,8,9,10,11,12

Five Per Cent Depreciation Costs for Each Type of Land Use

FI — $4,800	O — $1,800	R1 — $ 600
PI — $2,400	CS — $1,200	R2 — $1,500
	LS — $1,200	R3 — $2,400
		R4 — $3,600

Steps of Play

CLUG proceeds through a set of steps of play. Specific kinds of action and decisions are called for at each step. Transition from one step to another is determined by the instructor; return to a previous step is not allowed. Players who have not accomplished all their activities during the appropriate step in a given round must wait until the next round before these tasks may be completed. Play begins on Step 1 and proceeds sequentially through Step 11, at which time Step 1 of the next round begins.

1. *PURCHASE LAND:* Offers may be made for purchasing land from either the instructor or from other Teams. Each bid to the instructor must be written in a form that states both the coordinates of the parcel and the offered price to the nearest hundred dollars. The instructor will accept bids for any unowned parcels of land and award ownership to the highest bidder. Bids less than $1,000 are automatically rejected. Each team is allowed to bid on three pieces of unowned land in each round. Purchase of land and buildings from other teams may also be conducted during this step in any quantities desired.

2. *PROVIDE UTILITIES:* After consultation among all teams, proposals are made for the number and location of new utility lines desired by the community. Every new segment of a utility line to be placed on the board must be approved by a majority of the teams playing. A majority is always one team more than half the teams in play. After majority approval, the new lines are placed on the board by the instructor.

[3. *RENOVATE BUILDINGS:* This step is played only in the rounds divisible by five, e.g. fifth, tenth, fifteenth, etc. At this time, the age and depreciation of each building is announced and the owners are asked whether or not, and how much, they wish to renovate. Following the renovation decision on each building, a pair of dice are rolled and the possible condemnation of the building is determined. This continues until every building on the board has been covered.]

4. *CONSTRUCT BUILDINGS:* New buildings may now be built by each team on their own land. Full payment of the initial construction cost must accompany each new building. Buildings are allowed only on those parcels serviced by a Utility Line that runs along one edge of the parcel. Demolition of existing buildings is allowed at a cost to the owner of twenty-five per cent of its current Assessed Value.

5. *DESIGNATE EMPLOYMENT:* Formal contracts between residential owners and the owners of employing businesses are signed at this step. Employment is indicated by placing a matching marker on the employer building and on each employee residential building. *Employment contracts are binding until this step of play in the next round divisible by five.*

6. *SIGN TRADE AGREEMENTS:* Newly-constructed Local Stores, Central Stores, and Offices announce the prices they will charge for their particular goods until the next round divisible by five. Only one price can be offered by each commercial location. Owners of existing Local Stores, Central Stores, and Offices can change their prices only in a round divisible by five. Following the announcement of prices, owners of newly-constructed residential units indicate which Local and Central Stores they intend to shop at and so notify the appropriate store owners. A similar notification is provided to Offices by owners of Local Stores, Central Stores, Full and Partial Industries. Units shopping with the instructor should so notify him. *Shopping Agreements are binding until this step of the next round divisible by five.* However, purchase agreements with the instructor may be broken in any round at this step of play.

7. *RECEIVE INCOME:* The instructor makes payment from the outside world to owners of industries. Full Industries receive $48,000 per round

income if they have four employees. Partial Industries receive $22,000 per round income if they have two employees. In the event that full employment is not reached, income is prorated according to the number of employees.

8. *PAY EMPLOYEES:* Employers make $6,000 wage payments to each of their employees.

9. *PAY LOCAL STORES, CENTRAL STORES, AND OFFICES:* Owners of Stores and Offices should inform their customers of the payments owed for shopping that round according to the number of customers and the agreed-upon prices. And the instructor collects from those players shopping with him.

10. *PAY TRANSPORTATION:* The instructor collects payments from each team for Transportation Costs incurred by various building types owned by them.

11. *PAY TAXES:* The Accountant informs each team of the Taxes owed by the community and the instructor collects these amounts. The community is informed of the total amount raised in Taxes, the amount of expenses incurred, the interest paid on debts, and the surplus or deficit situation of the community. Players then discuss and vote upon a new Tax Rate for the next round.

Preparing To Play

At the back of this manual are duplicate pages of tables called the Player's Information Form that summarize all the basic information needed during CLUG play. These are provided on perforated sheets so that one of them may be torn out of the manual for convenient reference during play. Most players find that one reading of the rules given above together with this single page of tables is sufficient to answer most questions which arise during play. (The duplicate page of tables is provided as a "spare" in case the first sheet becomes lost or mutilated in use.)

Also provided are several pages of perforated coupons that are convenient for recording your bids on land and formalizing your shopping contracts with other players. In filling out a land purchase offer indicate the even numbered coordinates of the land parcel being bid on, together with your team color and the current round. The price being offered should be given to the nearest one hundred dollars since this is the lowest denomination provided in the CLUG materials.

A Shopping Contract provides a written agreement between the owner of a Residential property and the owner of a Local or Central Store to shop at that store at an agreed upon price until the next round divisible by five. In filling out these forms enter the coordinates of the residential unit involved as customer and the color of the team owning these residential units. Also to be entered are the coordinates of the store location, the price agreed upon (usually reported in a price per residential unit figure), and the color of the team owning the store. This shopping agreement form is usually filled out by the "customer" and retained by the store owner so that he may conveniently keep track of money owed him by each team during each round.

Also included are two copies each of the CLUG Tax Record and the Community Financial Status form. One of each of these two forms will be required by the Accountant for each experiment or game run. He will also need a copy of the Property Ownership Record provided in the *Instructor's Manual.*

After playing through five or ten rounds of the Basic CLUG game, most players have developed a clear idea of the mechanics of operation and are in a good position to take over the operation of the game from the instructor. A careful review of the *Instructor's Manual* will help at this transition stage. Depending on the interests of the players, it may be worthwhile repeating a run of the Basic CLUG model either from the beginning or from Round Five or Six of the already completed run. At this point, it is usually wise to elect a game manager from one of the teams to take over the management of the game in place of the instructor. The manager must then appoint an Accountant to take care of recording of property transactions, tax assessments, and levies. The teams from which the manager and the Accountant are elected and appointed, respectively, are usually paid $6,000 per round from the city funds. The manager comes up for reelection every two rounds with the power to appoint a new Accountant upon his election.

More elaborate and realistic representations of city government may be desired in a rerun of the Basic CLUG game, particularly if some form of planning or zoning is to be attempted. In this case Experiment I provides more appropriate mechanisms.

Except for special purposes, it does not usually appear worthwhile to continue any play of the Basic CLUG game beyond ten or fifteen rounds. Beyond this point, the game tends to become highly repetitive and much of the earlier difficulty in securing development of the community disappears as capital becomes readily available. The most interesting development in extended plays of CLUG centers around the fact that at some point the community will cease to grow, despite the availability of funds for new industrial construction. This will always occur unless new improvements in transportation facilities or new terminal locations are provided.

Following initial trial experimentation with the Basic CLUG model, players should turn to exploration of the experiments on community problems and developments which are given in the following pages. These experiments are designed to explore and demonstrate the characteristics of a number of additional features of urban growth and development. They may be played in any order, except that a few of the later experiments call for set up conditions demonstrated in the earlier experiments. They do increase in difficulty of set-up and operation as they progress; players unsure of themselves might best do them in the order in which they are presented. The full participation of the instructor in the conduct of each of these experiments should not be necessary, but referral to the suggestions provided in the *Instructor's Manual* is probably necessary in most cases. When conducted without the immediate supervision of an instructor, a game manager should be elected from among the players to help ensure orderly procedures within the group. The game manager and his Accountant should review both the experiment and the special operating instructions for each experiment provided in Appendix II of the *Player's Manual.*

Experiments with the Community Land Use Game

Experiment I: Urban Politics

Introduction

Newspaper, magazines and books are full of exposés, descriptions, defenses and condemnations of politics in America's cities. As members of a representative governing system, we are all victims or beneficiaries of these political processes. It is the purpose of this modification to provide the player with some insight into the motivations behind the political processes in our cities. In the game as in real life issues are not clear cut, they overlap; solutions are not easy, they help some while they hurt others; and the politicians, no matter how hard they try, cannot please everyone. This modification provides for a local governing body composed of representatives of the CLUG community. Each representative has a clearly identifiable constituency; and each constituency has a clear economic role in the community.

In CLUG, industry provides the economic base for the community, but in this modification the bulk of the political power is held by those with housing units. Therefore, players will tend to choose to play for either political or economic power. Coalitions often develop between a team with a lot of economic power and one with a lot of political power. These game coalitions are much like the kinds of political activities we see in real life when a candidate is backed openly or otherwise by business interests.

In this modification we are concerned with the interrelationships among economic growth, community good, and political power. It is important to understand how and why political decisions are made; and it is on this decision-making process that the experiment concentrates.*

Rules of Play

The political modification can be divided into three basic components: establishing the government; governmental responsibilities; and governmental funds. The rules of Basic CLUG are retained; and the modification is introduced in Round 2.

Establishing the Government

In the first round the instructor serves as the head of the government. He mediates the discussion on providing the initial utility lines and determines the placement of the lines in the same manner as in Basic CLUG., e.g. by majority vote of the teams. As in the basic game, the tax rate is set at five per cent in the first round and players do not vote on the rate.

In Step 2 of Round 2 the teams elect a Mayor. The candidate receiving the largest number of votes (teams now have weighted vote, see below) is elected. The Mayor holds office for three rounds, but he can be recalled

*This modification was originally developed by the Center for Simulation Studies, St. Louis, Missouri. Used with permission of Richard F. Tombaugh, Director.

25

within his term of office if, during a Council meeting, a team can show cause and a majority of the votes held by the teams is cast against him.

The City Council consists of all the other team members. Votes are allocated according to the land uses held by each team. Teams are not required to cast all their votes as a unit.

Votes are allocated on the following basis:

Land Use	Votes
R1	2
R2	4
R3	6
R4	8
LS	1
CS	1
O	1
FI	4
PI	2

A team owning an R3 and a LS thus has 7 votes, 6 for the R3 and 1 for the LS.

After construction, Step 4, of each round the Operator will post the number of votes held by each team, the total of votes for the community and the number of votes constituting a majority.

Government Responsibilities

The Mayor's responsibilities include running the city council meetings, breaking tie votes (the Mayor may vote only in the event of a tie), and making patronage appointments in specific public facilities. Council meetings can only be held during Step 2. The Mayor may run city council meetings in any manner he wishes. Most frequently, however, Robert's Rules of Order are followed.

Generally, it is best to have the Mayor begin a council meeting by having the group decide on how long the meeting should last. Usually a vote is taken. The instructor then calls the time when it is up. This prevents council meetings from tying up the game. If the council has not finished all its business when time is called, the incomplete business is delayed until the next council meeting. If the tax rate is not set, the Assessor should use the rate from the previous round.

Each council meeting has an agenda as follows:

> Provide utilities
> Old business
> New business
> Set tax rate

New business may include providing public facilities, establishing a planning commission, a zoning commission, a department of public works or any other advisory board which the group desires. Whatever the item of new business to be adopted, it must receive a majority of the votes. Provision of utilities and establishment of the tax rate are also determined by a majority of the votes.

In addition to establishing a means to provide utilities and set the tax rate, the government is responsible for determining what public facilities are needed by the community. By Round 6 the community must have an equivalent of ten per cent of its total assessed value invested in public facilities. If the community has built no public facilities or does not have its full ten per cent quota, the instructor will require that it build up to its full ten per cent quota in Round 6. The cost of construction is borne by the taxes; and the tax rate must be adjusted accordingly. The purpose of this ten per cent requirement is to force the council to consider what public facilities they want and why they want them. The issue of public facilities is seldom considered without the requirement. The failure to act is as significant as what and why a group may choose to build.

Table I-1. Characteristics of Public Facilities

Facility	Cost of Construction	Maintenance Cost per Round	Number of Employee Units	Who Decides on Employee
Parks	Land Cost	$7,000	1	Mayor
Recreation Center	$12,000	7,000	1	Mayor
Public School System	24,000	13,000	2	Council
Medical Services	16,000	8,000	1	Council
City College	16,000	7,000	1	Council
City Hall	12,000	7,000	1	Mayor
Library	10,000	8,000	1	Mayor

The Public School System is a typical public facility. Its initial cost is $24,000. It employs two workers which the city pays $6,000 each. All workers in public facilities are paid their wages by the instructor at Step 7, Receive Income. The council determines by majority vote which teams will provide the units of labor. In the case of public facilities like the City Hall the Mayor will determine which team shall provide the employee.

Like a utility line, once a public facility is built it must be maintained. The cost of maintenance, which is listed above (Table I-1), includes renovation. In rounds divisible by five the Mayor must roll the dice on each public facility. The public facilities are considered to always be fully renovated.

Government Funds

In Round 2 the Mayor begins his term of office with $20,000. This money is held in a special contingency account. The $20,000 accrues five per cent interest, compounded each round, and the Mayor may request part or all of this money from the instructor at any time. The use of this money is up to the Mayor's discretion, unless the teams decide, by majority vote, to limit the Mayor's fiscal power. The monies in the contingency account need not necessarily be spent for public facilities, utilities, or any other community project. The Mayor may use the funds for his own team's construction, may divide the money evenly among the teams, or may use the money as bribes for votes. If the Mayor is caught stealing by the other players, it is cause for council action which may result in recall and the election of a new Mayor. A majority of the votes must be cast against a Mayor for recall. What is significant is that only by majority vote can the Mayor's power to allocate funds be controlled.

The political modification requires only minor changes in the assessment sheet. Public facilities constructed are entered into the expenditure column under utilities. Like utilities, the cost of construction is entered the first round and the maintenance cost entered in subsequent rounds. Should the facility be lost during renovation, the city no longer pays maintenance costs and the employee(s) is(are) laid off.

The following steps of play review the changes in Basic CLUG for this political modification.

1. Purchase Land	Unchanged from Basic CLUG.
2. Provide Utilities	Decision by council headed by elected Mayor. Utility decision made by majority vote based on weighted vote. Council also considers construction of public facilities, appointment of advisory boards, and other new business. Council sets tax rate by majority vote. Elect Mayor every three rounds.
3. Renovate Buildings	Unchanged from Basic CLUG.
4. Construct Buildings	City builds public facilities. Instructor posts the number of votes.
5. Designate Employment	Use special pins for city employees.
6. Sign Trade Agreements	Unchanged from Basic CLUG.
7. Receive Income	Unchanged from Basic CLUG.
8. Pay Employees	Pay wages to city employees.
9. Pay LS, CS, and O	Unchanged from Basic CLUG.
10. Pay Transportation	Unchanged from Basic CLUG.
11. Pay Taxes	Tax rate set in Step 2, merely pay taxes in this step.

A summary of the new information and changes needed for this experiment is provided on a tear-out sheet at the back of this manual. It is entitled "Summary of Changes for Urban Politics Experiment."

Discussion

Six to ten rounds are recommended for the best results with the political modification. Players need not begin a new game with this modification; it may be introduced into any game by counting up each team's weighted vote and making the required changes in the other steps of play. The requirement to have ten per cent of the total assessed value invested in public facilities would then come in the sixth round of play after the political modification has been introduced.

Study Questions

After playing six or more rounds with the political modification the following questions might be considered by the players:

1. In what ways can the governing body of the city influence a city's growth or decline?
2. Must a government act to have an effect?
3. What was the balance of political and economic power in your city? Who had what kind of influence, and why?
4. Which had the most influence on the government's action: the personality of the Mayor, the political coalitions between teams, the general desire for community improvement or the desire to maximize economic profit? How was this influence on the government's actions expressed? Can you cite examples of city governments which behave as yours did?
5. Will you behave differently if you play the political modification again?

Experiment II:
Rural-Urban Interdependence

Introduction

An adequate understanding of urban growth and development cannot be divorced from consideration of a number of important developments in rural areas. Theorists concentrating on either urban or rural phenomena too often overlook the significance of each of these areas for the other. The importance of agricultural development for early urban growth has been noted by many urban historians, while the impact of urban expansion and technology on farming practices is being studied by a number of current observers of agricultural problems. Yet these phenomena must be viewed together in order to understand their mutual significance.

Early Stages of Urban Growth

Improvements in agricultural technology provided some of the first impetus for urban development. These improvements resulted in increased agricultural productivity and surplus farm populations. These combined surpluses of product and population provided both the workers and the sustenance base for early urban settlements. At the same time, the increased profitability of agriculture provided capital for investment in urban enterprises, hence further stimulating urban growth. The products of early urban industry in turn provided a further stimulus to agricultural development by providing goods, materials, and services for which surplus agricultural products could be traded. This cyclical pattern was reinforced substantially with the introduction of industrialization and improvements in agricultural technology.

In more modern times the direction of causality sometimes appears to have been reversed. The most obvious impact of continued urban growth is the gradual conversion of farmland near cities into urban uses, often on land with better agricultural soils. This has resulted in the abandonment of many farms as well as in increased costs for the provision of urban services to more extended and less densely settled areas. Substantial reduction in transportation costs have greatly increased the extent of this phenomenon.

Technological Changes in Agriculture

Improvements in seed, fertilizer, mechanical equipment, management techniques, and animal husbandry have had an additional impact on agricultural practices. The successful farming of much larger acreages by a single farmer has been facilitated through these improvements, although the increased capital cost of such improvements has made a larger-sized farm more necessary in order to utilize equipment and techniques with efficiency. The ability to farm poorer land more successfully has also been improved through these technological developments. The merging of small farms into larger units, together with increased mechanization of farm labor, has resulted both in the release of additional populations for urban settlement and in increased surplus productivity to continue feeding this new urban population.

Organizational Changes in Agriculture

As these developments have been occuring, several important innovations in the marketing system for farm products have emerged. The evolution of cooperative marketing arrangements and contract farming has provided an improvement in the stability and security of prices for farm products. Through cooperative marketing the individual farmer is able to combine his products with those of others. By strategically withholding products from the market, the cooperative can affect prices and help to stabilize and improve members' incomes. Contract farming allows a farmer to sell his produce even before it is planted, thereby guaranteeing his income well in advance of producing his product. Both of these organizational changes can benefit the small farmer, as well as the larger farmer, and may make it possible for a smaller farmer to survive longer in the face of large scale competition. Nevertheless, his lower capitalization and inability to acquire additional acreage and improved techniques of farm management leave him in a less advantageous position than the larger farmer.

The Readings and Experiment

This experiment provides an overview of the relationship between agriculture and urban growth during two stages of development.

Stage I reflects a period of early urban development when the gradually accumulated capital from farming was transformed into investments in urban development. Population shifts to urban settlement from farms are not represented in the game, however, except for the possible shift of a farm residential unit into urban employment. Surplus productivity is represented only in the profit level of individual farms.

In Stage II, significant improvements in transportation, technology, and farm equipment have occured which make larger farms more feasible and profitable, while stimulating increased expansion of urban land uses into adjacent farm lands. More highly stabilized and slightly more profitable levels of farm income are also represented.

The article by Hauser provides a broad historical review of the impact of agricultural technology and its associated changes in social organization on urban growth and development. The gradual build up of these changes, along with improved market mechanisms, resulted in the accumulation of surplus capital that was invested in urban enterprises. Thompson discusses "urban sprawl" in present day cities. He views this phenomenon primarily in terms of the increased costs of urban management; he does not view the associated losses of agricultural land as being so important.

URBANIZATION: AN OVERVIEW

Philip M. Hauser

The Bases of Urbanization

The origin of the urban agglomeration as a form of human settlement is not precisely known. There is, however, a literature on the origin and development of cities, based in part on legend, myth, and speculation, in part on archaeology, and in part on the known origins of cities that have emerged during the period of recorded history. It seems clear that the emergence and development of the city was necessarily a function of four factors: (1) the size of the total population; (2) the control of natural environment; (3) technological development; and (4) developments in social organization.[1]

Population size is necessarily a factor in urban development because to permit any agglomeration of human beings there must be some minimum number to sustain group life; and to achieve large urban aggregations relatively large total populations are required. Similarly, the environment must be amenable to control in the sense that it meets at least minimal requirements for aggregative living. Thus, although earliest cities apparently were located in river valleys and alluvial plains, the ingenuity of man has permitted the use of a wide variety of natural environments for urban development. In any case, the natural environment, by means of relatively primitive technology, provided the necessities for survival—food, shelter, protective clothing, and, of course, an adequate water supply.

Permanent human settlement had to await technological innovation—the inventions of the neolithic revolution. It was only with the achievement of domesticated plants and animals that it became possible for man to lead a relatively settled existence. Apart from these requirements, however, other techniques were involved and certainly played a major role in determining the size that the agglomeration could reach. Foremost among these was the development of agricultural technology to a point where a surplus was possible, that is, a food supply in excess of the requirements of the cultivators themselves. The emergence of the crafts and their proliferation was necessarily a function of the size of the surplus, permitting some persons to engage, at least part time, in activities other than agricultural. With improved technology, including the wheel, the road, irrigation, cultivation, stock breeding, and improvements in fishing, the surplus became large enough to support a sizable number of persons freed from the production of food. Certain it is that developments of this type were associated with the first units of settlement ten times and more the size of any known neolithic

From *The Study of Urbanization*, edited by Philip M. Hauser and Leo Schnore (New York: John Wiley and Sons, 1965), pp 1-5 and 41-42. Reprinted with permission of the publisher.

[1] Otis Dudley Duncan, "Human Ecology and Population Studies," in Philip M. Hauser and Otis Dudley Duncan (Eds.), *The Study of Population: An Inventory and Appraisal* (Chicago: University of Chicago Press, 1959), pp. 681ff.

villages, as revealed in the archaeological finds in Egypt, Mesopotamia, and the Indus Basin.[2]

The development of relatively large agglomerations of population required more, however, than an increasingly efficient technology. Relatively large aggregations of population required more complex social organization, including improved communication, and social and political mechanisms permitting some form of exchange among the emergent specialists, agricultural and nonagricultural. Chief among the social organizational requirements was a working arrangement between the population agglomeration and the hinterland, its source of food and raw materials. In the history of cities there is evidence of great variation in forms of organization by means of which integration and coordination of activities was achieved between city and hinterland and within the city. The rise and fall of empires, as recorded in ancient history, may be read in large measure as a chronicle of developments in social organization by means of which the ancient cities acquired a hinterland. The Roman Legion may be interpreted as a form of social organization enabling the city to achieve effective working arrangements with a hinterland.[3] The same function centuries later was performed by emergence of the market mechanism, including money as an instrumentality of exchange.

It was not until the nineteenth century that mankind had achieved both the level of technological development and social organization that permitted the relatively widespread appearance of very large cities. On the technological side the developments included techniques that greatly increased productivity in agriculture as well as in nonagricultural commodities. A critical factor in increased productivity was, of course, the utilization of nonhuman energy in production—the emergence of the machine, powered first by water or wind, then by steam, and now by mineral fuels or electricity derived therefrom, with atomic energy in prospect.[4] Technological advance proceeded at an exponential rate under the impetus of the "scientific revolution."

Social organizational developments paralleled the technological. Strong central governments evolved, bringing relative peace and tranquility to increasingly large areas and permitting the development of local, regional, national, and international markets. Increasing division of labor and specialization were accompanied by various forms of formal and informal organization providing essential intergration and coordination. New social institutions evolved or were invented to meet the needs of the increasingly complex and interdependent social and economic orders. A full account of the emergence of the large city in the context of its antecedents is yet to be achieved, if indeed it ever can be documented. But the available literature certainly provides a basis for at least pointing to the major factors associated

[2] Ralph Turner, *The Great Cultural Traditions*, Vol. I, *The Ancient Cities* (New York: McGraw-Hill, 1941), pp. 126ff.

[3] *Ibid.*, Vol. II, *The Classical Empires*, pp. 856ff.

[4] Fred Cottrell, *Energy and Society* (New York: McGraw-Hill, 1955).

with the emergence of the city and of relatively highly urbanized nations.[5]

In a neo-evolutionary approach, Gras has outlined with broad strokes the relationship between economic development and settlement or habitation patterns in his account of economic history.[6] He has fused historical ways of making a living with technological developments, on the one hand, and with developments in human settlement on the other. Gras writes the history of Western civilization in terms of this joint classification. He delineates five stages or periods: (1) the collectional economy; (2) the cultural-nomadic economy; (3) the settled village economy; (4) the town economy; and (5) the metropolitan economy.

The settled village economy was possible only with the development of agriculture as the dominant way of making a living. The town economy was a function of increased agricultural productivity, the proliferation of the crafts, more efficient transport, and the development of trade. The metropolitan economy was a product of the combination of technological and organizational changes associated with industrialization and the emergence of the metropolitan complex with the large city as a nucleus for an interdependent hinterland. Although Gras's five-stage scheme of urban development is open to serious question, a general neo-evolutionary interpretation of urban development has not been attempted since Gras, indicating, perhaps, a serious gap in the literature.

Economic history as seen by Gras is, in effect, an analysis of the pattern of human habitation considered as a dependent variable. Lampard approaches the problem in the same way in his treatment of urban-industrial development, following the stages, if not the language, of Geddes.[7] The antecedents of the preindustrial city may be seen in his description of cities in Europe and America toward the end of the sixteenth century: "Urban centers were court cities, cathedral cities, fortress cities, markets, ports, country towns, and mere villages. Many, of course, were composites of several types." The preindustrial European city was "limited (dominated) by the needs and capacities of the rural hinterland and a highly stratified society." The preindustrial European city was "essentially a loose-knit system of food economies centering on a few relatively large mercantile-administrative capitals, with a growing inter-regional commerce but no marked territorial division of labor."

The industrial city was the product of acceleration in agricultural productivity and industrial technology during the eighteenth century. It was "a major outlet for capital accumulated in commercialized agricultural production." Its development was facilitated by the emergence of coal and steam as sources of power and particularly by the centripetal force of the steam

---

[5] For example, Ralph Turner, *op. cit.*, Vols. I, II; V. Gordon Childe, *Man Makes Himself* (London: Watts, 1941), Chaps. 5–6; *What Happened in History* (London: Penguin Books, 1946), Chaps. 3–4; Robert J. Braidwood and Gordon R. Willey (Eds.), *Courses Toward Urban Life* (Chicago: Aldine, 1962); N. S. B. Gras, *An Introduction to Economic History* (New York: Harper, 1922); Lewis Mumford, *The City in History* (New York: Harcourt, Brace & World, 1961).

[6] N. S. B. Gras, *op. cit.*

[7] Eric E. Lampard, "The History of Cities in the Economically Advanced Areas," *Economic Development and Cultural Change*, 3 (January 1955), pp. 103–104.

engine. Factories and population piled up in the industrial city as is documented in the history of English industrial cities such as Manchester and Birmingham. This history was paralleled during the first half of the nineteenth century in France, the Low Countries, and northeastern United States. Major ingredients in the very rapid development of industrial cities in Europe and the United States included the utilization of new fuels as sources of nonhuman energy, new materials, mechanical aids, improved transport and communication, and a closer integration of productive and managerial processes.

The twentieth century "metropolitan city" was the product of the extensive application of science to industry, the diffusion of electric power and the advent of the automobile. The metropolitan city, as compared with the industrial city, was the product of the accelerating technological revolution that permeated virtually all phases of life. Whereas the steam engine and the belt and the pulley had set centripetal forces into motion creating dense population around factory plants, the combination of electric power, the automobile, and the telephone set centrifugal forces in motion which simultaneously diffused population and industry widely over the landscape and permitted larger agglomerations of both. The metropolitan city is a nucleus or core of a metropolitan area which has become a basic economic and social unit not only in regional and national economies but also in the world economy. It is a highly complex and interdependent unit binding centralization with decentralization and specialization and differentiation of function with integration and coordinating mechanisms.

The emergence of the metropolitan community as a basic unit of economic and social organization should not obscure the relation of the metropolitan city to the larger economy and society of which it is a part. Technological and social organizational developments which have produced the metropolitan city have also produced "systems" of such cities. Recognition of a "system" in the distribution of cities is manifest in the literature, both inductively and deductively. Central-place theory points to and attempts to explain the system in the location of cities as "functions of distance, mass production, and competition."[8]

· · ·

[8] August Lösch, *The Economics of Location* (New Haven: Yale University Press, 1954). Cited in O. D. Duncan et al., *Metropolis and Region* (Baltimore: Johns Hopkins Press, 1960), p. 25.

THE PRICE OF URBAN SPRAWL

Wilbur R. Thompson

Probably no recent phenomenon of urbanization has been more pointed to with alarm than urban "sprawl." Sprawl is used somewhat loosely to include both a haphazard intermingling of developed and vacant land on the urban-rural fringe and the siting of houses on lots of ever larger size.[1] Although there are some critics of big cities to whom size itself is an offense, the principal target of attack is not so much the growing total population and sheer land size of the urban area as it is the steadily falling density of residential development on the periphery where new building is occurring. Urban core areas tend, of course, to be solidly built up with very little vacant land available for new building and therefore they must grow by expanding centrifugally. But if the new residential subdivisions are too extravagant in their use of land—house lots too large—or if much usable land is skipped over in the march of urbanization outward, the urban area grows "unnecessarily large" and transportation, communication, utility services and local public services all become "unnecessarily" inefficient and uneconomical. A clear distinction between physical growth due to population growth and that due to low residential density should be made because it is density which is at issue in this country at this time, although in England aggregate size has been the subject of considerable thought and public policy for a couple of decades. How has this purported too extravagant use of land for urban dwellings come to be, if indeed such a problem really does exist?

Urban sprawl could be nothing more than a color word dramatizing an adverse value judgment on one particular urban living arrangement—a distinctive combination of land and structures. A group of confirmed urbanites, impassioned and articulate, may simply disapprove of suburbanites' taste patterns—the substitution of open space and privacy for frequency and ease of interpersonal contact—and seek to apprise the city deserters of the errors of their ways.

Perhaps the most impassioned protest against urban sprawl is the most questionable: the fear that the physical growth of cities is "devouring" prime farm land, with ominous long-run implications to our supply of agricultural products. Cities were founded and flourished, for the most part, in two contexts: as transportation centers and as market places for agricultural areas. In the former case, the city site was most often a good natural harbor and on land of mediocre quality at best. But in the latter case, the better the soil in the area, the more prosperous the local farmers, the faster their

From Wilbur R. Thompson, *A Preface to Urban Economics*, (Baltimore: Johns Hopkins, 1968), pp. 320-322. Reprinted by permission of the publisher. Published by The Johns Hopkins Press for Resources for the Future, Inc.

[1] While the antisprawl literature has stressed the leapfrogging of open land more than the trend toward large lots, the latter is probably more quantitatively significant and obviously has the greater long-run significance—the skipped-over places do usually fill in. For some feeling for the relative importance of various kinds of open space on the total size of an urban area, see Stanley B. Tankel, "The Importance of Open Space in the Urban Pattern," *Cities and Space, op. cit.*

market town grew, the greater the conversion of prime quality agricultural land to sites for homes, streets, stores, and factories.

Even so, the considered opinion of most land economists is that the loss of agricultural land is a small matter and the major economic impact of sprawl is to be found elsewhere. Technological advances in fertilizers, hybrid seeds, and farm machinery have greatly increased output per acre, while advances in contour plowing, terracing, and irrigation continually replenish our supplies of land. Mason Gaffney[2] argues:

> We run no danger of running out of cropland. Consider the most extreme case, the destruction of southern California's Valencia citrus industry by the insatiable subdividers of Los Angeles. It is tragic, it is largely unnecessary, yet there remain in California, in the southern San Joaquin Valley alone, something like one million acres with thermal conditions suitable for citrus, according to a recent report from the Riverside Citrus Experiment Station. The Central Valley Project, the Feather River Project, the San Luis Project, and a rash of Engineer Corps dams on San Joaquin Valley streams are bringing water to this land. Meantime Florida has run off with the lion's share of the U.S. citrus industry, easily filling the shortage left by Los Angeles. Italy and Israel are beginning to wonder where they will ever market the surpluses from all their new acreage soon to bear. The problem is going to be to find markets for the produce of all the new groves now coming into bearing—groves planted closer, with better stock, and managed more knowledgeably than the declining old Los Angeles groves they are replacing.

Homes, factories, stores, and theaters make very intensive use of land and these uses must be clustered because of the frequent movement back and forth and other heavy interaction. Farming, on the other hand, is an extensive land use, which suffers little from being isolated; the farmer makes relatively few trips to the various urban "buildings." It is not surprising then that farms will continually be displaced when they come in contact with expanding cities. The free market is, more often than not, doing its job very efficiently when it effects the orderly transfer of fringe land from rural to urban uses. This is no way denies that society may choose to subsidize the continuation of farming at the edge of a rapidly growing urban area to preserve "open space." But the farm becomes, in effect, an urban land use—its value lies in its spillover benefits as an urban amenity.

[2]Mason Gaffney, "Containment Policies for Urban Sprawl," *Approaches to the Study of Urbanization* (Lawrence: University of Kansas Press, 1964).

Rules of Play

This experiment retains most of the rules of Basic CLUG, along with the introduction of a new form of land use, the farm. Play begins at Round 1 with no urban land uses in existence; rather, each team owns a farm consisting of twenty-five contiguous parcels of land and a farm building, the FM unit. Figure II-1 illustrates the initial layout of Primary Roads, Terminal,

Figure II-1. Location of Primary Roads, Terminal, Utility Plant, Team Holdings, and Site of Each Team's FM Unit

	52	54	56	58	60	62	64	66	68	70	72	74
2	R	R	R		Y	Y	G	G	Hill	Hill	Hill	Hill
4	R	R	R	Y	Y	Y	G	G	R	R	R	Hill
6	R	R	Y	R	R	Y FM	G	G		R	R	Hill
8	R		Y	Y	R	Y	G	G	R	R	R	R
10	R	BL	Y		Y	R	R	R FM	G	G	G	G
12	BL	BL	Y	BR	Y	Y	R	G FM	G	G		G
14		BL	Y	BL	BR	BR	G	BR	G	G	G	G
16	Y	Y	BL	BL	BL	BR	BR	G	BR	BR	BR	BR
18	Hill	Y	BL	BL	BL	BL	BR FM	BR	G	BR	BR	BR
20	Hill	Y	Y	BL	BL	BL FM	BL	G	BR	BR	BR	BR
22	Hill	Y	Y	Y	BL	BL		BL	BR	BR	BR	BR
24	Hill	Hill	Hill	Y	BL	BL	BL	BL	BR	BR	BR	BR

R = Red
Y = Yellow
G = Green
BL = Blue
BR = Brown

—— Secondary Road (mode weight=2)
∎∎∎ Primary Road (mode weight=1)

Hill

□ Terminal

○ Utility Plant

Utility Plant, team holdings, and the location of each team's FM unit. Table II-1 (see page 40) gives the probable levels of income for different sizes of farms according to their probabilities of occurrence for the first stage of the experiment. Table II-2 (see page 41) gives the same information for the second stage of the experiment. The first stage of the experiment ends at the end of Round 9 and the Stage II innovations are introduced at the beginning of the tenth round.

STAGE I

The FM unit can be constructed at a cost of $20,000 and is assessed at this level. Its rate of depreciation is the same as other buildings in CLUG, five per cent per round. The unit is self-employed but has the same basic demands for LS and CS goods as a normal residential unit in CLUG. The FM unit represents both the farm population unit and the associated buildings and equipment, resulting in higher construction cost than for a comparable residential unit. It is provided with a Private Service Plant, so that construction on parcels not serviced by Utility Lines is now possible. The cost of construction of a Private Service Plant is $1,000 for a plant serving a single FM unit. The Maintenance Charge on such a plant is $500 per round. When a parcel of land containing an FM unit becomes serviced by normal Utility Lines the per round Maintenance Charge on the Private Service Plant need no longer be paid. In Stage I the Private Service Plant may only be used for very low density units, i.e., the FM unit.

Farms may operate in any of three sizes with a single FM unit: 20-24 parcels of land, 25-36 parcels, and 37 or more parcels. Any farm containing less than 20 parcels is considered inoperative and receives no farm income. Other size classes take effect in the second stage of the experiment.

Each team begins the game with a working farm, 25 contiguous parcels of land in farming, an FM unit provided with a Private Service Plant, and $35,000 in cash. Each farm parcel is assessed at $500, and the initial Tax Rate is set at 3 per cent in order to pay for the only community expense in effect at this time: the $1000 per residential unit charge for social services that also applies to FM units.

Step 1 (Purchase Land) functions in the same manner as in Basic CLUG except that the instructor will accept bids for land as low as $500 per parcel. To become part of an operating farm, a new land parcel must touch one parcel of the original farm on at least one corner. Teams may still buy as much land from each other as desired at whatever price they can agree upon.

Step 2 (Provide Utilities) remains the same—with the additional rule that any team may construct and pay for a Private Service Plant. Such a PSP can service only an FM unit. Utility Lines from the Utility Plant must be provided for any urban land use. Prior construction of a PSP on a lot does not in any way reduce the later cost of servicing that parcel with normal Utility Lines. Costs for PSP construction ($1,000) and maintenance ($500) are paid directly to the instructor by the Owner.

Step 3 (Renovate Buildings) and the chance of the loss of a building are the same as in Basic CLUG. If an FM unit is lost by the dice roll in a round divisible by five, the farm may be continued in operation only by the construction of a new FM unit and its associated Private Service Plant on a different parcel.

Construction in Step 4 is the same as in Basic CLUG, along with the additional possibility of constructing new FM units as desired at $20,000 each.

Step 5 (Designate Employment) follows Basic CLUG rules except that FM units are self employed.

Step 6 (Sign Trade Agreements) is unchanged from Basic CLUG.

Step 7 (Receive Income) remains unchanged for urban land uses; it also provides an additional income mechanism for the FM units. Each individual FM owner must roll a pair of dice to determine the level of income for his own farm. Table II-1 gives three levels of income for each of three sizes of farm unit and the probabilities of obtaining each income level together with the corresponding winning numbers on a pair of dice.

Table II-1. Farm Income Levels by Probability and Size of Farm — Stage I Technology

Probability	Winning Numbers	Size of Farm		
		20 to 24 Parcels	25 to 36 Parcels	37 + Parcels
.25	8,9	$8,000	$12,000	$18,000
.42	2,3,4,5,6	10,000	14,000	20,000
.33	7,10,11,12	12,000	16,000	22,000

Step 8 (Pay Employees) for urban land units is unchanged. As self-employed units, FM units have no payroll.

Step 9 (Pay LS, CS, and O) is identical with Step 9 in Basic CLUG. Each FM unit must purchase these items every round in the same fashion as a single residential unit, and has the same kinds of transportation costs if purchases are made from units on the board. An FM unit does not have any payments to O in Stage I.

Step 10 (Pay Transportation Costs) is operated in the Basic CLUG manner for urban uses. FM units must pay to ship their products to be Terminal at an Association Weight of $1000. The relative weights for Primary and Secondary Roads are set at 1:2 for State I.

Step 11 (Pay Taxes) operates under the same mechanisms as in Basic CLUG. The costs are somewhat lower until urban development occurs, however, since individual teams must pay their own utility costs through payments for construction and maintenance of Private Service Plants. Payment for maintenance of individual PSP's is made at this Step. Following Step 11 of Round 9, the Stage II innovations are introduced.

A summary of the new information and changes needed for Stage I of this experiment is provided on a tear-out sheet at the back of this manual. It is entitled "Summary of Changes for Rural-Urban Interdependence Experiment—Stage I."

STAGE II

At the beginning of Round 10, a number of changes are introduced to provide a pattern of growth more approximate to developments in this century. Changes in transportation technology result in a general upgrading of all North-South roads. Mode Weights between Major Highways and Primary Roads are set at a ratio of ½:1. An additional Major Highway is added to intersect the existing road at the Terminal. Technological improvements in farming make the construction of FM units more expensive, allow the operation of larger farms, increase the level of farm income, and make the operation of very small farms impossible. Organizational changes in marketing have provided increases in farm income and have decreased the variations in income between individual farmers. R1 residential units are now allowed to be serviced by a Private Service Plant.

No further changes in **Step 1** (Purchase Land) occur in this stage.

Step 2 (Provide Utilities) is unchanged, but the cost for maintenance of a Private Service Plant is increased to $800 per Round and R1 units may also use Private Service Plants.

Step 3: The same Basic CLUG provisions for renovation and depreciation of buildings apply. If the owner of an FM unit wishes to operate his farm at the new technological level, he must fully renovate his FM in Round 10, as well as pay the increased capital costs of $20,000 in order to bring his unit up to Stage II technology.

Step 4 (Construct Buildings) is unchanged other than the increased costs ($40,000) for constructing new FM units.

Step 5 (Designate Employment) remains the same as in Basic CLUG.

Step 6 (Sign Trade Agreements) continues in the same manner but transportation costs are reduced by half or more due to improvements in transportation.

Step 7 (Receive Income) is unchanged for urban uses from Stage I and Basic CLUG. Farm income depends on both the size of the farm and the level of technology at which the farm is operated. Those farms which are not brought up to the new level of technology continue to operate under the provisions of Table II-1. A single roll of the pair of dice now determines income for all farms at once regardless of age or technology. Farmers who have advanced to the higher level of technology are governed by the income provisions of Table II-2. Note that farms of less than twenty-five parcels are no longer productive.

Table II-2. Farm Income Levels by Probability and Size of Farm — Stage II Technology

Probability	Winning Numbers	Size of Farm		
		25 to 36 Parcels	37 to 49 Parcels	50 + Parcels
.11	9	$10,500	$13,000	$24,000
.39	7,8,11,12	11,500	14,000	25,000
.50	2,3,4,5,6,10	12,500	15,000	26,000

Step 8 (Pay Employees) is unchanged. FM units continue as self-employed activities.

Step 9: Payments to LS and CS continue unchanged. FM units must now make a payment for Office services. The instructor's price is $1,000 a round for an FM unit. The FM Association Weights to Offices are the same ($100) as for LS and CS to Office.

Step 10: Transportation costs are lower due to improvements in transportation technology represented by the Major Highway: Primary Road Mode Weights are set at ½:1. All Association Weights are unchanged except for the new cost for travel to Office for FM units.

Step 11 (Pay Taxes) is substantially the same, with the Maintenance Charge for Private Service Plants now increased to $800 for an R1 or FM unit using such facilities.

A summary of the new information and changes needed for Stage II of this experiment is provided on a tear-out sheet at the back of this manual. It is entitled "Summary of Changes for Rural-Interdependence Experiment— Stage II."

Discussion

During Stage I, several rounds will probably pass with almost no activity other than gradual acquisition of farm land and the accumulation of capital through farm incomes received. The beginnings of urban growth will appear when a few teams have accumulated enough capital for the fairly substantial costs of Partial or Full Industries. The need for Utility Lines and increased social service costs for urban residents will probably result in increasing Tax Rates. Both higher Tax Rates and the use of farm land near the Terminal for urban development may cause some teams to drop out of farming even before Round 10 and the beginning of Stage II. A more rapid expansion of urban development and increased "sprawl" will probably become apparent early in Stage II at the same time that farms still in existence are moving toward larger size and higher levels of technology and income. The stabilization of market prices among all farmers represented by the single dice roll, together with their higher levels of income, may produce changes in the competition among farm teams for any remaining farm land.

Study Questions

Questions appropriate for discussion during play and at the end of Stages I and II include:

1. To what degree is "urban sprawl" evidenced during Stage I and Stage II? Does this phenomenon seem to have more impact on urban management and taxes or on farm operation?

2. What factors were important in decisions by individual players to move out of farming? Did the increasing level of taxation with urban development have any relation to these decisions?

3. Would a separate taxing district for urban and rural areas have had positive or negative effects on retaining land in farming?

4. Did some farm owners take large profits on the sale of farm land for urban uses or from developing these parcels for urban uses themselves?

5. Were these profits reflected in assessed values of nearby properties? Who earned this profit—the original farmer, or those who created the urban growth? Did these profits bear upon the accumulation of capital for urban investment and the decision to move out of farming?

6. As technological and organizational changes continue will farming become more important or less important as a form of investment competitive with urban investment?

7. Are the levels of farm income sufficient to justify the increasing capital and operating costs of farming? If increases in farm income due to increased productivity were not great enough, who would pay for additional increases? What effect might this produce on LS and CS prices charged by the instructor?

Experiment III:
Transportation and Technology

Introduction

Technological innovation has played a major role in the growth and development of cities and regions throughout the world. While improvements in technology have not been sufficient causes of city growth, they have certainly been necessary components in the evolution of today's urban society. Changes in the technology of transportation have opened new avenues of inter-regional trade and significantly altered patterns of development within regions. Advances in the technology of energy production and consumption have decreased the costs of power while increasing energy availability and usage. Industries have become more efficient, more independent of the natural environment, and better able to orient to a variety of external markets. Commercial activities have expanded their local service areas by attracting customers from wider and more extensive developed areas. Households have spread to previously rural lands. Technological innovations have, in general, lessened the dependence of cities on the natural environment, and expanded considerably their opportunities for growth.

Transportation

Three developments in transportation have been of particular historical significance in the United States.

Prior to the 19th century, the major means of transferring goods and persons across space was by horse or other animal driven conveyance along trails and roadways only marginally improved over the open countryside. Inter-regional trade was minimal except between a few sea and river port cities. Cities were limited in both size and area by the high cost of transport. At the beginning of the 19th century, with the construction of canal systems new markets were opened and trade between regions increased. Though port and handling costs were high, canals were well suited for shipping heavy goods long distances. Tightly compacted cities developed at intervals along these new lines of communication.

Rail transport was the second major innovation to influence the rate of city growth. Less fixed to naturally favorable sites than water transport and having lower construction costs, railroads further expanded the external markets available for locally-produced goods. Like water, rail transport had high terminal and loading costs relative to costs for shipping heavy goods to distant markets. The tightly compacted pattern of city structure was maintained though growth increased due to additional economic activity.

The third, and the most influential, advance in transportation technology was the invention of automobile and highway transport. With even less dependence on favorable natural sites and lower construction costs than previous technologies, highways were constructed extensively. External markets were thus further increased, yielding accelerated rates of urban growth. Particularly important has been the effect that the automobile has had on the internal structure of the American city. While previously clustered around water and rail loading points, development has been allowed to expand along highways and secondary roads into previously rural hinterlands. Figure 1 in the reading by Hoover clearly illustrates the explosive character of these developments.

Energy

Three equally important innovations in the production and consumption of energy have also occurred which have influenced the rate and pattern of urban growth in the United States.

The first major source of energy for industrial production was water power. This derivation of power directly from natural water movement meant that economic activity was confined to a limited number of naturally-favored locations. At these sites, limited and highly localized urban development took place.

The adoption of steam as a source of power was a second advance in the technology of energy production. While requiring substantial amounts of fuel, coal could be transported, unlike water power. Some flexibility in location was thus granted to industry.

Electrical power was the third and most important advance to occur in energy production. Because electricity can be generated in large quantities and cheaply transported along lines for great distances, this advance has had important consequences for the location of economic activity. On a local scale, energy has been made available to virtually all sites, thus removing the locational constraints imposed by water power and, to an extent, by steam power. At the same time that unit production costs for energy have been declining, industry has altered its production methods to use increasing amounts of energy, though at a lower total cost, resulting in more efficient operations.

The net effect of these advances in production and consumption of energy has been to allow industry to expand its realm of possible locations by orienting increasingly toward markets rather than energy sources. This general outward reorientation of industry, along with concomitant developments in transportation technology, has made rapid rates of urban growth and area expansion possible. Many of the basic characteristics and problems of cities in the United States today are reflections of these technological evolutions.

The Reading and Experiment

The reading which follows presents a more extensive discussion of some of the points made above. Although Hoover identifies two additional technological innovations—changes in materials usage, and maturation of industries—this experiment will restrict consideration to the factors of transportation (transfer, in Hoover's terms) and energy. The experiment is divided into three stages that represent three technological periods. Stage I deals with water transport and water power; Stage II with rail transport and steam power; and Stage III with highway transport and electrical power. The experiment is designed so that stages can be played either separately or built up sequentially playing one upon the end results of another in an evolutionary fashion.

TECHNOLOGY AND LOCATIONAL CHANGE

Edgar M. Hoover

1. Effect of Improved Transfer Service

Changes in transfer costs and services play a peculiarly significant part in locational evolution. Each innovation (turnpikes, canals, railroads, steamships, telegraph, telephone, electric transit, automobiles, radio, or aircraft) cheapens transfer and at the same time alters the whole structure of transfer costs and the locational significance of distance and volume. The consequent recasting of the over-all locational pattern makes some locations economically obsolete but opens up investment opportunities in new areas and is thus closely associated with variations in the total *amount* as well as the *location* of investment and economic activity.[1]

Let us first consider the effects of the general downward trend in transfer costs. Not only have rates fallen, but the quality of transportation and communication service has steadily improved.[2] In the absence of any other changes, the effect of all-round cheaper transfer is to give greater locational influence to differences in processing costs.[3]

Transfer costs link the production of consumers' goods and services to the pattern of consumer demand and link the earlier stages of processing to the pattern of extractive activity. In both cases, these costs have a decentralizing influence, since consumer markets and most kinds of extractive activity are relatively scattered. Exploitation of the advantages of concentrated processing is impeded by the necessity of keeping distribution and procurement costs down. In terms of the economy of areas, transfer costs encourage self-sufficiency by protecting local industries against outside competition.

Cheaper transfer means some relaxation of these constraints. Industries distributing to relatively scattered markets find they can now serve them just as well from a greater distance and concentrate their operations in fewer,

---

[1] See Walter Isard, Transportation Development and Building Cycles, *Quarterly Journal of Economics*, vol. LVII, No. 1, November, 1942, pp. 90–112, and The Transport-Building Cycle, *Review of Economic Statistics*, November, 1942; Caroline and Walter Isard, Economic Implications of Aircraft, *Quarterly Journal of Economics*, vol. LIX, No. 2, February, 1945, pp. 145–169. Isard ascribes six major waves of investment and locational change in the United States to transport innovations as follows: canals (beginning about 1830); railroads (1843, 1862, 1878); electric railways (1895); automobiles (1918); and foresees a comparable structural change coming from the development of aircraft in the immediate future. He is concerned only with goods and passenger transport and does not consider the effects of innovations in communication apart from air mail.

[2] For further details see 79th Congress, 1st Session, Senate Document No. 76: Board of Investigation and Research, "Technological Trends in Transportation," 1944.

[3] This statement ignores possible changes in the *structure* of transfer costs, which are taken up in Section 2. It is also to be noted that the locational effects of improved transfer can be offset if processing-cost differentials are reduced at the same time by enhanced mobility of labor and capital or by technical developments favoring small-scale production.

larger, and more efficient processing units, each with a larger market area.[4] Correspondingly, industries collecting materials from relatively scattered sources now find it possible to concentrate processing operations in fewer, larger, and more efficient units, each with a larger supply area.[5] Any particular community or region becomes less self-sufficient, and interregional trade grows on the basis of specialization according to processing advantages.[6]

2. Effect of Changes in the Structure of Transfer Costs

The level of transfer costs does not change simultaneously everywhere. Each advance in methods of transfer favors routes particularly well suited to the new techniques, and these routes may constitute a very limited network. Thus the introduction of canals in the United States in the early nineteenth century put increased emphasis on relative transfer advantages, favoring a small number of locations. The development of new means of transfer with different cost and rate structures alters cost relations between long and short hauls, between large and small shipments, and between different kinds of traffic. All these changes have important locational implications.

Railroads and Shipping Services. Their terminal costs are high, but line-haul costs are low, so that rates per ton-mile drop off sharply for longer hauls. The route networks, also, are much less dense than highway networks.

---

[4] ". . . the general improvement in transportation service has operated to permit manufacturers to consolidate their warehouse stocks at the more important distribution centers. . . . The time on carload shipments [between Chicago and Minneapolis] has been reduced from 3 or 4 days to 36 hours. As a result in some lines it is no longer necessary to carry stocks of merchandise in both Chicago and the Twin Cities." R. S. Vaile and A. L. Nordstrom, "Public Merchandise Warehousing in the Twin Cities," University of Minnesota Studies in Economics and Business, *Bulletin* 3, p. 40, Minneapolis, 1932; quoted in National Resources Planning Board, *op. cit.*, p. 76n.

[5] "In the past it was the custom to establish cheese factories from 2 to 4 miles apart. This was no doubt due partially at least to the bad condition of roads over which milk had to be hauled in wagons. A short hauling distance was necessary in order that the farmer might deliver his milk to the factory in a suitable condition for cheese making. Under such conditions, the small factory may serve satisfactorily; but where roads have been improved and the automobile truck is extensively used, few and larger factories are being built. At present factories operate very successfully in warm climates and collect the milk in trucks within a radius of 20 to 25 miles of the factory." Points to Consider in Establishing a Cheese Factory, *U. S. Department of Agriculture Miscellaneous Publication* 42, Washington, 1928, p. 5. *Cf.* also the parallel case of sugar-beet collection, noted in the discussion of Fig. 3·2, [in Edgar M. Hoover, *The Location of Economic Activity*].

[6] For local industries previously sheltered from outside competition, this involves a sometimes painful readjustment. Danish wheat growers, for instance, converted to dairying when transport improvements brought cheap New World wheat to Europe in the latter nineteenth century. More recently, improvement of milk transport into United States cities has widened milksheds and forced some readjustments on the nearer dairymen, as the following quotation shows: "Decreased cost of transportation and preservation of good quality in milk shipped by tank car is opening up new areas of potential supply and developing competition such as the highly specialized diarymen in the most northern part of the state [Indiana] have never experienced before. . . . The identical milk market conditions that have caused many dairymen in extreme northern Indiana to become greatly discouraged and pessimistic concerning the outlook for the future have caused dairymen around Francesville and in similar grain producing areas to take a new lease on life." "What is Happening to Agriculture in Northwestern Indiana?", *Purdue University Agricultural Experiment Station Bulletin* 321, p. 8, 1928.

Railroad and waterway transport development, as a result of these characteristics, has been especially significant for *interregional* specialization. Individual regions have been enabled to concentrate on certain branches of production, serving widespread markets and using materials gathered at a distance, but the *local* pattern of towns and cities and within small districts was not radically changed by the advent of these means of transport. Trains and ships are large transport units, particularly adapted to cheap transport in bulk; consequently they favor the concentration of production in large plants. Finally, their high proportion of costs other than those of line haul is the basis for a large latitude of discrimination in the rates on different classes of traffic. It has already been indicated in Section 3·5 that this discrimination usually runs in favor of materials as against their products, on account of the lower unit value of the materials and consequently greater elasticity of demand for transport. This discrimination, by inflating delivery costs relative to procurement costs, encourages orientation to markets.

Automobile Transport. This has a higher proportion of costs varying with distance and therefore a more nearly proportional progression of costs with length of haul. The investment required for establishing a route is small. It is particularly adapted, then, to short hauls between a great number of points over a very dense network of routes.

Consequently the principal effect is not upon interregional specialization but upon the structure of metropolitan and other local areas. Retail shops can draw customers and factories can draw labor from greater distances; so both are enabled to expand in size. Still more important is the fact that necessary movements and contacts within the metropolitan area no longer call for such close crowding as before. A notable loosening, sometimes graphically described as "explosive" growth, has been observed in American cities in the past two or three decades. Residence has been greatly decentralized by the automobile; business establishments seeking the advantages of the local labor market or close contact with other local manufacturing, servicing, or distributing enterprises can retain these advantages with a more suburban location than before.

. . .

At this point, we may glance at some graphic evidence of the "explosive" character of the change. Figure 1 shows the built-up areas of Baltimore, Washington, and Chicago before and after (or during) the explosion. It will be observed that the outward extension has followed the radial pattern of main highways but has left interstitial areas vacant. Many gaps are caused by rapid settlement just outside municipal boundaries, to avoid taxes and building restrictions, before the territory within the city itself has been fully built up.

The effect upon agriculture in the zones immediately tributary to cities is complex. Direct trucking of produce to urban markets offers little or no cost reduction in the remoter parts of large supply areas where the long-haul

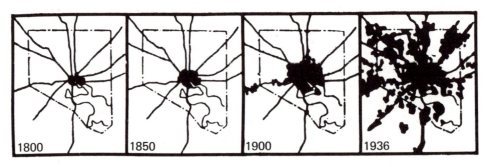

BALTIMORE

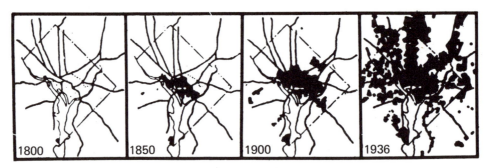

WASHINGTON

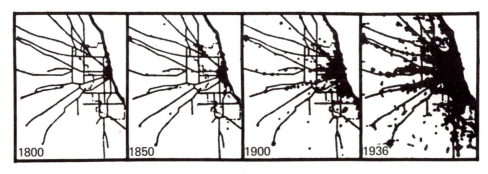

CHICAGO

Figure 1 Expansion of the built-up areas of Baltimore, Washington, and Chicago. The main highways that appear in the series of diagrams for each city have been unchanged in location throughout the period covered. Different scales have been used in mapping the three cities. (*Reproduced from Interregional Highways, message from the President transmitting report of National Interregional Highway Committee, Fig. 26, p. 55, 78th Congress, 2d Session, House Document No. 379, Washington, 1944.*)

advantages of railroads come into play.[7] For shorter hauls the use of trucks has tended to equalize distribution costs as between large and small producers and as between producers near railroad stations or processing plants and those more distant from such points. It seems likely, then, that a comprehensive examination of the development of local supply areas around cities in the past few decades would show an increasing correspondence to actual distance from the city, with particular kinds of production such as fluid milk developing more and more coherent doughnut-shaped production zones.[8]

Air Transport.[9] This method too has characteristic economic features that determine its locational effect. Advantages are high speed, low costs of route establishment and maintenance, small unit of movement, *i.e.*, the capacity of a single plane as compared with that of a train or a ship, and almost complete freedom of movement in direct lines regardless of terrain. Its handicaps, which are being reduced, are high line-haul costs, extensive terminal-space requirements, dependence on weather, and the dangers and difficulties of use by nonprofessional pilots.

The high line-haul costs seem likely to prevent air freight from competing with existing rail and water carriers on anything but valuable and urgent express shipments during the foreseeable future. No direct effect upon the location of heavy manufactures or the most important branches of extractive industry is to be anticipated.[10] Indirectly, however, air transport is already greatly accelerating the industrialization of undeveloped areas by carrying key personnel, equipment, and supplies as well as some compact materials and products and providing that contact with industrialized areas which seems to be necessary to boost backward regions over the threshold of industrialization.[11] The great advantages of air transport in such areas are its

---

[7] It was found some years ago that in the New York City milkshed, "tank trucks have a decided advantage over the railroads on short-haul traffic, but the advantage decreases with distance. Apparently truck costs are about equal to rail rates at 200 miles. Beyond that, rail transportation usually is cheaper." H. R. Varney, Transportation of Milk and Cream to the New York Market, *Cornell University Agricultural Experiment Station Bulletin* 655, p. 40, Ithaca, N. Y., 1936.

[8] R. D. McKenzie, in "The Metropolitan Community," p. 80, McGraw-Hill Book Company, Inc., New York, 1933, envisaged a trend toward more compact local agricultural supply areas. The greater emphasis on perishable products (milk and fresh vegetables) and rapid direct marketing does work in that direction, offsetting to some extent the reduction in transfer costs for any given haul.

[9] For further details see the informative and stimulating article by Caroline and Walter Isard, Economic Implications of Aircraft, *Quarterly Journal of Economics*, vol. LIX, No. 2, February, 1945, pp. 145–169, and W. F. Ogburn, "The Social Effects of Aviation," Houghton Mifflin Company, Boston, 1945.

[10] In terms of tonnage, air-freight traffic is still negligible. Only about 0.01 per cent of the total intercity commodity traffic in the United States in 1946 was carried by air [table cited here]. The relative significance of air freight is, of course, much greater in countries where surface transport is less well developed. In 1938 the top five countries in air-freight tonnage were the USSR, New Guinea, Canada, Honduras, and Colombia (Isard, *op. cit.*). For long-distance passenger transport the air lines are already competing advantageously with railroads and ships. For analyses of the potential market for air transport see Air Transport of Agricultural Perishables, *U. S. Department of Agriculture Miscellaneous Publication* 585, 1946 and Ogburn, *op. cit.*, Chap. 8 and *passim*.

[11] Such problems of regional transition are discussed in the next chapter.

disregard of surface barriers and the low capital requirements for establishing routes. Indirectly, then, air transport may pave the way to an earlier development of the surface-transport facilities necessary to exploit the bulkier resources of undeveloped areas like the interiors of China and Brazil.

As an improved means of maintaining personal contacts over long distances, the airplane will thus speed the integration of backward regions into the more advanced industrial economy. Within and between more developed regions as well, it facilitates the extension of control over branch plants and the maintenance of contacts with distant suppliers or customers. Some further expansion of market and supply areas, then, should result even in cases where the materials or products involved are not themselves shipped by air. The mobility of capital and enterprise is being rapidly increased. Without air transport for key personnel, it seems doubtful that so many industrial firms could have been induced in the period 1940 to 1944 to take on the operation of new war plants making unfamiliar products at great distances from the center of operations of the firm.

The design of cities must, of course, make provision for airports and their connection with the local surface-traffic system. Whether or not air transport will really revolutionize metropolitan structure, as Isard and others have suggested,[12] seems to depend on the extent to which present handicaps of runway requirements and difficulty of nonprofessional operation can be overcome. If the family helicopter becomes a reality, it will have just as revolutionary locational effects as the family automobile. Effects upon metropolitan structure analogous to those of the automobile, but greatly magnified in distance terms, are to be expected. Residence and some services, light industry, and trade may decentralize explosively. Industrial centers with some tributary resident population will remain, as will likewise the principal centers of finance, administration, and specialized trade. Particular significance will attach to the points or zones of connection between air and ground transport—perhaps a ring of air stations and parking spaces surrounding the city centers.

Means of Communication. The concept of "transfer," of course, includes more than just the transportation of goods. Personal contact is a vital part of many commercial relations and involves passenger transport by any or all of the agencies already discussed. Those offering the greatest speed and frequency of service (associated with small units of traffic movement) naturally are of the greatest importance in facilitating contact at a distance, which accounts for the fact that automobile and air transport have already attained preeminence in this regard out of all proportion to their relative importance as carriers of tonnage freight.

Contact is also effected by the transmission of messages alone, which likewise puts a premium on speed rather than low tonnage rates. The fastest medium of carriage, aircraft, seems about to take over completely the job of carrying nonlocal letters. Instantaneous communication by telegraph, telephone, radio, and television has progressively made easier the coordination

---

[12] Isard, *op. cit.*, and references there cited.

of economic activity and the standardization of tastes, which in turn facilitate both the spread and the specialization of industries.

3. Technical Maturing of Industries

Changes in labor requirements, generally as the result of a modification of processes, exert profound effects on the locational patterns of industries. As indicated in earlier chapters, an industry requiring specialized or highly trained labor generally has a concentrated and rather stable pattern, clustering at points where such a labor supply has gradually developed. But eventually the processes of almost any industry become routinized, through technical and managerial improvements, so that ordinary labor without special training can be used. [13] The normal result is that the industry spreads or moves to other areas, its dispersion from the original centers being sped by the relatively high wages and inflexible conditions that have become established there by the skilled elite. [14] Some technical changes involve so much mechanization as to make labor supply an inconsequential factor, in which case the industry may reorient itself in relation to whatever other considerations were next in importance.

The locational histories of individual industries have very often—one may almost say "typically"—involved an early stage of increasing concentration followed by a later stage of redispersion. [15] This sequence can be explained largely on the basis of the supply of labor and management personnel. When an industry is young and its problems unfamiliar, it prospers best in those few places which provide the combination of appropriate basic skills (generally developed in preexistent similar industries), together with experienced managers and some venturesome enterprises and financial backers. The product is then perfected and standardized, the best methods of cheap large-scale manufacturing are worked out in those places, and the economies of mass production and geographical concentration assert themselves. The rise of Detroit to preeminence in automobile manufacturing is an example.

Ultimately the industry and its main production center "mature," in the sense that the rate of growth of market has slackened off, the fundamental questions of product design have been settled, and the necessary specialized machinery has been devised. It is then that a dispersion phase often sets in. When the technical uncertainties of production and the commercial uncertainties of market development are reduced to a point where other locations may successfully cope with them, independent outside competition may arise. Even before that, however, the labor skill requirements may have been so reduced that established firms in the main center of the industry are free

---

[13] "Routinization" means merely the standardization and simplification of the individual worker's task so as to make less demand on his skill. But once a process has been resolved into repetitive operations, it becomes possible to do most or all of those operations by machinery. Routinization thus normally leads in practice to a considerable degree of mechanization.

[14] Cf. Section 7·4 [of Hoover, *The Location of Economic Activity*].

[15] This historical pattern was stressed by Malcolm Keir in "Manufacturing," The Ronald Press Company, New York, 1928.

to consider branch plants in areas of lower labor cost or closer to market and in extreme cases, *e.g.*, the New England cotton-textile industry, may gradually move the bulk of their operations elsewhere.

This common association of decentralization with maturity does not by any means imply, however, that industry *as a whole* will or should progressively decentralize. New industries are continually being born. In their early stages, before they become fully mechanized, these are especially likely to be dependent on versatile labor and venturesome capital. It is found that the larger and better established industrial centers play a leading part as germinating grounds for new industries. [16] Some evidence on this point is provided by D. B. Creamer's analysis of census data:

> In view of the abundant evidence of an ever-decreasing share of wage jobs located in the principal cities [of industrial areas], it is of interest that the highest birth rates in both durable and semidurable goods industries have been in the principal cities. On the other hand, despite the relative growth in manufacturing importance of the industrial peripheries, these communities have a relatively low [industrial] birth rate. The data on relocated establishments suggest that the periphery towns have grown chiefly by the immigration of manufacturing plants and their expansion subsequent to relocation. . . .
>
> Another result that seems very clear is that the bulk of the loss of wage jobs due to relocated establishments has been sustained by the principal cities of the industrial areas. . . . This loss has been shared to a lesser extent and with exception of 1930–1931 by the large satellite cities (B) of the industrial areas. The chief recipient of the gains in each case has been the industrial peripheries (C). The next largest gains were in the communities in the "All the rest" category (G) with the exception of 1928–1929 when the second largest share of the gains was received by the important industrial counties (F). [17]

4. Changes in Material Requirements

Improvements of processing methods have altered the balance of advantage between market and material orientation in specific lines of production. The locational effect of a technical change increasing the yield of products relative to materials is, of course, generally an enhanced attraction toward markets. Thus in the coke industry, the replacement of beehive ovens by by-product ovens has shifted most of the industry from the coal towns to the vicinity of the iron- and steelworks where the coke and by-product gas are used. The bulkiness of the chief additional product, gas, is the principal reason for this shift.

---

[16] There is food for thought in the contrast shown here between the behavior of industrial enterprises and that of people. Human beings seem to reproduce more bountifully in a rural than an urban environment, which gives rise to a characteristic current of cityward migration. New businesses, on the other hand, spring up in the more densely settled areas in greater numbers, and such migration as occurs is more often outward.

[17] Carter Goodrich and others, "Migration and Economic Opportunity," pp. 334, 340–341. University of Pennsylvania Press, Philadelphia, 1936.

In cases where one material is substituted for another, the locational effect depends on the importance and sources of the materials involved. The substitution of extracts and synthetic tanning agents for crude bark and other vegetable materials in the leather industry has freed tanneries from dependence on nearness to forests and allowed them to concentrate at points better located in relation to hide supply and markets. Where the bark supplies themselves are close to hides and markets, however, they are still a basis for tannery location.[18]

Another important basis of change in material requirements and in location is the fact that large-scale production or concentrated and specialized production in general calls for materials that can be supplied in large quantities and over long periods to a single processing point. Wood charcoal and bog iron ore are adequate materials for isolated local ironworks operating on a small scale, but output equal to that of a large blast furnace would quickly exhaust local supplies of this character. The replacement of extensively produced by intensively produced materials is reflected in a greater concentration of the industries oriented to those materials.

The third major change in process requirements is a very rapid increase in the use of nonhuman energy. It would seem that this must increase the locational importance of energy sources, but that has not always been the case. The changing locational significance of energy use is important and complex enough to warrant discussion in a separate section which follows.

5. Energy Utilization and Transmission

New techniques of energy utilization and transmission always affect the location patterns of at least some industries. Not only are costs of energy lowered, but the newer forms have generally been more transportable than the old and either more or less adaptable to the needs of small users. Thus the whole pattern of costs with reference to location and scale is changed for each industry.

Although the consumption of energy in production has rapidly increased, energy sources have not necessarily become a more important factor of location. In some periods the contrary has been true. Energy has become steadily cheaper; moreover, it has become progressively easier to transport fuels and electricity, which means that geographic differences in energy costs have diminished. No two new developments in energy have had quite the same effect on the over-all locational pattern.

Water Wheels. These were the first device used on a considerable scale for the conversion of nonhuman energy and naturally attracted industries to natural water-power sites. As long as the energy secured was nontransportable, the plants concerned had to concentrate at the site itself. The growth of textile manufacturing along the streams of New England is well known,

---

[18] See E. M. Hoover, "Location Theory and the Shoe and Leather Industries," Chap. IX, Harvard Economic Studies, vol. LV, Harvard University Press, Cambridge, Mass., 1937, and L. C. Brown, S.J., "Union Policies in the Leather Industry," Harvard University Press, Cambridge, Mass., 1947.

the largest developments being those at Lowell, Manchester, Lawrence, Holyoke, and Lewiston before the Civil War.[19]

Steam Engines. This form of power provided a means for converting fuel into mechanical energy and could be set up wherever fuel was obtainable. Since in this case the material (though not the energy itself) was transportable, the locational effect was more elastic. Energy costs reflected primarily the costs of transporting coal from the mines.

This pattern of energy costs contrasted sharply with that set by water power. Especially before the coming of the railroad, coal was cheapest along navigable water rather than in the back-country locations where small and easily exploited water-power sites abounded. The locational effect was to concentrate industry on navigable water as well as in the coal regions themselves. To refer again to the history of the New England textile industry, the application of steam power to cotton spinning and weaving led to the rapid growth of the industry in the Fall River—New Bedford area after the middle of the nineteenth century.[20] In the same period, a rapid growth of heavy industry occurred near the Pennsylvania coal mines. Steam also provided an indefinitely expansible energy source, permitting manufacturing agglomerations much larger than could have been sustained by direct use of water power. Steam power and its application to transport in the railroad locomotive were the principal factors in the revolutionary concentration and urbanization of industry that occurred in the nineteenth century in Europe and North America.

It should be noted, though, that continued improvement in the utilization and transport of fuel has reduced the importance of nearness to fuel sources, so that only certain groups of industries (notably ferrous metallurgy, heavy chemicals, cement, ceramics, glass and primary metal processing) are still influenced significantly by geographic differences in fuel costs.[21]

[19] T. R. Smith, "The Cotton Textile Industry of Fall River, Massachusetts—A Study of Industrial Localizations," Table 8, p. 42, King's Crown Press, New York, 1944 (processed).

[20] "Fall River's rise to the position of the leading textile center in New England was the beginning of the shift of the locational center of gravity in the industry toward the southern coast of New England. This was in large measure made possible by the changing competitive position of coal and water as sources of power for the expanding industry .... Competitive equality between the two as sources of power for new plants had been reached before 1870. This was the result of two closely related developments which took place during the 20 years prior to the Civil War. The first of these was the increasing scarcity of large, easily developed, conveniently located water privileges upon which such an important part of the textile capacity of 1850 had been based. The second was the improvement of the steam engine and its more successful adaptation to the power requirements of the textile industry." Smith, *op. cit.*, pp. 40–41. Still a third reason, less important, was the higher atmospheric humidity of the coastal district.

[21] For further discussion see National Resources Planning Board, "Industrial Location and National Resources," Chap. 7, Government Printing Office, Washington, 1943.

Electricity. [22] The conversion of mechanical energy into electricity (and perhaps even more important, the development of transmission in high-voltage alternating currents) has likewise had important locational effects, though less revolutionary than those of steam. Energy transmission in the form of electricity over distances of as much as 300 miles gives added flexibility of location in relation to both water-power and fuel resources. In the case of water power, which would otherwise not be transportable at all, this advantage is very important and has restored some of the locational attraction of water-power sites. Hydroelectric power generated at the best sites and used in the immediate vicinity is sold to continuous users at rates less than those for any other form of energy, and this type of location has consequently attracted those processes which need the largest amounts of energy relative to other requirements. [23] These include some operations involving electrolysis (as in aluminum reduction) and some involving heat (as in ferroalloys and special steels and abrasives). No processes are attracted to such sites for savings in costs of mechanical energy.

In the meantime, changes in fuel-burning equipment have steadily increased the energy yield (in terms of mechanical and electrical energy) of fuels. The average amount of coal burned to produce 1 kilowatt-hour of electrical energy in the United States in 1902 was 6.4 pounds. By 1920 this had fallen to 3.4 pounds and by 1944 to 1.3 pounds, [24] while in large plants built in recent years it runs well under a pound. Where fuel is cheap, such plants can produce electricity at costs comparable to those of large hydroelectric developments.

[22] Nearly a decade ago it was estimated that the use of nonhuman energy in the United States was equivalent to the continuous utilization of about 33 horse power per person. This came from the following primary sources:

Source	Per Cent
Bituminous coal	48
Petroleum	32
Natural gas	10
Anthracite coal	6
Water power	4

National Resources Committee, "Energy Resources and National Policy," pp. 8–9, Government Printing Office, Washington, 1939. These primary sources of energy are used to some extent directly (the fuels in combustion and other chemical reactions, the water power as physical energy). But nearly all the water power is converted into electricity first. About an eighth of the coal is used in generating electricity for sale, and manufacturing and mining establishments supplement their purchases of electricity by generating over half as much themselves for their own use. The mechanical energy used in manufacturing in the United States is now provided mainly from electric motors.

[23] Cf. Federal Power Commission, "Power Requirements in Electrochemical Electrometallurgical and Allied Industries," Washington, 1938. Further information on electric energy requirements in specific manufacturing industries is given in National Resources Planning Board, "Industrial Location and National Resources," Chap. 7, Washington, 1943.

[24] "Statistical Abstract of the United States," 1946, Table 531, p. 475. Fuel oil and gas consumed have been converted into coal equivalent, accounting in 1944 for about 19 per cent of the total electric energy generated. Similar economies have been recorded in cement making, metallurgy, and other direct heat-using processes.

It is certain that the rate of energy yield from coal and oil will continue to improve as already proved devices such as the gas turbine are put into wider use. Locationally, the effect is to diminish the importance of nearness to fuel sources but at the same time to encourage production techniques and products that call for large amounts of energy.

Many persons have thought that the availability of electricity in small or large quantities anywhere on the distribution system [25] would produce a general scattering of industry to small rural plants or even back into workers' homes. [26] No such shift has occurred or seems likely. Energy rates are considerably lower for large users and are a significant element in location for only a few large-scale chemical and metallurgical processes.

One significant locational effect has arisen, however, from the easier transmissibility of energy *within industrial plants* when electricity is used. The nineteenth-century large factory building was a blocky structure several stories high, built in this fashion partly in order to minimize the distance over which power had to be transmitted by belts and shafting from the steam engine or water wheel. By contrast, large modern factories using electric motors can be low and extensive, since power travels on wires. Frequently they are only one story high. This change in plant design has played a part in the choice of more suburban locations for new industrial plants—though motor transport of materials, products, and workers has probably been a still more important cause.

Atomic Energy. Controlled nuclear disintegration in atomic piles is a new source of heat energy, the importance of which it is difficult to assess in the light of the scanty information thus far available. A few general observations, however, may be ventured.[27]

Piles of present types operate at moderate temperatures. The principal use of the heat is envisaged as the raising of steam for generation of electricity in conventional power plants, and there is no indication that the high temperatures needed in metallurgical processes can be economically developed under suitable conditions. We shall assume, then, that atomic energy means essentially a new fuel for steam power stations.

Heat will probably be developed and converted into electricity at two kinds of pile installations, apparently of roughly equal importance in terms

[25] General practice of utility companies is to change a uniform rate over a wide area, the only concession to near-by customers being an occasional special rate to large continuous users who take off their power at the generating site before it is stepped up to transmission voltage.

[26] For a rather extreme view on this point see Laurent Dechesne, "La Localisation des diverses productions," pp. 81–82, Les Editions Comptables, Commerciales et Financiéres, Brussels, 1945.

[27] These comments are based primarily on the following sources: H. DeW. Smyth, "A General Account of the Development of Methods for Using Atomic Energy for Military Purposes under the Auspices of the United States Government, 1940–1945," Government Printing Office, Washington, 1945; Atomic Energy: Its Future in Power Production, *Chemical Engineering*, October, 1946; reprinted with an appended summary of the report transmitted to the United Nations Atomic Energy Commission by the United States representative on Sept. 7, 1946; S. H. Schurr, Economic Aspects of Atomic Energy as a Source of Power, *Bulletin of the Atomic Scientists*, April—May, 1947; Walter Isard, "Some Economic Implications of Atomic Energy," *Quarterly Journal of Economics*, vol. LXII, No. 2, February, 1948, pp. 202–228.

of potential electrical energy output. These are "primary" units using puri-fied uranium and "secondary" units using plutonium produced by the primary units. In both cases the weight of transported materials required is negligible: a 500,000-kilowatt primary pile unit would consume only about 5 tons of purified uranium in a year.

The use of primary units is subject to two probable limitations: They can more easily make explosives and are thus likely to be under more stringent control than the secondary units; their efficiency depends on very large size. Cost estimates have been made for capacities on the order of 500,000 kilowatts for the primary units [28] and 20,000 to 100,000 kilowatts for the secondary.

The prospective costs of electric power generated from atomic heat are difficult to estimate, since they depend to a considerable extent on how much of the total cost of the plant is charged to military purposes and how much to the production of radioactive "tracer" isotopes. This is the same problem of cost allocation that confronts any multiple-use energy develop-ment but is particularly full of uncertainties in the present stage. The consensus is, however, that in a few decades secondary-pile installations will become competitive with ordinary coal-burning power stations except in areas where coal is unusually cheap, while the more efficient primary units will match the costs of the cheapest coal-burning power stations and all but the cheapest hydroelectric plants.

The outlook, then, is that almost any region on earth may soon be able to generate electric energy from secondary-pile units at costs comparable to present costs in those regions of the United States which must bring coal considerable distances by rail. Any region in which there is a sufficiently concentrated potential demand to use, say, 500,000 kilowatts of new capaci-ty from a single source can (if regulatory authorities permit a primary unit) get electricity at a generation cost lower than that of present coal-burning stations but still not so low as the best hydroelectric sites.[29]

Atomic energy does not seem to portend, then, any revolutionary locational changes. It will be as if every country on earth were to be endowed, at the possible discretion of an international authority, with coal resources similar to those of the United States, subject to the important

[28] To visualize this size, it may be helpful to know that 500,000 kilowatts represents about 0.8 per cent of the total electric generating capacity in the United States, including both utility and industrial installations. It is roughly equal to the capacity of public-utility generating plants alone in any one of the following states: Kansas, Florida, Kentucky, Louisiana, or Oklahoma.

[29] The report printed in *Chemical Engineering (loc. cit.)* concludes that this restricts the use of primary units to a few of the largest metropolitan areas of the world. This may be going too far. It should be remembered that electricity is being transmitted as far as 300 miles. A circle of even 200 miles radius has an area of more than 125,000 square miles; for such an area, a primary pile capacity of 500,000 kilowatts would be equivalent to only 4 kilowatts per square mile. Taking the United States as a whole, we now have about five times that much generating capacity per square mile. Each of the nine census regions of the United States has at least 3 kilowatts of capacity to the square mile; only the Mountain region is below 7 kilowatts. The total potential demand of any of a great many regions, then, would probably absorb the output of such a plant, although many years might elapse before full utilization could be attained. Experience in such areas as the Tennessee Valley shows that the long-run elasticity of demand for electric energy is very large.

qualification that this coal could be used only in large electric power plants. The new source of power will not significantly affect transport costs (except possibly those of water transport, which are already extremely low). It will have little effect on the retail cost of electric power to domestic and other small users, where the main item is distribution cost. It is unlikely to replace good hydroelectric sites. Direct use of atomic heat in metallurgical processes does not appear imminent. Apart from metallurgy and the electroprocess industries now oriented to superior hydroelectric sites, *e.g.*, aluminum, magnesium, and artificial abrasives, most manufacturing industries are not greatly affected in their locations by energy-cost differentials, since those costs are small in proportion to other items of procurement, distribution, and processing costs.

Summary

Technological improvements have affected locational patterns through changes in transfer costs, labor requirements, materials requirements, and energy costs.

Cheaper transfer has enlarged market areas and supply areas, allowing further concentration of market-oriented and material-oriented industries but at the same time a loosening of the structure of metropolitan communities. Each new transfer medium developed has had a different effect on location, reflecting its own characteristic of cost structure.

In individual industries, technical "maturity" makes labor requirements less specialized and exacting and permits a spread or decentralization to new centers of production after the initial concentration phase.

Technical improvements which increase product yields lessen the attraction of material sources; but for modern large-scale industry, size and permanence of a materials source are increasingly important.

The vastly increased use of nonhuman energy in production has been offset by improved techniques that make energy cheaper and more transmissible and tend to equalize the advantages of various locations in respect to energy cost. Atomic energy development, as now foreseen, is unlikely to produce radical locational changes. It can lower electricity costs in areas where they are now high but probably cannot compete with the best hydroelectric sites. The lowest cost atomic power is likely to be available only in areas of fairly concentrated demand, and its location and development may be primarily dictated by strategic and political considerations.

Rules of Play

Stage I

Water transportation and power are the two major factors dealt with here that differ significantly from Basic CLUG. Play of this stage should cover three to ten rounds or continue until growth has ceased as a result of the constraints imposed by this level of technology. A river runs down one

Figure III-1. Board Setup

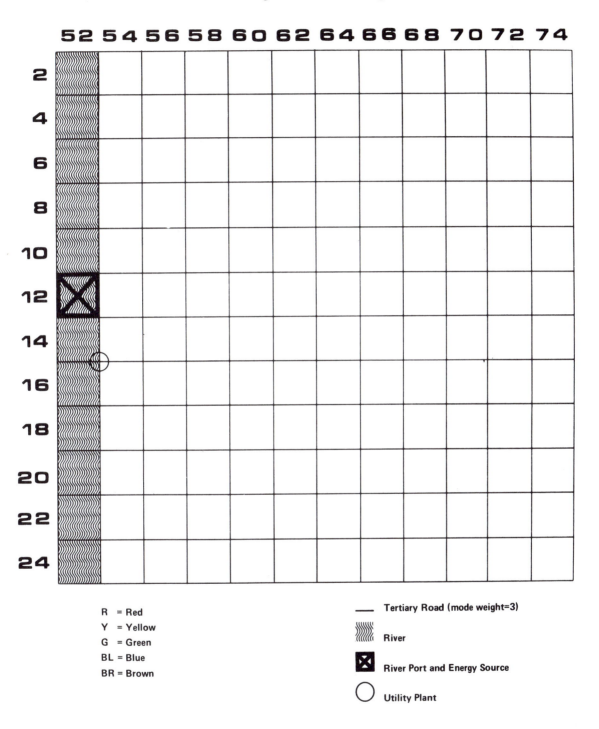

R = Red
Y = Yellow
G = Green
BL = Blue
BR = Brown

—— Tertiary Road (mode weight=3)

〰 River

▨ River Port and Energy Source

○ Utility Plant

side of the playing board as play begins. One square of the river will function both as a River Port and as an Energy Source. Figure III-1 depicts these initial parameters. Each of five teams begins play with $100,000 cash and play begins in Round 1 on Step 1.

Step 1 (Purchase Land) is unchanged from Basic CLUG.

Step 2 (Provide Utilities) is unchanged from Basic CLUG.

Step 3 (Renovate Buildings) is unchanged from Basic CLUG.

Step 4 (Construct Buildings) is identical to Basic CLUG exept that Full and Partial Industry may be built only on the three parcels touching the Energy Source (the same square as the River Port).

Step 5 (Designate Employment) is unchanged from Basic CLUG.

Step 6 (Sign Trade Agreements) is unchanged from Basic CLUG.

Step 7 (Receive Income) is changed in that gross industrial income is increased in this experiment to $65,000 for FI and $32,000 for PI. Table III-1 indicates these new levels of income to be paid to industry in Step 7.

Step 8 (Pay Employees) is unaltered from Basic CLUG.

Step 9: The normal procedures are followed for paying Local Store, Central Store and Office. In addition to these transactions, the instructor should collect Energy Costs of $10,000 from each FI and $5,000 from each PI as indicated in Table III-1.

Table III-1. Unit Characteristics for Industry — Stage I

	Full Industry	Partial Industry
Construction Cost	$96,000	$48,000
Number of Employees	4	2
Payroll	$24,000	$12,000
Maximum Office Cost	$ 4,000	$ 2,000
Energy Cost	$10,000	$ 5,000
Gross Income	$65,000	$32,000

Step 10 (Pay Transportation) contains a number of procedural changes from Basic CLUG. For the level of transport technology represented in this stage, a Mode Weight of 3 has been assigned to all Tertiary Roads on the Playing Board. Transportation Costs for the following trips are computed using the usual formula: R to work; R to LS; R to CS; LS to O; CS to O; PI to O; and FI to O. Industry, since it is located on the River Port, pays no cost to transport goods to the Port. Industrial shipping costs instead include River Port Fees and the cost to reach external markets is determined in accord with Table III-2.

Table III-2. Transportation Costs for Industry to Market — Stage I

	Location of Market				
	Near	Inter- mediate	Far	Port Fee	
Die Number	1	2,3	4,5,6		
Full Industry	$5,600	$5,800	$6,000	+ $5,000	= Transportation Cost from Port to Market
Partial Industry	$2,800	$2,900	$3,000	+ $3,000	

To use Table III-2 a single die is rolled once per round by the instructor; the result determines the location of industrial markets for that round. The Cost of Shipment is then added to the Port Fee to yield the Transportation Cost for each Full or Partial Industry to be collected by the instructor.

Step 11 (Pay Taxes) is conducted as in Basic CLUG. After Step 11, recycle to Step 1.

A summary of the new information and changes needed for Stage I of this experiment is provided on a tear-out sheet at the back of this manual. It is entitled "Summary of Changes for Transportation and Technology Experiment—Stage I."

Discussion

An absolute minimum of five rounds are required in order to adequately explore the possibilities and implications of Stage I. Ten rounds are far preferable in order to note the marked tendency of the community to cluster closely along the river front and to exhibit relatively high densities as a result of the costly levels of intra-urban transportation characteristic of this period in history. The levels of transportation technology represented include not only river transport and mechanical means of distribution of water power but also the highly restrictive travel possibilities present for travel within cities which existed prior to the development of the street railway system and later the automobile. The result has been historically a form of city very similar to that developed under Stage I of this experiment.

Study Questions

After completing play of Stage I, several questions might be considered based upon the experience generated with it:

1. Is the maximum size of a city in part determined by the level of transportation technology in existence at a given point in history? In what manner is this limit imposed?

2. Is the pattern of development of a city determined by the quality and type of available transportation within the city? Does this pattern appear to be different from that found in contemporary cities?

3. When the major means of shipment to an external market is by water does the distance traveled to an external market play an important part in the total cost of external transportation?

Stage II

Rail transport and steam power are the major technological innovations introduced in this portion of the experiment. Stage II can be played independently or continued upon the earlier city developed in Stage I. Figure III-2 indicates the layout of the playing board which contains a Railroad Line and a Rail Siding. The Utility Plant is sited as in Stage I and now also provides the new Energy Source. If Stage II is continued from

Figure III-2. Location of Railroad Line and Rail Siding

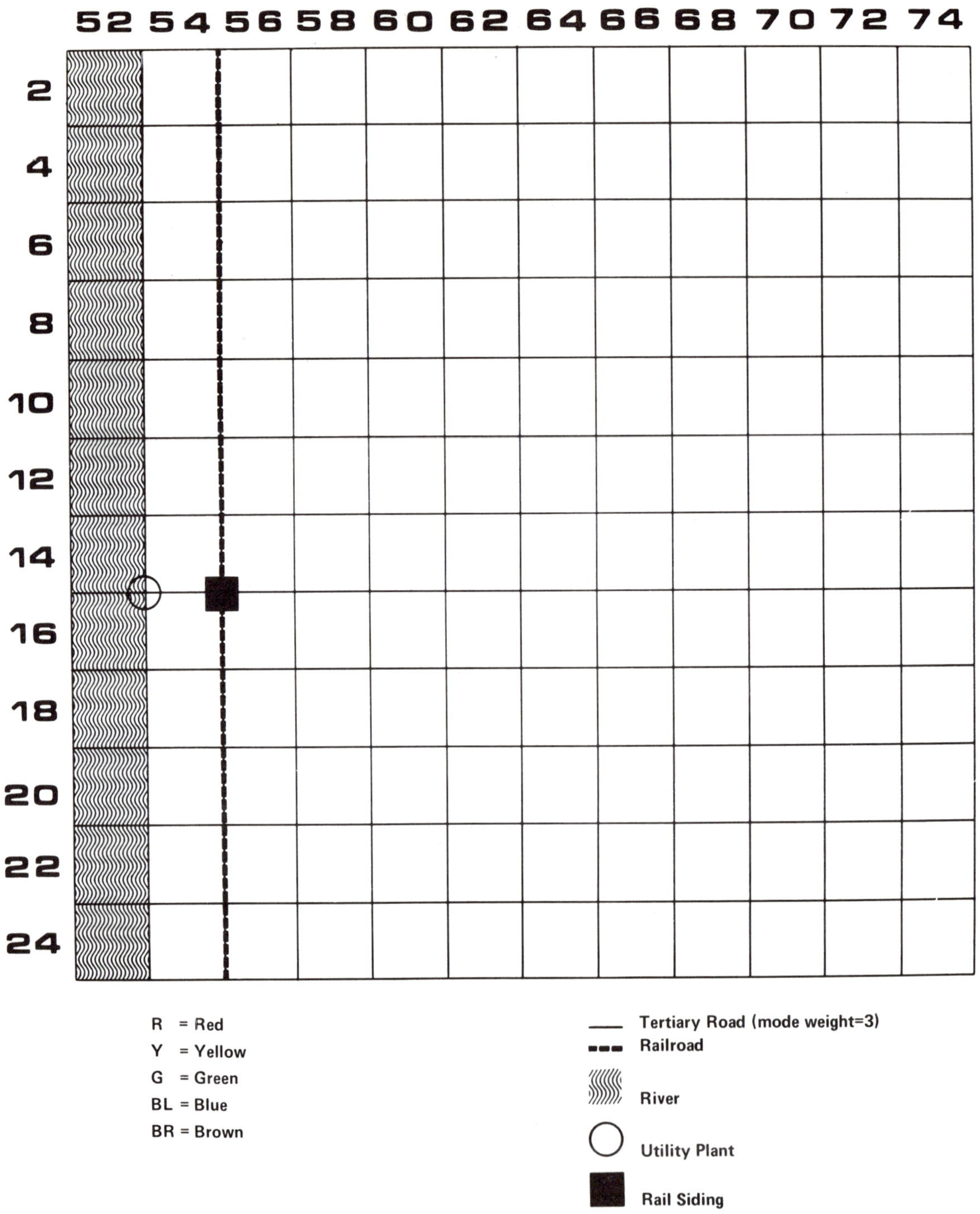
52 54 56 58 60 62 64 66 68 70 72 74
2
4
6
8
10
12
14
16
18
20
22
24
R = Red
Y = Yellow
G = Green
BL = Blue
BR = Brown
Tertiary Road (mode weight=3)
Railroad
River
Utility Plant
Rail Siding

Stage I, the layout in Figure III-2 is simply added to the existing playing board. If Stage II is played independently, then each team should begin play with $100,000 cash. Of course if Stage II continues upon Stage I developments, play begins with each team holding the cash, land, and buildings in existence when Stage I was completed. Community finances are treated accordingly in either case.

Step 1 (Purchase Land) is unchanged from Basic CLUG.

Step 2 (Provide Utilities) is unchanged from Basic CLUG.

Step 3 (Renovate Buildings) is unchanged from Basic CLUG if Stage II is played independently. However, if Stage II is developed upon the historical base of Stage I, then the age and Renovation status of a Full or Partial Industry determines the level of its technology. If any older industry is to take advantage of the level of technology offered in Stage II, it must be fully renovated up to that round in which the change in technology occurred. Older industries which are not renovated up to this point must continue to operate under the Stage I conditions. Thus, for example, if Stage II begins in Round 10 and an industry is still in existence which was built in Round 4, it must continue to operate upon its original basis of technology until and unless it is fully renovated up to Round 10, thereby improving its level of technology and equipment to match the current conditions. Any newly built industries will, of course, operate under the new level of technology.

Step 4 (Construct Buildings) is now more fully identical to Basic CLUG in that new industries may also be located on any parcel because energy is transportable from its source, the Utility Plant. Transportation costs for energy and for movement of industrial goods to either the River Port or the railroad are high, however.

Step 5 (Designate Employed) is unchanged from Basic CLUG.

Step 6 (Sign Trade Agreements) is unchanged from Basic CLUG.

Step 7 (Receive Income) is the same as in Stage I of this experiment.

Step 8 (Pay Employees) is unchanged from Basic CLUG. Note that Residences are not technologically constrained except for transportation costs and any Residential Unit may be employed in any Industry without respect to matching levels of technology between employer and employee.

Step 9 (Pay Stores and Office) is conducted as in Stage I except energy costs for new or fully renovated industries are reduced to $6,000 for Full Industry and $3,000 for Partial Industry as indicated in Table III-3.

Table III-3. Unit Characteristics for Industry — Stage II

	Full Industry	Partial Industry
Construction Cost	$96,000	$48,000
Number of Employees	4	2
Payroll	$24,000	$12,000
Maximum Office Cost	$ 4,000	$ 2,000
Energy Cost	$ 6,000	$ 3,000
Gross Income	$65,000	$32,000

Step 10 (Pay Transportation) once again involves most of the changes required for this stage of the experiment. The Mode Weight for all roads

remains at 3 and most transportation costs to work, to shop and to office are computed as in Basic CLUG. The fundamental changes from Basic CLUG and from Stage I involve industries. Industrial transportation costs involve four basic components: the cost of getting manufactured products to either the Rail Siding or the River Port; the Siding Fee or Port Fee; the cost for shipment to external markets; and the cost of transporting energy from the Utility Plant to the industrial site. Distances are computed as in Basic CLUG from nearest corner of origin to nearest corner of destination and Mode Weights for all within the community are 3 on the tertiary roads.

Table III-4 gives the Association Weights used for computing the cost of moving manufactured goods to the Rail Siding or River Port and for moving Energy from the Utility Plant to the industry. Thus a Full Industry one parcel away from the Rail Siding and two parcels away from the Utility Plant operating at Stage II technology would pay: 1 (Distance) × 3 (Mode Weight) × $1,000 (Association Weight) plus 2 (distance) × 3 (Mode Weight) × $400 (Association Weight) for its cost of movement of goods to the Siding and its cost of transporting energy.

Table III-4. Association Weights for Industry — Stage II

Purpose of Trip	Full Industry	Partial Industry
Goods to Siding or Post	$1,000	$500
Energy Transportation	400	200

Table III-5 provides the additional information necessary to compute the additional components of transportation cost for an industry at Stage II of development using the railroad as its means of shipment to external markets. The comparable table from Stage I should be used if the industry continues to ship from the River Port regardless of its stage of technological development. *The die should be rolled only once for all Full and Partial Industry regardless of age.* Industries still operating under Stage I technology use Table III-2 to calculate the Transportation Cost to Market. Industrial Transportation Cost is the sum of all four components and is collected by the Instructor or Game Manager each round.

Table III-5. Transportation Costs for Industry to Market — Stage II

	Location of Market			Siding Fee	
	Near	Inter-mediate	Far		
Die Number	1	2,3,4	5,6		
Full Industry	$4,400	$5,000	$5,600	+ $1,500	= Transportation Cost from Rail Siding to Market
Partial Industry	$2,200	$2,500	$2,800	+ 800	

Step 11 (Pay Taxes) is unchanged from Basic CLUG.

A summary of the new information and changes needed for Stage II of this experiment is provided as a tear-out page at the end of this manual. It is entitled "Summary of Changes for Transportation and Technology Experiment—Stage II."

Discussion

Stage II should be played for at least five rounds and preferably for ten rounds depending upon the degree of development of the city which is desired. The changes in locational preferences of industry should become apparent quite early after the change in technology has occured. If based upon an earlier Stage I development, a movement away from the river front should be apparent with some slight shifting outward of the corresponding residential and commercial developments. In time, the earlier industries located on the river may actually be abandoned by their owners in preference for better sites near the Rail Siding. Greater sensitivity to the importance of the dice roll is also likely to occur as the increasing importance of distance to market under rail transportation becomes apparent.

Study Questions

At the end of this stage of the experiment, the following questions may serve as a guide to discussion and evaluation.

1. What similarities or differences in rate of growth of the cities developed under Stage I and Stage II technologies are apparent? Are there other differences which seem likely to influence the maximum size which the city may obtain under these two conditions?

2. Is the spatial pattern of development different under the two different technologies? Would these differences be more marked if the railroad had been located more closely to the river or more distant from the river? What effect would a location further from the river have upon the location of the commercial center of the city?

3. If the upcoming location of the railroad had not been precisely known, would this have affected your land buying patterns? Do you think you would have bought more or less land under these circumstances and do you think the price would have been higher or lower? How valuable to you is it to know in advance the forthcoming location of the railroad?

4. How do water and rail transportation costs compare? Were you more or less sensitive to the location of the external market when shipping by rail? What factors contributed to this change of attitude?

Stage III

Highway transportation and electrical energy represent the third major set of technological innovations to be modelled in Experiment III. As was the case previously, Stage III can be played independently or continued upon the existing development from play of Stage I and II. If run independently, each of five teams begins play with $100,000 cash or; if run cumulatively with previous Stages, cash is determined by balances at the end of the prior play. The setup of the playing board is indicated in Figure III-3, which includes the location of the Major Highway and Interchanges, and the Utility Plant.

Step 1 (Purchase Land) is unchanged from Basic CLUG.

Step 2 (Provide Utilities) is unchanged from Basic CLUG.

Step 3 (Renovate Buildings) is the same as Basic CLUG except that any older industries remaining from previous technological stages must be fully renovated to the round at which Stage III begins to take advantage of the new technology.

Step 4 (Construct Buildings) is completely restored to the status of Basic CLUG. Energy is equally available at no additional cost to any sites serviced by Utility Lines.

Step 5 (Designate Employment) is unchanged from Basic CLUG.

Step 6 (Sign Trade Agreements) is unchanged from Basic CLUG.

Step 7 (Receive Income) is the same as in Stage I of this experiment.

Step 8 (Pay Employees) is unchanged from Basic CLUG.

Step 9 (Pay Stores and Office) is conducted as in Stage I except that energy costs for FI and PI are now reduced to $2,000 and $1,000, respectively.

Step 10 (Pay Transportation Cost) is now computed with Mode Weights of ½ and 2 on the Major Highway and Secondary Road, respectively, replacing the uniform value of 3 used in Stages I and II. Major Highways are not limited access and may be entered at any point but transportation costs of industrial products to market are computed from one of the three interchanges and within city costs must be computed from the industrial site to one or another of these interchanges. All other normal transportation costs may be computed as in Basic CLUG using the Association Weights given there together with the Association Weights for industries given in Table III-6.

Table III-6. Association Weights for Industry — Stage III

Purpose of Trip	Full Industry	Partial Industry
Goods to Siding, Port or Interchange	$1,000	$500
Energy Transportation	0	0

Table III-7 provides data for determining Interchange Fee and shipping cost to external markets. The instructor rolls a single die to determine the location of external markets for all industry regardless of the age of each building. Stage I and II industries use the previous tables. No Transportation Cost is paid by industry in Stage III for transport to energy as indicated in Table III-6.

Figure III-3. Location of Major Highway, Interchanges, and the Utility Plant

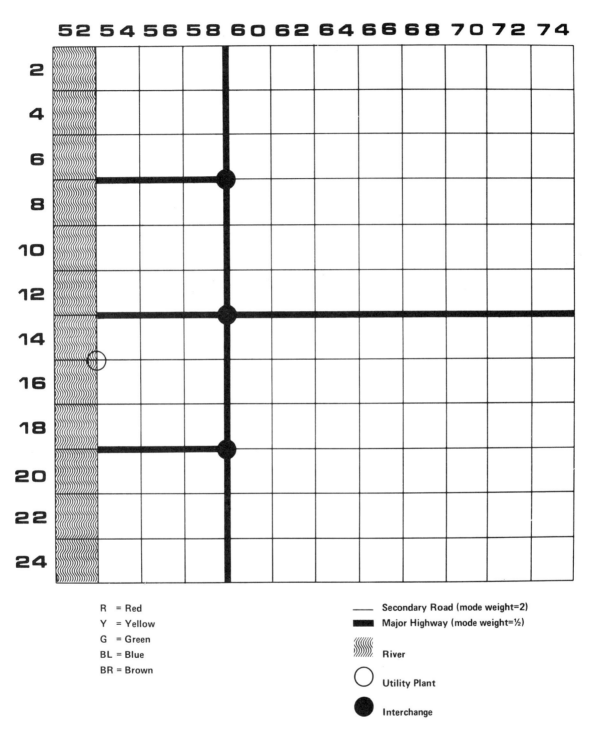

R = Red
Y = Yellow
G = Green
BL = Blue
BR = Brown

——— Secondary Road (mode weight=2)
▬▬▬ Major Highway (mode weight=½)
〜〜〜 River
◯ Utility Plant
● Interchange

Table III-7. Transportation Costs for Industry to Market — Stage III

	Location of Market			Loading Fee	
	Near	Inter-mediate	Far		
Die Number	1,2,3	4,5	6		
Full Industry	$1,600	$3,000	$4,400	+ $200	Transportation Cost from Inter-change to Market
Partial Industry	$ 800	$1,500	$2,200	+ $100	=

Step 11 (Pay Taxes) is played as in Basic CLUG.

A summary of the new information and changes needed for Stage III of this experiment is provided as a tear-out page at the end of this manual. It is entitled "Summary of Changes for Transportation and Technology Experiment—Stage III."

Discussion

Stage III could be played almost indefinitely except that calculations become increasingly difficult after fifteen or twenty rounds. Once the growth of urban sprawl becomes apparent with the change in transportation costs and the new Interchanges, the game manager or instructor may reasonably terminate the experiment. A substantial departure from the earlier densely built up urban settlement should become apparent within a very few rounds of the introduction of the new levels of technology. Although the Interchanges provide a mild focus for industrial location, the much reduced transportation costs within the city make almost any site at all appropriate for an industrial location. At the same time, the general availability of cheap energy at all sites further reduces any limitations on industrial location.

Study Questions

At the end of this stage of the experiment, the following questions may serve as a guide to discussion and evaluation.

1. Under each successive stage of technological development how has the role of transportation changed as a determinant of the pattern of urban growth? Under Stage III levels of technology can transportation costs any longer be considered to be an important factor in determining urban patterns? If they are now unimportant, what other factors now help to determine the growth pattern?

2. Given the loss of structure due to lessening of transportation costs, is public policy and land use control likely to be more or less important in guiding and determining the growth patterns of cities?

3. What might the consequence be of combining different sets of costs for transportation and energy technologies, e.g., water transport and electrical energy, highway costs and water power, etc? Do these considerations have any bearing on urban growth patterns in developing countries?

4. Are there other costs involved in the stage III technologies which are not recognized in this experiment? Would these additional costs and disbenefits effect urban growth patterns in other ways which are not illustrated here?

5. What limitations now exist on the maximum size to which a city can grow under Stage III technology? If no limits exist, would you be willing to play and operate a CLUG game for fifty rounds under Stage III technology? What kinds of management and accounting problems would be likely to arise and what are the implications of these problems for maximum city size in the real world.

Experiment IV: Land Use Regulation

Introduction

Experience with a laissez-faire policy of urban growth has demonstrated the need for governments to play an active role in regulating private land development decisions. The results of unguided growth have made it clear that all too often the private developer fails to consider the interests of the larger community in his attempts to profit from his own investments. Numerous community problems have resulted from such a policy. Poor location and siting of buildings, traffic congestion, sprawl, inflation of land values, and unbalanced growth serve as familiar examples.

Most city governments have recognized these problems, and through city planning departments, have attempted to regulate land development. Their records of success, however, are generally less than admirable. John Reps has argued that this failing is due not necessarily to the quality of our city plans, but to inadequacies in the means by which planners attempt to implement their plans.

The most fundamental of these means are the simple tactics of advice and persuasion. While heavily relied on by planners, these techniques rest on no legal authority. In some cases, persuasion is enhanced by the offering of incentives to developers, but again cooperation is voluntary and the planner has no guaranteed ability to influence private decisions. The most powerful technique widely available to planners today is that of public regulation and control, through devices such as zoning, subdivision regulations, housing and sanitary codes and official maps. A further strategy, discussed at length in the reading by Reps, is that of public land acquisition.

Zoning

Zoning is by far the most widely employed and relied upon means for legally regulating private land development decisions in the United States today. Since the reading to follow presumes some familiarity with this technique, it is briefly described below.

Zoning is a police power measure granted by state legislatures to local municipalities. Zoning rests on the constitutional power of government to restrict and regulate actions which might injure the public health, safety, morals, or welfare. When adopted by a municipality, a zoning ordinance divides the city into a set of homogeneous land use districts based on the appropriateness of land parcels for different types and densities of development. Residential, Commercial, and Industrial are the basic land use categories for which districts are determined.

Districts may be defined either inclusively or exclusively. Under an inclusive zoning scheme, land use categories are ranked according to their potential noxiousness: Industrial, Commercial, Residential. The most potentially undesirable use is then limited to development on parcels where this use is explicitly permitted and prohibited from development elsewhere.

Residential uses may locate in any district, while Commercial uses are prohibited only from Residential districts. Inclusive zoning ordinances, then, allow Residential uses to locate in Commercial and Industrial districts but don't allow Industrial or Commercial development in Residential zones. On the other hand, under an ordinance devised with exclusive development districts each land use category is permitted to locate only in those districts where explicitly allowed. Thus, Residential and Industrial uses are each prohibited from locating in districts specified for the other. Most munici-palities have adopted the exclusive form of zoning ordinance because of its greater power to control development and its greater ability to implement the protective logic of the police power.

When a municipality has chosen to adopt a zoning ordinance, future development must conform to the regulations in the ordinance. Non-con-forming uses which exist at the time of adoption are generally allowed to continue though not to expand. If a builder cannot meet the prescribed restrictions, he may either apply for a variance or judicially challenge the validity of the entire ordinance. Variances may be granted to particular parcels of land if it can be shown that the existing regulations cause undue hardships and practical difficulty to that parcel. In those instances when entire ordinances — not just their applications to a few parcels — have been taken to court, the judiciary has invalidated them when it can be shown that their provisions amount to confiscation or complete prohibition of the right to use private property without due process and compensation as required by the Fourteenth Amendment of the Federal Constitution.

Public Land Acquisition

Another alternative governments might pursue as a means of regulating urban land development is suggested by Reps. In this scheme, a public corporation would be established with the ability to purchase land on the open market, or to condemn land not otherwise for sale. Condemnation would rest on the power of eminent domain and would operate in a fashion similar to current urban renewal efforts. Corporation-acquired land could be provided with the necessary improvements and then offered either for sale or lease. In either case, provisions restricting land use would be included as part of the title or the lease. These provisions guide the pace and pattern of development.

The Readings and Experiment

Two readings by Reps are included in this experiment. In the first, a series of criticisms is levelled at zoning as one of the principal methods for implementing development plans. In the second, the Metropolitan Land Corporation is described and proposed as a supplementary or alternative technique. It should be noted that both readings are addressed to an audience of professional planning officials who are both familiar with and committed to zoning as an important aspect of urban planning. Reps' arguments, therefore, are intended to provoke critical thought. The reader, who may not be so familiar with zoning, is advised to bear this fact in mind while considering Reps' assessment of zoning.

REQUIEM FOR ZONING

John W. Reps

The year 1966 [was] a significant one for American Planning. It [marked] two anniversaries: the beginning of the fifth century of the oldest city in the United States and the ending of the fifth decade of comprehensive zoning. It is a nice question which is less obsolete—the St. Augustine plan of 1565 or the comprehensive zoning ordinances of this country based on the New York City Zoning Resolution of 1916. The quaint, narrow streets of the old Spanish town serve at least to attract the tourist dollar; the quaint, narrow provisions of our zoning ordinances, judging from current comments, attract only the lawyers.

Zoning is seriously ill and its physicians—the planners—are mainly to blame. We have unnecessarily prolonged the existence of a land use control device conceived in another era when the true and frightening complexity of urban life was barely appreciated. We have, through heroic efforts and with massive doses of legislative remedies, managed to preserve what was once a lusty infant not only past the retirement age but well into senility. What is called for is legal euthanasia, a respectful requiem, and a search for a new legislative substitute sturdy enough to survive in the modern urban world.

The powers of zoning and all of our other techniques for controlling urban development appear grossly inadequate when measured against the often radically different development patterns which modern metropolitan plans propose. I am not here judging the desirability of such alternative urban configurations as advocated by the Dutch in their Rim City plan, the Danes in their finger plan for Copenhagen, the British in their satellite city and greenbelt design for Greater London, or the radial corridor scheme for Washington, D. C. I am contending only that our existing system of development guidance permits us to hope for nothing better than partially controlled sprawl and that such bold plans now have little chance of success.

My concern today is with only one of the means of planning implementation, but it is necessary first to view its position in the matrix of urban shaping devices. In another context I have suggested, as have others, that the mechanisms for directing the urban pattern might be regarded as a guidance system.[1] Like the components of the machinery that places a satellite into a planned orbit, this urban guidance system comprises a number of subsystems that can be used to steer a metropolis through time to a predetermined goal.

* * *

. . . What are these methods by which the patterns of urban growth and change can be shaped? I suggest that all of our activities in this direction can

From *Planning, 1964: Selected Papers from the ASPO National Planning Conference* (Chicago: American Society of Planning Officials, 1964). Reprinted by permission of the publisher and the author. The full text is available from the publisher.

[1] John W. Reps, "Mechanism for Directing and Controlling Future Development Patterns," Barclay Jones and Burnham Kelly (eds.), *Long-Range Needs and Opportunities in New York State* (Ithaca: Cornell University Center for Housing and Environmental Studies, 1962), pp. 306-337.

be classified under one of the following: advice, controls, inducements, and development. The order in which I have listed them is roughly the order in which they have been employed in our attempts to assert greater public leverage in constructing urban patterns.

When the first public planning agencies were created, their sole power was that of advice: advice to governmental departments and officials, to other levels of government, to civic organizations, to individuals. Advice, and the closely related techniques of persuasion and inspiration, still play important roles in guiding development. Indeed, at the metropolitan scale this is the chief technique on which we rely. But the power of advice necessarily has its limits, especially where advice runs even faintly counter to the dictates of the marketplace.

Next in point of time came our inventions of various kinds of control devices—zoning, subdivision regulations, official map techniques, and building, housing, and sanitary codes. But controls are negative instruments—they can prevent but they cannot compel, and their usefulness proved limited.

We then turned to various types of inducements or incentives as a method of attracting private building of types and in locations and under conditions that contributed to the public good. Through low-interest loans, tax exemptions, aids in land acquisition, direct subsidy payments, guarantees against financial loss, and other techniques, public bodies began to influence the urban pattern by combining the carrot of inducements with the lash of controls. Early redevelopment projects resulted from programs extending such financial incentives. The cluster sub-division concept provides another example.

Finally, direct public development has now taken on its place as an urban forming force. In one sense, of course, this is nothing new. Vast public construction of streets and utilities in advance of need during the 1920's made possible the land boom of those wild years and certainly influenced the form of cities. But acquiring, planning, and selling land in central redevolopment areas to reshape the city's core is employing public development powers in a new way. Expressways, rapid transit routes, trunk utility lines, and major public buildings have powerful influences on the growth patterns of cities, and coordinated planning of these and other city-shaping elements offers great promise as an effective guidance mechanism.

I would go much farther in the direction of public development and use some modification of redevelopment techniques at the urban fringe. To be specific, some public agency with metropolitan jurisdiction might acquire raw land, plan it, provide street, utility, park, and other needed improvements, and then convey lots, blocks, or neighborhoods to private builders for development as planned and as controlled by deed restrictions. This would accomplish three things: it would provide a public yardstick operation against which purely private land development activities could be measured, it would establish a more precise tool of environmental control and guidance, and it would, paradoxically enough, aid private enterprise and the competitive market by making it possible for small builders who cannot afford the uncertainties and costs of the modern scale of land development to stay in business.

I hope my position is clear that the incentives and public development components of the urban guidance system need much further examination and expansion. I am convinced that in the long run these are the areas in which much of our intellectual resources should be invested. It should also be clear that what I shall now have to say about zoning and its future deals with a minor, although far from unimportant, aspect of urban planning implementation.

Having narrowed the subject for discussion while at the same time placing it in its larger context, let me now attempt a working definition of zoning for purposes of analysis. I suggest the following: zoning is a police power measure enacted by units of local government under permissive state legislation. Zoning regulations establish, in advance of applications for development, groups of permitted uses that vary from district to district. These regulations are not necessarily related to other regulatory devices or to any community plan. They are administered by officials having only limited discretionary powers. Ultimate review of the regulations and the actions of administrative officials under them is by appeal only and is a judicial function.

Now let me challenge the wisdom of zoning as so defined. This is, frankly, an effort to free your minds of whatever convictions you may have that our present system of zoning is somehow the only or the best method for controlling the bulk, use, intensity, location, and density of development. The sanctity of half a century of tradition stands between me and this goal, but let me make the attempt. A number of propositions will elaborate on the elements of my definition, against each one of which I will pose a question for your consideration.

One: Zoning is a police power measure. It follows that the impact of zoning regulations must be reasonable and that their effect must not be so burdensome that they amount to a taking of property instead of a mere restriction in the interests of protecting or promoting the public health, safety, morals, or general welfare. Regulations found to be unreasonably burdensome are invalidated by court action. Constitutional rights are protected, but the community is stripped of this power to guide land development, and the public at large may suffer unfortunate consequences from the assertion of private rights in land. *Question:* Would it not be desirable to introduce a system of compensation to supplement the police power where severe limitations on land use are deemed essential or desirable to shape and guide community development?

Two: Zoning is permissive. While much state legislation requires municipalities to carry out specified services or to provide certain facilities, the choice of regulating or not regulating land use is optional under American enabling statutes. *Question:* Would it not be desirable for state legislation to require all communities or those having certain characteristics to enact such regulations?

Three: Zoning is enacted by units of local government. Zoning regulations are intensely parochial. Standards required in any single metropolitan area may vary enormously depending on the whims of local legislators. We make much of the principle that land similarly located must be similarly zoned within a given municipality, but this concept is cruelly violated when a homogeneous area is zoned for industry on one side of a municipal boundary line and for high-class, low-density residential uses on the other side. Standards of enforcement vary equally widely. The possibility of achieving coordinated and balanced metropolitan development under such a situation, insofar as land use regulation is effective at all, can be written off as a mere fiction. *Question:* Would it not be desirable to deny zoning powers to the smaller units of government and place this responsibility at the county level, or as a duty of some metropolitan government or agency, or as a function of the state government?

Four: Zoning establishes regulations in advance of applications for development permission. As Daniel Mandelker has so well put it, "One difficulty with American legal techniques is that they borrow constitutional trouble by making land-use decisions with constitutional impact before the fact. Thus, exclusive agricultural zoning is restrictive immediately upon its enactment. It immediately raises a constitutional issue throughout its area of application regardless of the fact that many affected landowners would be quite happy with an exclusive agricultural restriction. But under the present system, an attack by a few will affect the entire ordinance."[2] *Question:* Would it not be desirable to have a method of control which avoided this difficulty and left the issue of legal validity to be raised when dealing with each application to develop land or to change its use?

Five: Zoning establishes groups of permitted uses that vary from district to district. In our understandable attempt to simplify in a complex and bewildering world we have done three things. We have attempted to prepare detailed standards for development which are supposed to cover all conceivable situations. We have Balkanized our cities into districts with precise and rigid zone boundary lines. We have established categories of uses that have segregated rather than integrated functional portions of cities and which have often disregarded the interrelationships between rather widely separated categories of uses. *Question:* Would it not be desirable to do away entirely with, or at least place far less emphasis on, the creation of districts and lists of supposedly compatible uses?

Six: Zoning is not necessarily related to other regulatory devices. Forget the theory here, and look at the facts. There is a multitude of regulatory measures—zoning, subdivision regulations, building codes, sanitary restrictions, housing ordinances, official map regulations, and others—enacted at different times, often by different bodies, enforced by different sets of officials, and reviewable by different administrative tribunals or courts. It is a rare zoning ordinance that does not in several ways conflict with the community subdivision regulations. It is a rare community that has not omitted some vital provision from both. It is a common necessity for the developers of all but the most routine and standardized projects to deal with

[2] Daniel L. Mandelker, "What Open Space Where? How?," American Society of Planning Officials, *Planning 1963* (Chicago: ASPO, 1964), p. 25.

several boards or officials and to secure amendments, approvals, waivers, or variances from the provisions of a number of ordinances and codes in order to proceed. *Question:* Would it not be desirable to consolidate all or most regulations dealing with control of urban growth into a single development ordinance that provided a sensible and efficient system of administration and enforcement, and which was purged of ambiguities, conflicting provisions, and redundancies?

Seven: Zoning is not necessarily related to any community plan. Again, forget the theory and look at the facts, including the depressing but understandable record of judicial review on this point. There are few communities that can claim with much justification that their regulations stem directly from any comprehensive, long-range plan. Charles Haar has demonstrated, in perhaps the most frequently court-cited law review article on zoning ever written, that whatever we think state legislation says about the necessity to ground zoning in a well-considered or comprehensive plan, the courts by and large have interpreted such a plan to be the zoning map itself.[3] This circular reasoning will prevail until new legislation changes the rules of the judicial game. *Question:* Would it not be desirable for statutes to require any local development regulations or discretionary administrative decisions reached on development proposals to be clearly based on a community plan, expressed graphically and/or as meaningful statements of development policy?

Eight: Zoning is administered by officials with limited discretionary powers. I am not here concerned with the scandal of unwarranted discretionary decisions by boards of appeals or such comparative novelties as floating zones or site plan approval procedure, but with the amount of discretion normally exercised by administrative officials in reviewing applications for zoning or building permits. It is in the nature of controls by districts, use lists, and bulk and density standards that present administrative review is essentially mechanical and requires only a check-list mentally. *Question:* Would it not be desirable to construct a system of development controls in which, as is the case of subdivision review, informed discretionary judgment plays the dominant or at least a much larger role in the process of reviewing applications to build or develop?

Nine: Ultimate review of the regulations and the actions of administrative officials under them is by appeal only. Only a person who feels aggrieved and who has the ambition, time, and money to appeal can obtain some kind of review of the wisdom or legality of a zoning enactment or administrative decision. State governments, which have conferred regulatory powers on localities, have failed to provide any form of central review of the regulations as originally established or as amended or of administrative actions taken under them. There is no county or metropolitan review of local regulatory activities except the most peripheral. *Question:* Would it not be desirable to establish a system of state or metropolitan review of zoning-type regulations that could insure conformity with state or metropolitan

---

[3] Charles Haar, "In Accordance with a Comprehensive Plan," 68 *Harvard Law Review* 1154 (1955).

development objectives and, in the case of local appeals situations, conformity with standardized fair procedures that would insure adequate attention to due process requirements and would curb both excessive restrictiveness and undue liberality on the part of administrative officials exercising wide discretionary powers?

Ten: Ultimate review of zoning regulations and administrative action is a judicial function. Courts are more and more being called on to decide issues which are increasingly technical and complex. Most courts have taken refuge in the doctrine of the presumption of legislative validity, but as the thrust of regulations becomes more vigorous it is unlikely that courts can refuse to decide issues on their merits. Yet, courts are ill-equipped to make decisions on technical matters, and it is far from clear that the adversary system provides the best approach to decision-making. *Question:* Would it not be desirable to create state administrative tribunals, assisted by an expert staff, authorized to obtain evidence in a variety of ways, and empowered to decide appeals or claims arising from the application of land use controls?

· · ·

At this stage of our urban development we badly need imaginative experimentation in our fifty legislative laboratories. Where are the states that have placed metropolitan decision-making power at the metropolitan level, that require state or metropolitan approval of local plans, that provide for state or metropolitan review of local appeal decisions, that have reorganized the fiscal systems of municipalities so that land use decisions can be freed from the shackles of tax and revenue implications, that permit zoning-type regulations based on a community plan instead of a zoning map? And where have been the planners who should have been in the front ranks of those demanding reforms at the metropolitan and state levels?

For half a century we have engaged in a kind of legislative Shintoism, worshipping at the shrine of the Standard State Zoning Enabling Act. Zoning served us well during a period when urban life was simpler and less dynamic. We should honor those who were responsible for its birth and early care—the Bassetts and the Bettmans and, later, the Pomeroys of our professions—all of whom demonstrated a fertility of intellect that we have failed to imitate. But we do these men, and ourselves as well, ultimate honor not by tending their legislative monuments at the end of the by now well-worn legal road they constructed but by carving new trails toward new frontiers to serve an emerging new urban America.

THE FUTURE OF AMERICAN PLANNING:
REQUIEM OR RENASCENCE?

John W. Reps

Three years ago in sounding a requiem for zoning I analyzed the shortcomings in our methods of regulating urban development and suggested an alternative system of land use control.[1] That address included a statement that the regulatory elements in a system of planning implementation possessed only limited effectiveness and far greater emphasis should be placed on more positive measures.

Time has only strengthened my conviction that this assessment was correct. A year of residence abroad has since provided an opportunity to observe closely planning systems which differ from our own in this respect. I propose now to explore this subject in greater depth.

Let me make clear at the outset that, while a member of ASPO's board of directors, what I have to say is not in any way to be construed as a declaration of organization policy. Nor does it represent the views of Cornell University or my colleagues there in the department of city and regional planning.

I start from the premise that the American urban environment is grossly unsatisfactory when compared to what we are capable of achieving. It is inefficient, inconvenient, unattractive, uneconomical, and unloved. The tragedy is that this condition is also unnecessary. There are just enough examples in America of good urban design to demonstrate the existence of this planability gap. From the Riverside, Illinois, of a century ago to the Reston, Virginia, of today we can see that under exceptional circumstances high quality, attractive, convenient, safe, healthful, and efficient neighborhoods and communities lie within our technical grasp.

Europe furnishes even more impressive examples to demonstrate what contemporary urban planners can achieve under more favorable conditions: Tapiola, Välingby, and Amsterdam West, to name but three of the many soundly conceived and brilliantly executed projects abroad.

I am not suggesting that planners know all the answers or that all the answers can be supplied only by planners. Indeed, planners and professional colleagues from other fields have not yet even identified all the meaningful questions. But I do maintain that public plans, deficient though they may be in many respects, far exceed in quality in almost every case what actually emerges as the built urban environment.

Between vision and reality stands our antiquated, ineffective, and endlessly frustrating system of planning implementation. It is to this area of research and innovative thinking that we should channel our major invest-

From *Planning, 1967: Papers from the ASPO National Conference* (Chicago: American Society of Planning Officials, 1967). Reprinted by permission of the publisher and the author. The full text is available from the publisher.

[1] Reps, John W., "Requiem for Zoning," *Planning, 1964: Selected Papers from the ASPO National Planning Conference.* Chicago: American Society of Planning Officials, 1964, pp. 56-67.

ment of intellectual resources. It is what comes after a plan and not what comes before that should receive greatest current emphasis, because it is precisely here that the planning process is weakest.

Our public rhetoric is completely misleading on this subject. Three general positions taken by planners can be identified. The traditionalists propose long-range master plans looking forward to some target year. They tell the community at large and its public officials that by a combination of good zoning, vigorous use of subdivision control, the adoption of capital improvements programing, and implementation of urban renewal this kind of plan can be carried out.

A second school of planners, correctly perceiving that this approach has not and cannot work, especially at the metropolitan scale with our present chaotic pattern of governmental boundaries, suggests another approach. The really important determinants of urban form, they assert, are lines of communication and notes of employment. Locate them strategically, and the future shape of the metropolis will automatically follow. This position may be somewhat more realistic than the first, but its flaw lies in its disregard for the character and quality of the development which would inevitably be attracted along the corridors of communication and around the concentrations of commerce and industry. We could follow this strategy and be successful in shaping the broad lines of the future metropolis only to find that the details of the resulting environment would be no better than at present.

A third group disdains the idea of a long-range physical plan as mere utopianism. Their doctrine is disjointed incrementalism, to borrow a term used in the field of public administration. Seek not the optimum solutions to urban development because it is impossible to weigh and assess the implications of all possible alternative courses of action. Strive only for a solution to a given problem representing an improvement over the present. This is a sophisticated elaboration of the doctrine of muddling through. Applied to urban physical planning this strategy might lead to results almost the opposite of the second. We might very well achieve a series of acceptably designed individual elements but which in the aggregate would yield an over-all metropolitan form which would prove unsatisfactory.

To sum up: the first strategy is not working well and is not likely to produce any better results in the future. The second concentrates on those aspects of urban growth which are essential to urban life but neglects all those vital details which make that life worth living. The third focuses on details of development but disregards the need for attention to the fundamental structure of the metropolis. All three strategies are basically conservative in that they do not rely on or even contemplate substantial changes in our outlook toward the raw material of the subject—land and its institutional setting.

I now suggest a far more radical approach. It is radical, however, only in the modern American context. It is a system of urban development guidance long employed in certain European countries, producing there far happier results than anything we can offer by comparison. It has been suggested before in the United States, and modest programs similar in nature have been experimented with in Canada and Puerto Rico since 1949. Let me first summarize my general proposition and then proceed to explain and elaborate on its details.

I propose that land at the urban fringe which is to be developed for urban uses should be acquired by a public agency. Acquisition, in fact, should run well ahead of anticipated need and include the purchase or condemnation of idle or agricultural land well beyond the present urban limits. The public agency, therefore, should be given territorial jurisdiction which includes not only the present central city and the surrounding suburbs but a wide belt of undeveloped land.

Land scheduled for early development should be designed in detail, conforming to a general, comprehensive, and long-range metropolitan growth plan. The public agency, directly or indirectly, should install all street and utility improvements and should identify and retain all sites needed for such public facilities as parks, schools, and other neighborhood and community needs. The remaining land should then be disposed of to private builders by sale or lease, the aggregate price to reflect full acquisition and improvements costs but no profit. The terms of the sale or lease should include adequate safeguards to insure development only in conformity to the detailed plans prepared for the area. In short, I am suggesting that a municipal, metropolitan, or state agency enter the field of land development in suburban or rural locations in a manner similar to that used in central city redevelopment projects.

Let me now turn to the details of this scheme.

I visualize the creation, under state enabling legislation, of a metropolitan land corporation. This might be a wholly public enterprise, but I see no objections and some possible advantages to a mixed public-private venture. This would be similar to COMSAT, the public-private satellite communication corporation already established under federal sponsorship or the proposed public-private body to undertake renewal projects recently discussed in the press.

To speed the creation of such agencies and to hasten the passage of appropriate state legislation, I suggest an expanded federal loan and grant program. This might combine and broaden some of the features of present federal aid activities for acquiring open space and advance site acquisition for public facilities. Financial assistance should be made available for land purchases on a larger scale and not limited to parks or public buildings as the ultimate use of the sites.

The metropolitan land corporation would possess authority to purchase land in the open market as well as the power to condemn land. These powers would be subject to the normal due process constraints applying to more traditional municipal bodies. I would hope that eventually this corporation could be attached to a general purpose metropolitan government and become its real estate arm, but this is not essential to the proposal.

Federal loans and grants, plus possible additional state financial assistance, would provide the basic financing. In the initial years of operation, capital costs and operating expenses might exceed revenues derived through land sales or rental income. In the not so long run, however, as European experience conclusively demonstrates, the financial operations would become self-sustaining. Income from land sales and rentals would add to a revolving fund which would be invested in low-priced outlying land. This publically-owned undeveloped land need not lie idle. It could be leased back to present occupants for farming or other non-urban purposes. Again, European experience proves the feasibility of such a system. The Ottawa greenbelt is a North American example.

A variety of land disposal methods could be employed to provide flexibility in meeting various kinds of needs and to avoid stereotyped design.

In certain cases, raw land could be conveyed to a developer under an approved plan. Developers in this case could be selected as the result of design competitions, the submissions being guided by broad specifications as to such factors as density, permissible mixture of uses, and general types of allowable structures.

In some situations, the metropolitan land corporation need only provide major essential and form-giving public improvements, such as principal roads, trunk sewers, main water lines, and community open spaces. Individual developers could then be selected to fill in the detailed structure subject to corporation approval.

Or, probably in the majority of situations, the corporation could carry out all detailed site planning, install or schedule for construction all of the services and facilities, and reserve specific areas for public and semi-public building locations. Improved sites could be disposed of in individual lots, urban blocks, or entire neighborhoods.

Site planning design need not be done entirely by the corporation staff. As at Harlow, perhaps the most successful of the British new towns from the design standpoint, private firms of planners or designers could be retained by the corporation for individual sections, subject only to the broad outlines of the metropolitan plan or the somewhat less general plan for the expansion of a major sector.

The most important advantage of such a system, which alone justifies its adoption, is that it would provide effective public control over the strategic elements of urban growth—the location, the design, the sequence, and the tempo of development. Our present control mechanism, relying chiefly on police power regulations, does not. Decisions about land use in this country are those of private individuals tempered only slightly by the public interest. The proposed system would place these essential decisions in the hands of an agency charged primarily with promoting and safeguarding the public interest but directed as well to devote appropriate attention to the needs and interests of private parties.

Traditional subdivision control procedures would be eliminated. Types of police power regulations, such as now embodied in zoning ordinances, building regulations, and housing codes would still apply in areas previously developed, but in these new urban extensions would exist chiefly as standby protective devices.

Let me now mention some of the other benefits this system of urban guidance would provide. First, this policy of public land acquisition and site development would largely overcome the evils and dangers of land speculation which distort the growth patterns of our cities and which add unnecessarily to the costs of housing and other elements or urban development. It would reduce somewhat the cost of urban land, partly through the nonprofit nature of the operation, partly because of lower interest rates on capital borrowed for land purchases, and partly through advance acquisition of land at lower cost.

Second, the present statutory and constitutional difficulties that arise in requiring dedication of public sites as a condition of plat approval would be avoided. While courts are now looking with more favor on these impositions, many problems remain. All these would be eliminated through a policy of acquiring land to be developed and then simply withholding from subsequent sale or lease those sites needed for a wide variety of public uses.

Third, the system could provide a constant flow of improved building sites to the housing market. At the present time, buildable land becomes available only erratically, subject to the vagaries of personal whim, the owner's tax position, the availability of development capital, the often uninformed appraisal of the probable market, and a host of other uncertainties. Often a paradoxical shortage of building sites exists even at times of high market demand, thus hindering the activities of builders and frustrating those who are seeking homes. Probably the most often repeated complaint of builders—both large and small—is the shortage of land.

Fourth, the proposed method of directing urban expansion would promote contiguous development rather than the wasteful, discontinuous pattern which now prevails and which results very largely from the whimsical characteristics of the peripheral land market. In order to find land on which to build, the developer must often leap-frog over near-in tracts which are held off the market for one reason or another. The expense of public services and facilities becomes unnecessarily high, and the cost to individuals in time and money is increased by this useless and unessential dispersal. The proposed system would normally place on the market only land contiguous to the existing network of services, but it could also be employed to create new towns or detached satellites where this is found desirable.

Fifth, as programs of urban renewal gain momentum, the method of urban expansion which I advocate can be used to provide land for persons displaced from renewal operations. Public bodies have an obligation here far greater than they now accept. Much of the pain of renewal can be eased and some of the opposition reduced by a policy of providing attractive sites for relocation.

. . .

I have already observed that essentially similar systems of guiding urban land development have long been in operation in certain European cities. Political democracy and a free enterprise economy are as highly prized there as in the United States, but land is rightly regarded as a community resource and not a commodity for private speculation. Let me briefly describe the experience in two cities which must surely rank as among the best planned in the world.

Large scale advance purchase of land around Stockholm began in 1904.

It was this policy which has made it possible for the city to shape its physical destiny over the years in such a remarkably effective way. As the director of its department of planning and building control recently stated: "Stockholm's ability to plan its physical, economic and social development must be attributed mainly to one all-important factor: public ownership of the land."[2] It is no accident that the 1967 land-use map of Stockholm is virtually identical to the 1952 general development plan which called for the creation of a series of separate and defined satellite communities. Vällingby, Farsta, and the 21 other superbly planned urban districts that have been created in the past 15 years did not result from advisory plans or the application of police power regulations. Their planning, and their speedy development as planned, were made possible only because of municipal land ownership of their sites and the disposal of that land only under conditions that guaranteed the implementation of public decisions for their use and design.

Amsterdam's record is even longer. Modern wholesale land acquisition started in 1902, but the unique ring canal plan of the inner city dates from 1610 when the city acquired most of the land needed for expansion, drained and filled the area, and constructed the necessary canals and streets. Building sites were then sold subject to appropriate restrictions. The result is universally regarded as one of the greatest accomplishments in city building of all time.

The achievements of this century are also noteworthy, beginning with the great design by Berlage for Amsterdam South, planned for a site purchased by the city to assure planned expansion. More recently an enormous new district, Amsterdam West, has been virtually completed, following in all its essential details the proposals first shown on the official comprehensive plan of 1934. This, too, was made possible only because of municipal ownership of the site. And the next great sector of development, the Bijlmermeer area to the southeast will be developed in precisely the same manner on land already in public ownership and awaiting construction. It is worth noting that although Dutch and Swedish cities possess adequate powers of condemnation, most of their land has been acquired through purchase rather than by eminent domain.

I have singled out but two cities in Europe among many which are guiding urban growth in the only effective way. To the list can be added, among a number of others, Oslo, Helsinki, Hamburg, Rotterdam, The Hague, and Utrecht, to mention only those of which I have some personal knowledge. This brilliant record stands in sharp contrast with the sorry story of modern American city planning. Nowhere in this country can one find a major city the expansion of which in the present era has taken place as planned. It is not a case of an occasional departure from an officially adopted plan. It is not even a situation where a majority of cities do not grow as planned. It is, rather, a record of complete and consistent failure. There is obviously something fundamentally wrong with a planning system

[2] Sidenbladh, Göran, "Stockholm: A Planned City," *Scientific American*, CCXIII, No. 3 (September, 1965), p. 107.

which never works as we say it should. We are being dishonest with ourselves and our clients—the community at large—when we think, talk, or write otherwise.

It was not always so in the United States. As an historian of American urban planning, I have been probing for historical precedents of what I am now advocating. Among other cities, in Savannah, in New York, in Detroit, and in San Francisco, the municipal governments once owned extensive tracts of land which now have been urbanized. Only Savannah, of these four, wisely used its opportunity to plan its growth with care and consistency. From 1733 until 1856, when the supply of public land was exhausted, the public authorities of the city created one or more new wards as population increased and additional land was needed. Each contained an open square around which were 40 house lots and four sites for public and semi-public buildings and uses. All but one of more than 30 of these squares still exist. Equally important, during this period of growth the city expanded in a contiguous pattern which is the direct opposite of the sprawling and discontinuous configuration of the modern city.

Let me offer in evidence a more important and better known example from our history.

A decision was once made that a major project of urban development should be undertaken, that the public interest dictated this should occur on vacant land, and that a careful plan should be prepared to guide this growth. It was no small project. The area involved was enormous—more than 5,000 acres of land. All this land was in private ownership. The owners were speculatively inclined. Most of them yearned to enrich themselves out of this project.

Largely as the result of the remarkable vision of two men, this entire site was acquired by a public agency. Both men knew from long and immediate experience the prevailing conditions of this country's land market as well as anyone before or since. Both were large land owners themselves and were ardent supporters of political democracy and a free enterprise economy. Yet both adopted the position—and acted accordingly—that only if the land to be developed came entirely into public ownership could a comprehensive urban plan be carried out.

After the site was acquired and the plan completed, whole blocks as well as individual building sites were sold for development subject to controls over the character of the buildings. Land for streets, squares, open spaces, and public buildings were retained for eventual community use. The result was what is still the most notable city planning project in the United States and ranks with the best in the world. Hundreds of thousands of visitors each year experience its unique urban environment unaware of the only reason that made its existence possible in its present planned condition—that once all its land was in public ownership, making feasible the transition from plan to reality.

I am describing Washington, D.C., the national capital. The two men most responsible for its founding and development as a planned city on public land were George Washington and Thomas Jefferson. The most active supporter of the legislation which made it possible was Representative James

Madison. If those of us who now support public land acquisition to cope with even more pressing problems of urban development than were faced in 1791 are to be branded as socialists, we stand with distinguished company.

One more historical footnote may be of interest. In 1839, a newly independent but underdeveloped country of the Western Hemisphere determined that a new capital city was required in the interests of national unity and to stimulate development beyond the existing frontier. The legislature passed an act creating a special commission with powers to select a site and to purchase the necessary land, or to acquire it by eminent domain if existing owners were unwilling to sell. Condemnation was, in fact, necessary and a special court was convened to determine adequate compensation. The law provided that the President should then appoint an agent to plan the city and that before selling any lots he was to "set apart a sufficient number of the most eligible for a Capitol, Arsenal, Magazine, University, Academy, Churches, Common Schools, Hospital, Penitentiary, and for all other necessary public buildings and purposes." The legislators who passed this law and the President who administered it were, like Washington, Jefferson, and Madison, vigorous advocates of both free enterprise and political democracy, as are their descendants. But, like the founders of the United States capital some years earlier, they realized that public ownership of urban land was essential to carry out sound city development. Like Washington, the new city was called after a national hero, a name which it still proudly bears. I refer, of course, to the planning of the city of Austin, once capital of the Republic of Texas, and the seat of government of the state.

I include these historical references believing that in studying history we are but looking backwards into the future, and that the past can serve as a guide to what might lie ahead. History would seem to indicate that what I am advocating is neither un-American or un-Texan. It is a policy which lies squarely in our national tradition. When applied intelligently, it has worked well. Washington, Austin, and Savannah are not isolated examples. In the 17th century, public land acquisition for urban development was widely used in Virginia and Maryland where a total of 77 sites were originally designated. Two of the most elaborately planned towns of Colonial America resulted from this program: Annapolis and Williamsburg.

Other examples of cities planned on land acquired for the purpose or located on sites from the public domain include Raleigh, North Carolina; Tallahassee, Florida; Jackson, Mississippi; Columbus, Ohio; Indianapolis; Indiana; Detroit, Michigan; and Chicago, Illinois. Further historical research would doubtless reveal many others. We lost this once firmly established tradition in the later 19th century when America abandoned the concept of city planning as an essentially public enterprise. This vital community function fell into the hands of private speculators who cared little for the public interest then and who, if their attitudes have changed somewhat over the years, can scarcely be relied on now or in the future to place public goals ahead of private gain.

To summarize: I argue that effective implementation of urban plans in the United States requires large-scale public land acquisition. I suggest that virtually all land to be urbanized should come into public ownership and then be made available for development as needed, where required, and under conditions that will assure building only in conformity with public development plans. I contend that leasehold disposition would better serve the public interest in both the short and long run while recognizing that sale of land subject to appropriately detailed covenant controls may be satisfactory. I assert that such a system is in our own tradition of fashioning empirical solutions to problems of this magnitude without regard for doctrinaire dogma, and that it is wholly compatible with our fundamental political beliefs and an economic system which puts heavy emphasis on private initiative and profit. I submit that evidence from the past in the United States and from current practice abroad fully supports my case and that there are no substantial arguments to refute it. While I claim that this major change in land policy is absolutely essential to the satisfactory control of urban growth, I would also point out that this alone will not guarantee sound planning and its implementation. We will need as well the intellectual capacity to make wise plans, the political courage to abide by them, and the administrative skills to carry them out.

I believe firmly that we can make this system work and that without it there will be neither a renascence of planning nor a hopeful future for urban America.

Rules of Play

This experiment is divided into two parts: Variation I will deal with zoning; Variation II will involve a Metropolitan Land Corporation.

Variation I

This portion of Experiment IV will involve play under the existence of a City Zoning Ordinance. The Ordinance is of the exclusive type: each land use may be developed only on those parcels designated for that use. Play begins with some parcels developed, some land owned, and with an existing utility system. Figure IV-1 illustrates the setup of the Playing Board. Table IV-1 lists team holdings while Table IV-2 gives each team's financial standing. Table IV-3 lists the community financial position.

Figure IV-1. Setup of the Playing Board

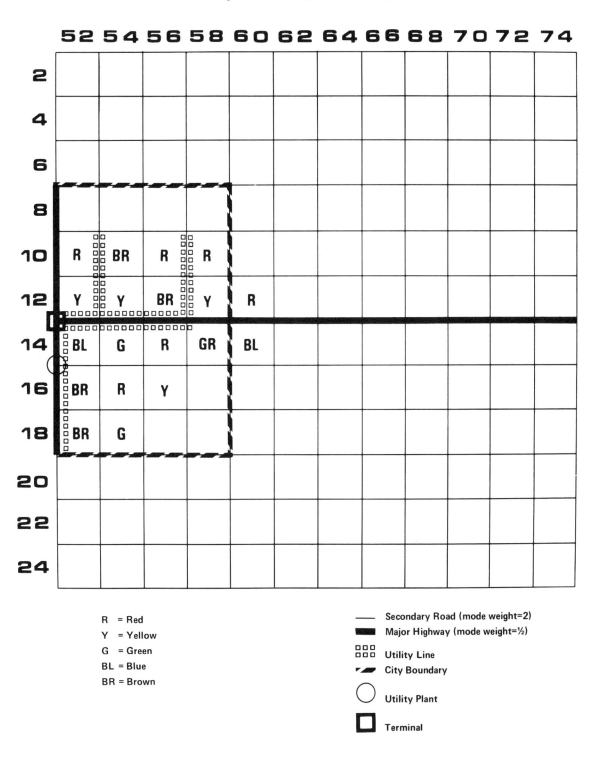

R = Red
Y = Yellow
G = Green
BL = Blue
BR = Brown

—— Secondary Road (mode weight=2)
■■ Major Highway (mode weight=½)
▫▫▫ Utility Line
◣◤ City Boundary
◯ Utility Plant
▢ Terminal

Table IV-1. Team Holdings — Variation I

| | Land | | | | Building | | |
| | | | | | | | |
Coordinates	Team	Purchase Price	Assessed Value	Type	Round Built	Assessed Value
10-52	R	$3,000	$2,500	PI	3	$48,000
12-52	Y	3,000	3,300	FI	1	96,000
14-52	Bl	4,000	3,100	FI	2	96,000
18-52	B4	1,000	1,800	R1	2	12,000
10-54	Br	1,500	2,200	R3	1	48,000
14-54	G	2,500	2,700	R4	2	72,000
14-56	R	1,800	1,900	R1	1	12,000
10-58	R	1,000	1,200	R1	3	12,000
16-52	Br	3,000	1,500			
12-54	Y	3,200	2,500			
16-54	R	1,800	2,000			
18-54	G	1,500	1,600			
10-56	R	1,200	1,400			
12-56	Br	2,500	2,000			
16-56	Y	1,000	1,500			
12-58	Y	1,500	1,500			
14-58	G	1,600	1,500			
12-60	R	1,000	1,200			
14-60	Bl	1,000	1,200			

Table IV-2. Team Standings — Variation I — Round 4

	Team R	Team Y	Team Bl	Team G	Team Br
Property Assessed Value	80,300	103,300	100,300	77,800	67,500
Cash	39,700	16,700	19,700	42,200	52,500

Table IV-3. Community Financial Standing — Variation I — Round 4

Total Assessed Value	$429,200
Tax Rate	5%
Total Taxes	21,500
Utility Lines (8 old, 2 new)	12,000
Residences	10,000
Interest on Deficit @ 5%	500
Total Expenditures	22,500
Round Surplus or Deficit	(−1,000)
Total Surplus or Deficit	(−11,000)
Debt Limit @ 10%	42,900
Tax Rate for Round 5	5%

Play begins in Round 5 at **Step 1** (Purchase Land). In this experiment, each team may bid on only one parcel per round. Bids are submitted and awarded in the conventional manner.

Step 2 (Provide Utilities) is unchanged from Basic CLUG.

Step 3 (Renovate Buildings) is unchanged from Basic CLUG.

During **Step 4** (Construct Buildings) the instructor or game manager will be responsible for the administration of the Zoning Ordinance and its provisions. This responsibility includes prohibiting development which does not conform to the designated use, prohibiting expansion of existing non-conforming uses (e.g., PI to FI or R2 to R4), and granting variances. Table IV-4 is used in determining the success or failure of variance requests.

Table IV-4. Variance Success Probabilities and Dice Numbers

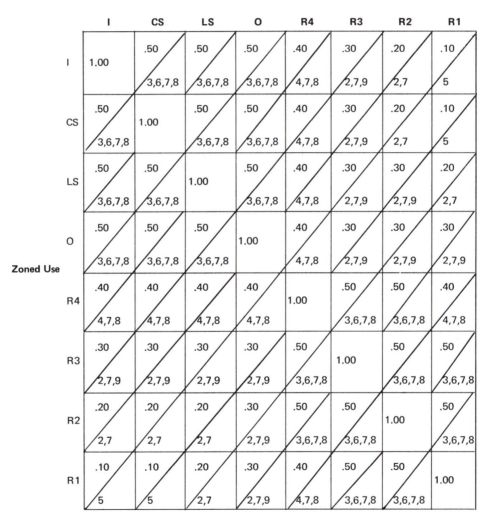

		I	CS	LS	O	R4	R3	R2	R1
	I	1.00	.50 / 3,6,7,8	.50 / 3,6,7,8	.50 / 3,6,7,8	.40 / 4,7,8	.30 / 2,7,9	.20 / 2,7	.10 / 5
	CS	.50 / 3,6,7,8	1.00	.50 / 3,6,7,8	.50 / 3,6,7,8	.40 / 4,7,8	.30 / 2,7,9	.20 / 2,7	.10 / 5
	LS	.50 / 3,6,7,8	.50 / 3,6,7,8	1.00	.50 / 3,6,7,8	.40 / 4,7,8	.30 / 2,7,9	.30 / 2,7,9	.20 / 2,7
	O	.50 / 3,6,7,8	.50 / 3,6,7,8	.50 / 3,6,7,8	1.00	.40 / 4,7,8	.30 / 2,7,9	.30 / 2,7,9	.30 / 2,7,9
Zoned Use	R4	.40 / 4,7,8	.40 / 4,7,8	.40 / 4,7,8	.40 / 4,7,8	1.00	.50 / 3,6,7,8	.50 / 3,6,7,8	.40 / 4,7,8
	R3	.30 / 2,7,9	.30 / 2,7,9	.30 / 2,7,9	.30 / 2,7,9	.50 / 3,6,7,8	1.00	.50 / 3,6,7,8	.50 / 3,6,7,8
	R2	.20 / 2,7	.20 / 2,7	.20 / 2,7	.30 / 2,7,9	.50 / 3,6,7,8	.50 / 3,6,7,8	1.00	.50 / 3,6,7,8
	R1	.10 / 5	.10 / 5	.20 / 2,7	.30 / 2,7,9	.40 / 4,7,8	.50 / 3,6,7,8	.50 / 3,6,7,8	1.00

Caption: Use Desired (column heading), Zoned Use (row heading).

In order to apply for a variance a team informs the instructor of its intentions. After locating the parcel under consideration on the Zoning Map, Figure IV-2, and determining the permitted use, the Instructor refers to the appropriate cell in Table IV-4. The figure above the diagonal gives the probability of the variance being granted while the number(s) below the

Figure IV-2. Zoning Map

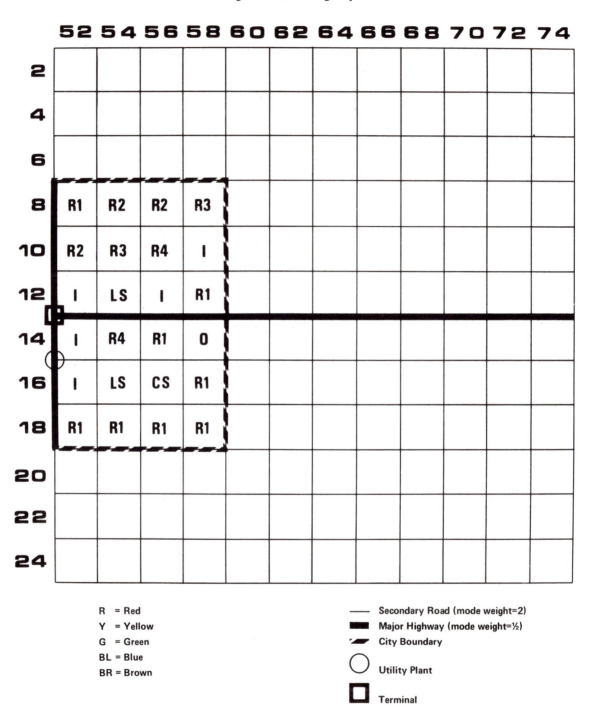

R = Red
Y = Yellow
G = Green
BL = Blue
BR = Brown

——— Secondary Road (mode weight=2)
▰▰▰ Major Highway (mode weight=½)
▨▨▨ City Boundary
◯ Utility Plant
◻ Terminal

diagonal are the corresponding numbers to be rolled on two dice for a successful application. If the variance is granted, the team proceeds with construction as desired or retains the variance for future use. If more than one variance is granted on a parcel, only the most recent variance is valid. A variance must be granted before an existing nonconforming use may be expanded. A parcel on which a variance has been granted is treated as if it had been rezoned, so that any change in land use requires a new variance application. A team may apply for only one variance per round. Judicial challenge of the validity of the ordinance will not be allowed in this experiment. In all other respects, Step 4 (Construct Buildings) is conducted as in Basic CLUG.

Step 5 (Designate Employment) is unchanged from Basic CLUG.

Step 6 (Sign Trade Agreements) is unchanged from Basic CLUG.

Step 7 (Receive Income) is unchanged from Basic CLUG.

Step 8 (Pay Employees) is unchanged from Basic CLUG.

Step 9 (Pay Stores and Office) is unchanged from Basic CLUG.

In Step 10 (Pay Transportation Costs) the costs are computed using Mode Weights of 2 for Secondary Roads and ½ for the Major Highway.

Step 11 (Pay Taxes) is unchanged from Basic CLUG.

After the initial set up of the board, the only special information required for running this Variation of the experiment is the Zoning Map and the Table of Variance Success Probabilities (Table IV-4). Since these are readily available in the text itself, a single summary page of information needed for the experiment in this variation has not been provided. A convenient summary of the new Steps of Play is as follows:

1. Purchase Land	Only one bid per team.
2. Provide Utilities	Unchanged.
[3. Renovate Buildings]	Unchanged.
4. Construct Buildings	All new construction or expansion of old buildings must be in conformance with the Zoning Ordinance or allowed by a successul variance. Teams are limited to one variance request per round.
5. Designate Employment	Unchanged.
6. Sign Trade Agreements	Unchanged.
7. Receive Income	Unchanged.
8. Pay Employees	Unchanged.
9. Pay LS, CS, and O	Unchanged.
10. Pay Transportation	Mode Weights are ½ and 2 for Major Highway and Secondary Road.
11. Pay Taxes	Unchanged.

Discussion

This variation of the experiment should be run for a long enough time to give players some understanding of the manner in which a zoning ordinance operates and a chance to evaluate its effectiveness in controlling land development. If possible, fewer than ten rounds from the Round 5 beginning point should be played for this purpose. It is important, however, that players gain some background in the major current method of land use regulation. It is not expected that players will be particularly impressed with the method under consideration or that they will have much to offer except negative comments on the manner of operation of the zoning provisions. The mechanism provided in the game is neither strong nor imaginative but in the opinion of the authors of CLUG and John Reps this is a reasonable characterization of most existing zoning ordinances.

Study Questions

A few study questions may help to guide discussion at this point but most questions and discussion should probably follow the completion of Variation Two.

1. To what extent was the Municipal Zoning Ordinance able to guide and direct the pattern of urban development?

2. In your opinion was the growth and development of the city aided or hindered by the existing zoning ordinance?

3. Were the city boundaries of any particular significance to you as you made investment and development decisions? In what way?

4. Assuming that the Municipal Zoning Ordinance presented represented a desirable pattern of final development for the city in terms of esthetic or other factors not considered in the game, what contradictory costs are incurred in its enforcement during play? Which set of factors is likely to be dominant in the growth and administration of a typical American city?

Variation II

This second part of Experiment IV will include the operation of a Metropolitan Land Corporation* and will explore the ability of this technique to guide land development. The Corporation will be operated by an Administrator chosen before play commences. In Round 1, the Administrator will be given a grant of $100,000 with which to buy, improve, and lease or sell land on a non-profit basis. Five teams also begin with $100,000.

In **Step 1** (Purchase Land) the Administrator may submit bids on nine or fewer parcels per round; each team is limited to bidding on one parcel per round. Bids are opened and competition resolved in the usual manner. At this step the Administrator may also condemn property by paying the owner the current Assessed Value plus twenty-five per cent for the land and/or building in question. The Administrator may not operate buildings but must

---

*Adapted from David L. Phillips, "Appendix D: A Modification of CLUG and CLUG-ALUM to Include the Policy of a Municipal Land Corporation," in Allan G. Feldt, *Community Land Use Game*, Ithaca, New York, 1968, pp. 111-128. Used with permission of the author.

demolish them before seeking agreement to redevelop the land in accordance with the Metropolitan Plan. There are no demolition costs in this variation.

Utilities are provided in the usual Basic CLUG manner in **Step 2.** In addition, however, the Administrator may construct Utility Lines to serve his own parcels. Each Line constructed by the Administrator must serve at least one Corporation-owned square of land. Before the Administrator constructs Utility Lines he must have the agreement of three teams that the community will maintain the Lines in all future rounds. If agreement is reached, the Administrator pays $2,000 per Line for construction to the instructor and the community is assessed $1,000 per line maintenance, to be taken out of Taxes in each subsequent round.

Step 3 (Renovate Buildings) is handled as in Basic CLUG.

Privately-owned land is developed as was done in Basic CLUG in **Step 4.** After consulting the Metropolitan Plan, Figure IV-3, the Administrator may offer parcels of his choice for lease or sale for specific land uses. The Plan is intended to serve as a goal for the pattern of development at approximately Round 15. The Administrator may depart from the Plan in the short run if this action would assist longer-run compliance. Leases are written for ten-round intervals and may be renewed at expiration. Both rent and sale price should be determined by the Administrator to be consistent with the intention of non-profit operation. Rents and sale prices should be as low as possible, yet cover the overall land acquisition, condemnation, and Utility Line costs of the Corporation in order to maintain the $100,000 worth of the Corporation in cash and property holdings. The rent or sale prices of a particular parcel may thus reflect costs not only directly attributable to that parcel, but also the cost of overall corporation operations. When lease or sale agreements are made between the Administrator and teams, development must take place within two rounds or the agreement is considered broken. Rent is not refundable, though the sale price minus ten per cent is returned if a purchase agreement is broken. If more than one team desires to lease or purchase a particular parcel, sealed competitive bids on rent or sale price are submitted to the Administrator, with the highest bid winning. The Administrator may make no loans to teams for any purchase.

Step 5 (Designate Employment) is unchanged from Basic CLUG.

Step 6 (Sign Trade Agreements) is unchanged from Basic CLUG.

Step 7 (Receive Income) is unchanged from Basic CLUG.

Step 8 (Pay Employees) is unchanged from Basic CLUG.

Step 9 (Pay Stores and Office) is handled as in Basic CLUG and the Administrator at this time also collects rents from those teams holding leases.

Step 10 (Pay Transportation Costs) is handled as in Basic CLUG with Mode Weights of ½ and 2 on the Major Highway and Secondary Roads, respectively.

Step 11 (Pay Taxes) is handled in the same manner as Basic CLUG for all players except the Land Corporation. Since this is supposedly a non-profit public corporation it should be tax-exempt. A record of its property holdings and their assessed value should be retained in the normal manner as

Figure IV-3. Metropolitan Plan

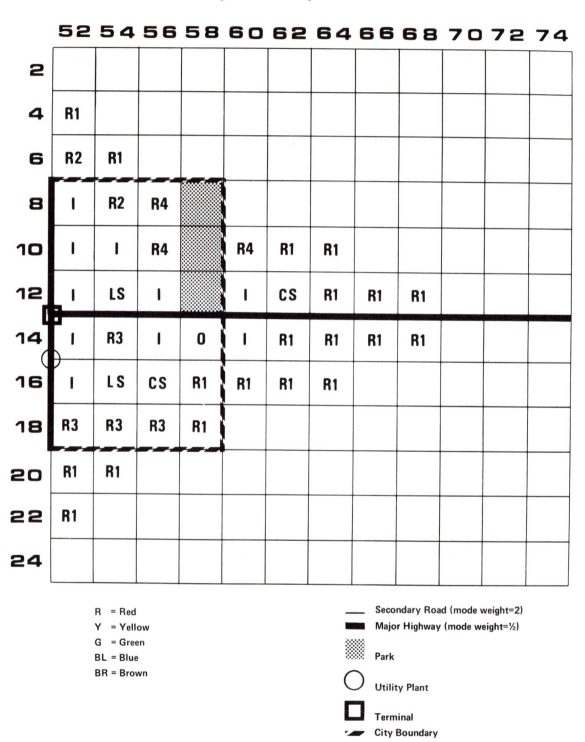

R = Red
Y = Yellow
G = Green
BL = Blue
BR = Brown

Secondary Road (mode weight=2)

Major Highway (mode weight=½)

Park

Utility Plant

Terminal

City Boundary

for other players, however. In each round divisible by five, the total assets of the Corporation should be evaluated and any value significantly greater than its original $100,000 should be declared a surplus and paid to the community as a tax credit to compensate for apparent overcharges on rents or land sales.

No special information is required for running this experiment other than the Metropolitan Plan given in Figure IV-3 and the special rules for managing the Land Corporation. Hence, no summary page of information is presented. A convenient summary of the Steps of Play is as follows:

1. Purchase Land	Only one bid per team in each round. Administrator may bid on nine parcels in each round and may condemn property.
2. Provide Utilities	Administrator may construct utility lines if community agrees to accept maintenance costs.
[3. Renovate Buildings]	Unchanged.
4. Construct Buildings	Unchanged except Administrator may sell or lease parcels for specific land uses.
5. Designate Employment	Unchanged.
6. Sign Trade Agreements	Unchanged.
7. Receive Income	Unchanged.
8. Pay Employees	Unchanged.
9. Pay LS, CS, and O	Administrator also collects rents.
10. Pay Transportation	Mode Weights are ½ and 2.
11. Pay Taxes	Unchanged except Administrator pays no taxes other than distribution of surplus in rounds divisible by five.

Discussion

In order that the Administrator be able to assume a target date for guiding development to conform to the Metropolitan Plan, it is recommended that this variation of Experiment IV be played until approximately Round 15. At this time, the Administrator and the Metropolitan Land Corporation can be evaluated and discussed. In general, the Administrator is evaluated in terms of the degree of departure he has allowed from the Plan and on his ability to minimize land costs while maintaining an acceptable rate of community growth.

The following specific criteria are suggested as aids to evaluation. Table IV-5 provides a scoring system for assessing deviations from the Plan. In order to score play, each parcel should be assigned 0 to 9 penalty points in accordance with the appropriate cell value. Scores should then be summed across parcels to yield a Total Penalty Score for the end of the game. In general, a Total Score of less than 20 is highly desirable with a score of 21 to 30 considered good.

A second criterion by which the Administrator and the Municipal Land Corporation can be assessed is average land value. Average values above

$3,000 can be considered excessive and due, at least in part, to land speculation and competition between players. The third criterion which can be suggested is that of assessing the rate of community growth in order to determine whether growth was sacrificed for the sake of conformity to the Plan. By Round 15, it would be reasonable to expect Total Community Assessed Value plus cash on hand for the five teams and the Administrator to be worth approximately $1.8 million or more.

For purposes of comparison it may be useful to compute these same three values for Variation I involving the City Zoning Ordinance. If this is done Total Penalty Points should be divided by the number of parcels developed in the appropriate jurisdictions.

Table IV-5. Penalty Points for Plan Deviations

Use Planned

		I	CS	LS	O	R4	R3	R2	R1	Park
	I	0	5	5	5	6	7	8	9	9
	CS	5	0	5	5	6	7	8	9	9
	LS	5	5	0	5	6	7	8	8	9
Use Developed	O	5	5	5	0	6	7	7	7	9
	R4	6	6	6	6	0	5	5	6	8
	R3	7	7	7	7	5	0	5	5	8
	R2	8	8	8	7	5	5	0	5	8
	R1	9	9	8	7	6	5	5	0	8

Study Questions

After completion of both variations of this experiment, a number of questions may be used for interesting discussions exploring the possibilities and mechanisms used in American cities.

1. How successful was the Metropolitan Land Corporation in guiding development policy of the city? Did it appear to be more successful than the zoning ordinance?

2. What impact did the Land Corporation have on land costs? Did this effect make development easier for private investors and developers? If land usually cost less under the Land Corporation variation who lost the higher profits on land and who gained through the lower costs? Who would be the counterparts of such players in the real world. Do the profits on land value properly belong to the public or to the private land holder who sells land at a speculative profit? What effect does zoning have on reducing or increasing such profits?

3. Compare the two methods of land use regulation with respect to their impact on the rate of growth of the community and their relative flexibility and availability of discretionary power. What controls does the

public have over malpractice or inefficiency on the part of the Land Corporation Administrator? How does this compare to public control over similar possible traits in zoning administrators?

4. If you were to attempt to implement a long range community plan in your own community, which of the two forms of control would you favor? What kinds of problems might you expect to encounter in gaining acceptance to a Metropolitan Land Corporation in an American city?

5. Aside from these two forms of land use regulation, what other forms do you know of which are used in this country or in other countries? How do you think they would compare with the two you have examined here?

Experiment V: Inter-Regional Relations

Introduction

The economic facts of urban growth can be viewed from two basic points of view: one emphasizing the characteristics of a community and its regional hinterland, and the other focusing on the community's relationship to a larger national economy. In the first case, the characteristics of a region or community are considered in response to their own wealth-producing potentials, internal supply. In the second case a community's trade relationship with an external economy becomes more significant in terms of external demands for the products of the community or region.

External Demand

On the demand side, the most widely known theory of urban growth is "export-base theory." As Thompson explains, the theory states that cities grow and decline on the strength and weaknesses of their industries that export to markets outside of the region. Following this logic, an analysis of the demand side would include the mix of an area's export industries and their vulnerability to cyclical and long-run trends in the national economy.

In Basic CLUG, industrial exports are represented by both Partial and Full Industry, but their markets are constantly expanding and not subject to the same external fluctuations to which real world industries are subject.

If one subscribed to the export-base logic as fully explaining urban growth, one would view the service sectors as mere adjuncts to the urban area's export economy. Some analysts, for example, have projected an urban area's future growth by carefully projecting growth of the base industries and multiplying by a constant ratio of service employees to export-base employees. The inadequacies of this premise are analyzed in depth by Thompson. Nevertheless, in Basic CLUG, the service sectors (LS, CS and O employment) can be projected fairly well by using the size of the labor force in Partial and Full Industry. This is the case because of the abstract and simplifying nature of the assumptions made to describe CLUG's economy. In Basic CLUG, the ratio remains constant primarily because the community's economy is not subject to the forces of supply and demand of the rest of the world.

Internal Supply

Thompson also discusses the four traditional aspects of the supply side of an urban economy: land, labor, capital, and entrepreneurship. Again, in Basic CLUG these factors are held constant by the abstract nature of the model and its simplifying assumptions. For example, the labor factor is undifferentiated. That is, it possesses one level of skill, education, consumption, and income, and is highly mobile. Entrepreneurship, the ability to create new products and new markets, does not exist in Basic CLUG. This is because demand for goods, which are only of one type, is unlimited. Capital in Basic CLUG is limited to the amount with which the game begins, the amount imported into the game economy through deficit financing of community services, and through export sales of industrial goods. Capital is completely mobile between teams, since borrowing between them is allowed and no team may borrow from the outside world. Lastly, land (or environment) has little meaning in Basic CLUG; there are no significant natural resources or environmental aesthetics represented. The costs of raw materials are merely "netted out" of Full and Partial Industry's income. Residents are totally indifferent to their environment.

The Reading and Experiment

The intent of this experiment is to expand upon several of the simplifying assumptions in CLUG's economy and compare the results of these several changes. A varying market for industrial goods and a national market for investment capital will be dealt with in this experiment. The results of these factors for urban growth are best observed by comparing two competing cities on the same game board, one with and the other without certain economic advantages.

Thompson covers much more than these two variations in his article, but to include more than these two changes would tend to make the game overly complex and comparisons among growth factors intractable. Having read the article, the student might imagine trying to use CLUG to display all the factors Thompson presents as being relevant to urban growth. This will give perspective to the complexity of this one aspect of the urban economy.

The player will be aided throughout if he views the processes of urban growth by thinking of the city as a system. Then, factors at work on city growth can be divided into those outside the city's control (exogenous) and those the city can directly affect (endogenous). This conception of the city as a system will aid both in reading Thompson's article and in playing and discussing the experiment.

ECONOMIC GROWTH AND DEVELOPMENT: PROCESSES, STAGES, AND DETERMINANTS

Wilbur R. Thompson

An Abridged Overview of the Urban Growth Process

The principal cause of the dramatic urban growth experienced by the United States since the turn of the century is the great rural to urban migration. By now, however, the significance of the continuing shift from farm to city is well appreciated; we need pause only briefly to recall its main characteristics as background for the principal concern of this chapter.

In brief, a steady advance in agricultural technology has greatly enlarged farm output per man-hour. The rate of annual increase has risen from a little over 1 per cent in the twenties to more than 5 per cent in the years since the Second World War. Our rapidly growing per capita income—the reflection of a generally advancing technology—has not, however, increased the demand for foods and fibers at anywhere near the same rate; food consumption is increasing only about half as fast as over-all productivity and per capita income, and not much more than half as fast as the productivity growth rate in agriculture itself. Thus, national economic development has required that the agricultural sector decline sharply in relative share. The percentage of the labor force engaged in agriculture plummeted from 12 to 6 percent between 1950 and 1960—while manufacturing and services absorbed expanding shares.

Farm to city migration was, then, dictated by national demand and supply forces and would have occurred even if demographic patterns had been neutral. But a farm birth rate considerably above the urban one resulted in more than proportionate manpower additions in agriculture, during a period when few additions were needed. In sum, the great shift from farm to factory and office is the most basic explanation of urban growth up to now.

But the nation's rural areas are rapidly emptying out; the great farm to city migration has about run its course and will soon belong to economic history. Today, the most challenging urban growth theory and the most compelling urban growth problems arise out of interurban competition for growth and the development of the national system of cities. It is in the size distribution and the spatial pattern of cities that the new vitality of urban economics lies. This chapter emphasizes, then, not the rural to urban migration of the past but the interurban interactions of the present and near future.

From Wilbur R. Thompson, *A Preface to Urban Economics* (Baltimore: Johns Hopkins, 1965), pp. 11-19, 21-33, 37-42, 44-47, 51-59. Reprinted with permission from the publisher. Published by the Johns Hopkins Press, for Resources for the Future, Inc.

The Many Lines of Linkage

Some appreciation of the fine web of urban growth forces can be gained by working through a much oversimplified presentation of the lines of linkage between a hypothetical urban area and the outside world, as outlined in Figure V-1. We arbitrarily break into the pattern of urban economic development by beginning with three local meat-packing plants (1) which sell outside the locality. These have been drawn together by the mutual advantages they enjoy in tapping a large local pool of specialized and skilled labor (2), created by their own *combined* demand. Because they have clustered together, these three plants have attracted a common supplier, a plant manufacturing meat cutting tools (3), and this integration of sequential operations has added to local exports, indirectly, by increasing the proportion of the meat products sales dollar that remains within the area. In other words, as vertical integration in the local export industries progresses, local value-added and income generated become a higher proportion of sales.

Local slaughtering produces hides as a by-product and this encourages shoe firms (4) to locate nearby to save transportation costs on their chief raw material. The horizontal agglomeration of shoe plants may be reinforced by the fact that shoes are subject to comparative shopping by wholesalers and retailers and an out-of-the-way shoe plant is at a severe disadvantage. All of this greatly increases the demand for local business services (5), such as transportation, financial, and marketing services, and thereby improves their quality and variety and lowers their cost.

As local business services become more varied and improve in quality, they steadily replace similar services (6) previously imported from larger, more highly developed neighboring cities. While the net effect is for the local economy to become ever more self-sufficient in business services, the growing complexity of the local economy will bring a need to import at least a modest amount of new, more esoteric business services (e.g., specialized financial and commercial services related to importing foreign steels for the meat cutting tool firm). Simultaneously, the addition of successive firms augments local payrolls and personal income of local households (7) which, in turn, enriches the consumer service sector (8). As successive consumer spending mounts, the variety store gives way to the department store, and then the "custom shop" and the "salon" are added.

Consumer expenditures rise faster than export industry payrolls as the "multiplier effect" takes hold and employees of the local service facilities (9) take incomes earned by servicing the households of employees of the export industries and the linked business service and cutting tool firms, and spend them for more locally produced goods and services. Parallel to the pattern developing in the local business service sector, as the local consumer service sector matures imports of consumer goods and services (10) will decrease, in relative terms, although the absolute amount of consumer imports will probably increase as the local economy grows in size and complexity.

Our hypothetical urban area is now moving up in rank in the hierarchy of cities. As it becomes first a provincial and then a regional capital, its rising status is explicitly recognized by an industrial structure which changes to

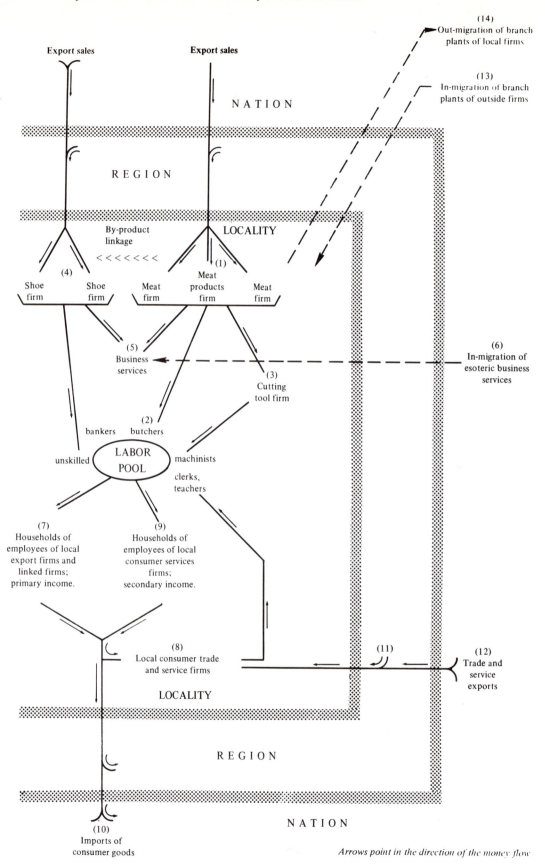

Figure V-1. The urban growth complex

reflect its new role: an exporter of services. A true metropolis as a "mother city" reaches out and renders the more specialized and skill-demanding administrative, financial, legal, educational, recreational, medical, and governmental services to its satellites. The first step, usually, is to export a growing range of services to nearby cities of the next smaller size (11), which in turn merchandise a somewhat abridged line of services to the next lower level of cities. With growth, however, the metropolis may extend its reach to embrace the whole nation or a very large portion of it (12) for a much narrower group of services: New York with finance, corporate administration, entertainment, and others; Chicago with nearly as broad a group; Miami, recreation and amusement; Washington, government and tourist services; Boston, education and research.

Even local manufacturing tends to become more diversified and self-sufficient, as the growing local market attracts the branch plants of outside firms (13), while the branch plants of the growing local firms are spun off in complementary fashion to the large and growing metropolitan areas elsewhere (14). Piece by piece, additional business and consumer services and manufacturing operations are added to the local economy, as the growing local market affords ever more economies of scale and cuts the cost of local production to the point at which the remaining cost disadvantage vis-à-vis the bigger and/or most efficient operations elsewhere is less than the transportation costs from each of them.

Finally, the metropolis, with its universities, museums, libraries, and research laboratories, becomes one big, spatially integrated "coffee house," where bright minds out of diverse cultures clash and strike sparks that ignite the fires of new products and processes—new export industries. We have now come full circle to where we began, or better, we have entered upon an endless and self-regenerative growth cycle.[1]

The Stages of Urban Growth

Can the many aspects of urban-regional growth be grouped and arranged in a time sequence of distinct stages?

We might identify, first, the *Stage of Export Specialization* in which the local economy is the lengthened shadow of a single dominant industry or even a single firm. This initial stage gives way with growth and size to the *Stage of the Export Complex* in which local production broadens to other products and/or deepens by extending forward or backward in the stages of production, by adding local suppliers and/or consumers of intermediate products. Next, the *Stage of Economic Maturation* (Local Service Sector Puberty) follows, in which the principal expansion of local activity is in the direction of replacing imports with new "own use" production; the local

---

[1] This summary and loose synthesis of the complex of forces underlying urban-regional economic growth and development draws liberally, of course, from innumerable sources, and only an unabridged history of doctrine in this field of thought would suffice to assign credits of authorship. The most comprehensive review of this literature and the most exhaustive bibliography published to date (or likely to be published for some time to come) is in Walter Isard, *et al.*, *Methods of Regional Analysis: an Introduction to Regional Science* (New York: John Wiley and Sons, Inc., 1960).

economy fills out in range and quality of both business and consumer services. Fourth, the *Stage of Regional Metropolis* is reached, when the local economy becomes a node connecting and controlling neighboring cities, once rivals and now satellites, and the export of services becomes a major economic function.

One more common phase is the *Stage of Technical-Professional Virtuosity;* national eminence in some specialized skill or economic function is achieved. This stage may succeed or precede the status of regional metropolis: Detroit was a national center of automotive design and engineering long before it became a regional metropolis, if indeed it is one now. Boston's acknowledged eminence in education and, more recently, research and development, followed its role as the capital of New England. San Francisco is a national cultural center, perhaps second only to New York, quite apart from its co-captaincy with Los Angeles of the West Coast region.

These purported stages of urban growth are, of course, highly impressionistic generalizations and deserve a hearing only as the most tentative hypotheses from which careful empirical work might be begun. Moreover, these growth sketches leave much too strong a feeling of the inevitability of growth and development—onward and upward forever. And yet we see many examples of local economic stagnation and decay and even demise. What are some of the dampening and restraining forces that surely must exist?

Failure of Momentum between Stages in Growth

Suppose the original growth stimulus—the economic environment at genesis—did not generate a sufficiently strong impulse to lift the economy to a level at which derivative growth forces could take over. For example: the local harbor and connecting waterways may not have been so superior or the local ore deposit so rich, given the current ore prices and the remoteness of the mine and so forth, to create a town large enough or a technology advanced enough to build an attractive labor force. Without this latter attraction, the local economy never drew the manufacturing plants which would have moved the local economy into the second stage of export diversification and into a state of general industrial enrichment, before the preferred mode of transportation changed or the vein of ore gave out. Or, if the small port or mining economy did manage to add a few manufacturing firms and limp through the second stage of growth, not enough of an industrial complex was created to develop the local market to a point where a strong surge of local service industry formation developed, replacing imports with local production. Thus the growth of a local economy may hesitate and stagnate between any of these stages if the momentum at the end of a phase is not strong enough to carry the economy to the point at which the mechanism of the next stage is activated.

An insufficiency of momentum may be relative rather than absolute, especially with reference to the fourth stage, metropolis formation. Typically, one city will rise from a group of rivals to become the "mother city" of the group. Whichever city gets the jump on the others and achieves early economic dominance usually finds that success breeds success as external economies of service industry agglomeration pave the way for progressive, cumulative coups.[2] The wholesale trade center for the group may stand in good way to become the financial center and the latter gain may commonly lead to administrative dominance and subsequent legal eminence and so forth. The sequence as sketched is purely illustrative because historical and/or statistical-empirical work on this facet of urban growth dynamics is scarce.[3]

Promotion up through the hierarchy of cities is, then, partly a matter of the right timing, usually an early lead amply fortified with local leadership. And we count, of course, more losers than winners in this interurban competition; too little and too late, relative to neighboring cities, is a powerful constraint on urban growth and development.

To be sure, a lagging city can forge ahead to dominance through some exceptionally fortunate circumstance, such as being the chance host to a firm which is destined to become the individual "success story" of *the* growth industry of the era (e.g., Ford Motor Company and Detroit) or through the discovery of great natural wealth (e.g., Houston). Ordinarily, however, success breeds success and the rich get richer, at least in the urban growth process.

. . .

If the rich always did get richer (and the poor poorer) in interregional competition, long-range urban forecasting would be much easier than it actually is. But victories can bring complacency and defeats can be challenges. We might postulate a crisis theory of human behavior in regional economic development: a community rises to the occasion in a variation on the Toynbee theme of "challenge and response."

When urban growth slackens or stalls—when the rate of growth of new jobs falls below the rate of natural increase in the local labor force—heavy, chronic unemployment creates local crises: personal, social and govern-

[2] For example, in the historic rivalry between Chicago and St. Louis for supremacy in the Middle West and as a gateway to the West, natural factors, such as the Mississippi River, as a north-south transportation facility and as an east-west barrier, and social factors, such as a river-minded leadership group in St. Louis and the disruptive effect of the Civil War on the border-state hinterland of St. Louis, all combined to edge Chicago past St. Louis. Cumulative forces in growth then widened the gap. See Lewis F. Thomas, "Decline of St. Louis as Midwest Metropolis," *Economic Geography* (April 1949), pp. 118–27, for a brief account, or Wyatt Winton Belcher, *The Economic Rivalry between St. Louis and Chicago, 1850–1880* (New York: Columbia University Press, 1947), for a more extended treatment.

[3] A number of static, cross-section studies have been made which classify cities according to their principal economic function—manufacturing, wholesale trade center, transportation center, seat of government and so forth. But dynamic analyses which take a city through a sequence of functions with sufficient analytical rigor to permit generalization are still to be done or lie hidden in fugitive materials. On the classification of U.S. cities according to economic function see Chauncy D. Harris, "A Functional Classification of Cities in the United States," *Geographical Review* (January 1943), pp. 86–99, and Howard J. Nelson, "A Service Classification of American Cities," *Economic Geography* (July 1955), pp. 189–210, both reprinted in Harold Mayer and Clyde F. Kohn (editor), *Readings in Urban Geography* (Chicago: University of Chicago Press, 1959), Gunnar Alexandersson, *The Industrial Structure of American Cities* (Stockholm: Almquist and Wiksell, 1959), and Otis Dudley Duncan, W. Richard Scott, Stanley Lieberson, Beverly Duncan, and Hal H. Winsborough, *Metropolis and Region* (Baltimore: The Johns Hopkins Press for Resources for the Future, 1960).

mental. Out-migration, the economist's solution, is often sluggish, especially in a time of ever more pervasive home ownership, tighter job seniority, and broadening unemployment compensation. (Millions for unemployment compensation, but not one cent for relocation expenses!) In depressed areas, sagging tax collections and soaring welfare costs upset municipal budgets and force politicians and public administrators to strain for more imaginative and incisive programs of area industrial development.

Agonizing reappraisals are made of local business taxes relative to competing urban areas, and the efficacy to tax concessions, subsidies in the form of rent-free use of vacant buildings, and other industrial lures are reviewed. One can almost predict the likelihood of "another" state-local tax study from the current rate of local unemployment relative to the current national rate. Comparative transportation facilities, wage rates, utility rates, and other leading plant location factors will also come in for close scrutiny during these trying times. If necessity is the mother of social, as well as technical, invention, the probability of imaginative and effective local action, both public and private, designed to improve the local business climate and nurture new industrial growth will be significantly increased in time of local stagnation.[4]

. . .

The Urban Size Ratchet

If the challenge of economic adversity does indeed beget the response of renewed community leadership and individual creativity, how can we explain abandoned towns and depressed areas?[5] The coal towns of Pennsylvania, West Virginia, and Kentucky have been challenged by chronic unemployment for decades now with little evidence or prospect of significant response; the smaller urban places in Nebraska, the Dakotas and Montana—the wheat belt—have been declining for decades and give every indication of continuing to do so.

But these illustrations are all of the smaller urban areas. Clearly a scale factor is at work: witness the difficulty of finding a similar illustration of an urban area of over half a million population, one which has suffered an absolute decline in population. How far down in population size must we go to name an urban area that has lost population? Perhaps some critical size

[4] Perloff and associates found a low *negative* correlation between the location of growth industries and the local growth rate. Harvey S. Perloff, Edgar S. Dunn, Eric E. Lampard, and Richard F. Muth, *Regions, Resources, and Economic Growth* (Baltimore: The Johns Hopkins Press for Resources for the Future, 1960), p. 68. Perhaps this is due to the tendency of invention, innovation, and promotion to come more than proportionately out of the industrially mature regions, a point they themselves make later in their work. This more than proportionate incubation of new industries in the older industrial areas may originate in their greater technological sophistication, and then again it may originate in purposeful desperation as local entrepreneurs rise to the challenge of heavy local unemployment and business losses.

[5] See *Distressed Areas in a Growing Economy*, A Statement of National Policy by the Research and Policy Committee of the Committee for Economic Development (New York, June 1961), and current unpublished memoranda on area redevelopment circulated by the Manpower and Social Affairs Committee of the Organisation for Economic Cooperation and Development (Paris). The former is directed to U.S. depressed area problems and the latter to the European counterparts.

exists, short of which growth is not inevitable and even the very existence of the place is not assured, but beyond which absolute contraction is highly unlikely, even though the growth rate may slacken, at times even to zero. In sum, at a certain range of urban scale, set by the degree of isolation of the urban place, the nature of its hinterland, the level of industrial development in the country, and various cultural factors, some growth mechanism, similar to a ratchet, comes into being, locking in past growth and preventing contraction.

A number of possible rationalizations of a hypothetical urban-size ratchet could be adduced. One argument would be that with growth and size comes industrial diversification, and even a random blending of young, mature, and decadent industries tends to produce local growth rates which deviate only slightly from the national average rate, or the rate applicable to the surrounding region. Freedom from rapid rates of decline, moreover, provides the large urban area a grace period in which to react to adversity. Finally, the rich industrial diversification of the large urban area is fashioned in part out of many small firms with extensive and complex linkages to other local businesses. Clearly, it is much harder for these firms to relocate than it is for the large self-sufficient plant characteristic of a small urban area.

A second possible basis for irreversible urban growth after achievement of some threshold size is simply power politics. With a larger population comes greater electoral strength at both the state and national levels and with reference to both executive and legislative bodies. True, political power may increase less than proportionately with population increase, as in malapportioned state legislatures and in the United States Senate; nevertheless, it does increase significantly. Thus, to the extent that federal and state financial aids and public works projects can revive faltering urban economies, the bigger urban areas are the gainers, for they can press harder for government support.

Third, and somewhat related, is the fact that tremendous amounts of fixed capital have been sunk in social and private overhead in the very large urban area—streets, sewers, schools, water mains, electric power lines, stores and housing—so that even if the area's productive facilities for export are worn out or technically obsolete, public service and utility costs are low enough to make it uneconomic to abandon so much immobile capital. No nation is so affluent that it can afford to throw away a major city.

Fourth, a greater and greater proportion of industrial activity is oriented to customers rather than to sources of supply, and the larger urban areas amass potential customers. A large local economy becomes almost self-justifying as a rich product market. New industries, born elsewhere, eventually reach a stage of development at which they are likely to establish branch plants in this large local market, sustaining local growth. Also, the current shift from manufacturing to service activity favors local market-oriented production. With growing size comes a steady improvement in an area's transportation position; every large urban area becomes a transportation hub regardless of its geographical position. In a day when the giant corporation engaged in nationwide operations is growing ever more dominant, the frequency of jet air service may be the critical factor in choosing an area for a headquarters or even a branch operation.

Finally, a large urban area is more likely to give birth to new industries at critical points in its life cycle than is a small urban area—an industrial birth which rescues it from the brink of stagnation or decline. While a large place may not produce more new ideas per thousand population per year than a small place—and some evidence will be cited below to suggest greater industrial creativity in larger places—a surer and steadier supply of invention, innovation, and promotion is to be expected in larger places. To illustrate, suppose that an entrepreneurial genius occurs only once in every 10,000 births, then a 50,000-population urban area with, say, 1,000 births per year will produce this key person only once every ten years, on the average. This area may not have a new industrial savior ready at the time of critical need, whereas the 500,000-population urban area, spawning a genius a year, almost certainly will. Gifted persons, moreover, born in smaller places tend to migrate to bigger cities. Sheer size may stabilize the supply of the key human resources necessary to economic growth and development.

In sum, if the growth of an urban area persists long enough to raise the area to some critical size (a quarter of a million population?),[6] structural characteristics, such as industrial diversification, political power, huge fixed investments, a rich local market, and a steady supply of industrial leadership may almost ensure its continued growth and fully ensure against absolute decline—may, if fact, effect irreversible aggregate growth.

Management as the Scarce Factor in Urban Growth

Absolute size may also be a brake on rate of growth as cities experience, after a certain critical level, increasing cost of public services due to density, congestion, bureaucracy, and so forth. Few statistical studies of public service production functions are available and even with a full portfolio of them one would have to exercise great care in generalizing across diverse urban areas. The principal diseconomy of scale may well turn out to be managerial efficiency, with a high variability between areas. The impression that management may be the limiting factor in urban scale is partly inferential by analogy from orthodox economic thought and partly intuitive.

In search of a theoretical constraint on size of firms, without which neither competition nor the self-regulating price system itself could be preserved, economists long ago found that they were forced to rely primarily on the limited expansibility of the managerial factor. The supply of land, labor, and capital does not seem to pose serious constraints on firm size. Apart from the managerial limitation, economists could rationalize firm-size limits only by turning to imperfect competition or the inability of a firm to sell an endless amount of a given product at a constant price (i.e., a

---

[6] Of the 212 Census-defined standard metropolitan areas, only seven experienced population losses between 1950 and 1960: Texarkana (92,000 population), Altoona (137,000), Wheeling (190,000), Scranton (235,000), Johnstown (280,000), Wilkes-Barre–Hazleton (347,000) and Jersey City (611,000). If Jersey City, N.J., is regarded as one of the central cities of the consolidated New York-Northeastern New Jersey metropolitan area, and it is alternatively classified that way by the Census, then we find no absolute declines in the one-half-million-and-over class and only two cases in the one-quarter to one-half million population class. U.S. Bureau of the Census, *Statistical Abstract of the United States: 1961*, Washington, 1961, Table 10.

"downward sloping demand curve").[7] If price cuts are necessary to sell additional product, the firm realizes steadily diminishing net additions to revenue and profit with each additional sale, even it its unit costs do not begin to rise. While the firm might continue to grow even here by adding new product lines, multiproduct operations pose even greater managerial demands. Sooner or later, management would come to be the principal limitation or scarce factor, albeit it later with multiproduct expansion.

The managerial factor may also be the critical limitation on city size. As the city grows in total population, density of population, and physical extent, a point may be reached at which the unit cost of public services begins to rise or the quality of the service begins to fall appreciably. If so, a force which tends to dampen urban growth will have come into being. Local export firms, with their costs of production rising, find themselves disadvantaged in interregional competition for shares of the national market; manufacturing firms must move their trucks through congested streets to cramped loading docks, while paying higher property taxes for the less efficient urban public services. The city size at which increasing public service costs first turn sharply upward is probably, in large measure, a matter of the current level of urban technology. While the state of the arts in such diverse fields as urban transportation, communication, governmental decision making, and personnel administration is common to all urban areas—for knowledge is freely available—the competency and creativeness of various sets of local public officials are not nearly so uniform. And it is the local public officials, elective and appointive, who are the principal instruments of urban efficiency, together with the private managers of a few key local service industries, such as the utilities, banks, and local transportation and communication systems.

The parallel to the multiproduct firm is the highly interrelated set of local public services that must be integrated or co-ordinated to preserve the efficiency of the city, seen now as a huge factory with its streets, power lines, and pipes as the assembly lines, and its complex of legal, financial, and technical services as a magnified version of the "front office." If we believe that success in business is closely tied to the efficiency and creativity of the firm's management, is it not equally likely that the efficiency of the local public economy will vary widely from place to place according to the quality of urban management? Just as efficient management of the General Motors Corporation can push back the point at which net diseconomies of scale take effect, so public service inefficiency and rising unit costs can be postponed considerably, even if not indefinitely, by able and experienced local public legislators and administrators.

But recruiting able public adminstrators at the local level is no easy matter. The Municipal Manpower Commission found:

---

[7] See the chapter on "monopolistic competition" in any standard Principles of Economics textbook. This idea dates back to the brilliant article by Piero Sraffa, "The Laws of Returns under Competitive Conditions," *The Economic Journal*, Vol. 36 (1926), reprinted in George J. Stigler and Kenneth E. Boulding (editors), *Readings in Price Theory* (Chicago: Richard D. Irwin, 1952), especially pp. 189 ff.

Low prestige of government employment adversely affects the quality of local government personnel. . . . Nearly half of the responses to a survey of local officials conducted by the Public Personnel Association said that low prestige was a major obstacle to recruiting persons to fill key positions in local governments. A still more striking manifestation of the effect of this low prestige of employment in local governments is found in the attitudes of municipal executives themselves. The Commission's study of 1,700 local executives revealed that only 17 per cent would recommend a career in local government.[8]

It is not enough to recruit talented people to serve as public officials, develop a science of local public administration, and professionalize urban management. The organizational and institutional framework within which all this functions is paramount. Even the most able urban managers may not be able to provide efficient government in a politically fragmented, unco-ordinated urban area. The problems of recruitment and political fragmenta-tion, moreover, interact, worsening the situation. The Municipal Manpower Commission also reported that:

A lack of clear-cut community-wide objectives and of permanent ma-chinery for area-wide planning and policy formulation. . . . The frag-mentation of the geographical area among numerous local governments and many leadership groups is a serious barrier to the solution of metropolitan problems which are beyond the capacity of any single jurisdiction or civic organization; it is a cause of frustration for munici-pal manpower. . . . Furthermore, the small-scale problems faced by such units do not offer much attraction to experienced and able personnel.[9]

Ultimately, then, diseconomies of scale in public services and quasi-public services, such as water supply, sewage disposal, electricity, gas and transpor-tation, may constrain the size of the city; but only if technological progress, political innovation, and administrative ingenuity do not keep pace. Despite the built-in frailties that have been mentioned, they have up to now.

Urban Growth Analysis: The Demand Side

One of the simplest and most useful analytical frameworks within which to view the urban economy is the highly popular "export-base" construct, an analytical rationalization of the urban economy first set forth explicitly in 1928 in Robert M. Haig's classic study of the New York region and more recently integrated into the mainstream of economic theory in the work of

[8] *Government Manpower for Tomorrow's Cities*, A Report of the Municipal Man-power Commission (New York: McGraw-Hill Book Co, Inc., 1962), pp. 44–46.
[9] *Ibid.*, pp. 30–32.

Charles Tiebout.[10] The urban area is depicted as a wide-open economy, heavily dependent on external trade, quite like the small, industrially advanced nation in the world market, only more so. Both Switzerland and Denver must export or die. A small metropolitan area (50,000–100,000 population) may devote as much as one-half of its economic activity to producing goods for sale outside of its borders, greatly surpassing even the most trade-oriented small nation in this regard.[11] With the proceeds of its "export" sales, complementary goods are purchased from outside ("imported"), roughly equivalent in dollar amount to the value of the area exports.

The Role of the Export Sector

Those who have tried to fathom the processes and patterns of small-area economic development—largely planners trying to anticipate the future and business groups promoting local industrial development, and only rarely economists—have gained valuable insights into the process of city formation and growth through these domestic, international-trade-type models. Because the city planners and area development people were most often concerned with long-range growth trends, the customary use of the export-base model was to project the future size and shape of the total local economy from the projected size and shape of the area's export sector. Since the export base of most urban economies is dominated by a relatively small number of manufacturing activities, the usual procedure was simply to estimate the number of manufacturing workers that would be employed locally at the target date and then add on the number of local service employees needed to accommodate the export industry workers and their families, and, of course, to serve each others' families.[12] Further, if the

[10] Robert M. Haig, *Major Economic Factors in Metropolitan Growth and Arrangement*, Vol. I, *Regional Survey of New York and Environs* (New York, 1928). The economic base or export-base logic of urban-regional growth has a long history of conceptual development traced through most thoroughly in the first of a series of articles by Richard B. Andrews, "Mechanics of the Urban Economic Base: Historical Development of the Base Concept," *Land Economics* (May 1953), pp. 161–67. The full series of ten articles together with eleven others are reprinted in Ralph W. Pfouts (editor), *The Techniques of Urban Economic Analysis* (West Trenton, N.J.: Chandler-Davis Publishing Co., 1960). Economic base theory was developed more rigorously in two articles by Charles M. Tiebout, "The Urban Economic Base Reconsidered," *idem*, pp. 279–89, and "The Community Income Multiplier: A Case Study," pp. 341–58, and reaches its height of elegance in Tiebout's *The Community Economic Base Study*, Supplementary Paper No. 16, Committee for Economic Development (New York: December, 1962).

[11] Exports may account for a full one-half of local economic activity in urban areas with as many as a quarter of a million people, in cases of heavy industrial specialization. For example, the Flint, Michigan, "urbanized area," with a total population of 278,000 and an employed labor force of 100,000, had over 51,000 workers in manufacturing of which close to 50,000 were producing motor vehicles or related intermediate products. Almost all of the automobile output, one-half of total local activity, is sold outside of the Flint area. Derived from the U.S. Bureau of the Census, *U.S. Census of Population: 1960, General Social and Economic Characteristics, Michigan* (Washington: U.S. Government Printing Office, 1962), Tables 32 and 75.

[12] With repeated handling, and the occasional intervention of economists, the export-to-service ratio became more sophisticated. An appreciation of the way in which it changes (decreases) with larger city size is most clearly conveyed in Irving Morrissett, "The Economic Structure of American Cities," *Papers and Proceedings of the Regional Science Association*, Vol. 4, 1958, pp. 239–56

projected export and service industry workers were summed and this number multiplied by the average number of dependents per worker, the future total population of the area fell neatly into place. (It is a fact, however, that the ratio of labor force to population does vary appreciably between urban areas, due to the availability of jobs for women, family income levels, and other factors.)

Applicability of the Export-Base Logic

Thus the export sector is cast in the key role as the active instrument of change, the point of contact between the national and the local economies; and national forces are presumed to be more powerful and more autonomous than local forces. "As the export industry goes, so goes the total local economy" might be the watchword. A typical characterization of the urban growth process, at least as it has evolved in the literature of regional geography and city planning, is that a given number of export workers "supports" a given number of local service workers. This has given rise to a long and sometimes bitter dispute over who "supports" whom. The export-base advocate argues that if the export jobs were to disappear, the local service jobs would also be lost—the very town would vanish—but if, instead, some part of the local service work were lost, say, through business failure, replacement service business would spring up automatically.

But this is not wholly convincing because one might also argue that replacement export firms could also be reborn on the base of a viable local service sector, if the reason of being for that industry in that place still exists; even new, unrelated export complexes might be generated if the town as a whole still has a *raison d'être*. Going behind local services, *per se*, an urban economy based on natural or persistent economic advantages (e.g., a good port and railhead, a pleasant climate and topography, the homes of skilled workers who resist migration) may give birth to wholly new export industries to replace lost ones with only modest labor pains. The champions of the local service sector, led by Blumenfeld,[13] rising to the challenge, have even argued that it is really the local service sector which is basic and enduring, and that this latter sector supports the chameleon-like export sector which, taking a very long view, is founded on transitory manufacturing firms. In short, a severed export appendage of the urban corporate body can, in time, be regenerated by a viable and efficient local service sector.

The phrase "in time" is critical. In the analysis of local business cycles the export-base logic is employed, quite legitimately, under the reasonable assumption that the industrial composition of the export sector of an urban economy is highly unlikely to experience any substantial amount of structural alteration in the short space of time within which business cycles take place. Not only the same industries but even the precise firms will probably remain intact. The local service industries, moreover, are probably not going to alter the competitive position of the local economy in any major way through increases or decreases in the cost or quality or availability of services

---

[13] See especially Hans Blumenfeld, "The Economic Base of the Metropolis," in *Journal of the American Institute of Planners* (Fall, 1955), pp. 114-32, reprinted in Pfouts, *op. cit.*, pp. 230-77.

rendered. Therefore, in analyses which extend over periods of time so short that the industrial structure—both export and local service—is largely fixed in kind and quality, the primacy of the demand for export products in effecting change seems clear and incontestable.

When the time dimension is extended, however, circularity sets in. The demand for local services is derived indirectly from the external demands for the export products of the area and directly from the local spending of payrolls and profits generated by that export production. In that sense the export sector is primary. On the other hand, local services are important inputs in export production and the efficiency of the local service sector is critical to export firms. An abiding electric utility and commercial bank that successively serve the firms and employees of, first, a wagon maker, and then an unsuccessful automobile firm, and then a railroad car firm, and so on, have strong claims to be counted "basic" in the local economy. But in order to avoid flagrant bias in the argument, we should note that the area exporter could well have been the same steel plant, year after year.

We observe the opening of an iron mine in Minnesota (export industry) stimulating the growth of a whole town (with its complex of derivative local service industries); alternatively, we observe the existence of a farm service center in Iowa with an efficient and pleasing local service sector (e.g., schools, utilities, shopping centers) attracting a manufacturing plant (exporter) which, of course, generates more local services. In a growth context, this is a chicken-and-egg problem which, if treated at the level of gross generality, can become a fool's game. When treated in a specific context, such as the emphasis on external demand and the export base in local business cycle analysis, selective emphasis can be both proper and incisive.

Urban Economic Projection as Demand Analysis

Still, the complexity of urban-regional growth does not completely vitiate the value of the simplistic export-base logic. One important element in any long-range growth prognosis is a projection of the demand for the area's current mix of export products—the lengthened shadow of the sales charts of a handful of key industries. While the export-base lines of causation in the growth process become adulterated with larger city size, demand projections for the current export mix still provide as good a place as any at which to begin.

One can begin an analysis of the trends in demand for an area's leading exports with a standard economic concept: income elasticity of demand, the ratio of the per cent change in spending on a good to the per cent change in disposable income. A 10 per cent increase in income might increase cigarette sales by only a couple per cent—an income-inelastic good—while sales of fashion dresses might increase by 20 per cent—an income-elastic good. We are interested here in identifying which are the "inferior" goods from which the consumer turns as his living standard rises secularly (e.g., grits and rice, bus and rail transportation), and which are the "superior" goods to which he turns in response to a steadily rising income (e.g., beef and wine, automobile and air transportation). The critical concept in our growth context is the *long-run* income elasticity of demand, a consumption-to-income trend line that abstracts from cycle swings. [14] Time is clearly on the side of those urban areas which are producing goods for which the long-run income elasticity of demand is greater than unity, the "luxury" goods, and the reverse. And this is obviously an operational concept, although precise measurement is difficult.

A second set of factors which bears on the growth prospects of an urban area, via the demand for its exports, is changes in the relative prices and availabilities of the principal substitutes for the local exports. Rising costs of production in rival urban areas, due perhaps to a growing scarcity of raw materials in their hinterlands relative to local environs, would tend to raise the prices or lower the quality of these competing goods, thereby shifting demand toward the local product. Of course it cuts both ways: improvements in the resource position of competing areas act to lower their prices or improve their quality relative to that of the local economy, and shift demand adversely. [15]

The adverse effect of the depletion of the natural resource base on which a town is built is a clear and obvious case. But mining towns may face more subtle threats too. A coal town stagnates when households in the areas it serves shift to oil or gas heat as supplies of these fuels increase or become more accessible. In the near future, electricity, an even more cleaner and more flexible form of heat, may become competitive in price for space heating as it already has for cooking. At that time, the gas and oil areas may slump a little and, in certain circumstances, the coal towns could revive. New coal mining techniques—such, for example, as pumping coal slurry through pipes to electricity generating plants—might underlie the falling electricity costs, or long-distance transmission might be accomplished with much less fall in voltage. And in the more distant future, as the huge public investment in atomic power technology pays off, plants using fission fuel may replace those using fossil fuel, in which case the outlook for coal towns darkens again.

Next, changes in tastes—autonomous changes now, not changes in consumption patterns in response to higher income or altered relative prices

[14] One must take care to distinguish between the deliberative reaction of buyers to the slow, steady increases in per capita income which come with economic development and the quick, first response of buyers to sudden (cyclical) fluctuations in their income. The distinction is a major one. In cycle analysis the durability of the good—the ease of postponing the replacement of an aging automobile or refrigerator—is the single most critical factor in determining income elasticity of demand, but in growth analysis the durability-postponability characteristic is of little interest. The time period spanned by a growth study is much too long to reflect the transitory postponements and accelerated purchases of durable goods that are part of the buyers' business cycle strategy. Compare the treatment of income elasticity of demand in any standard text on business cycles or national income with its treatment in any standard text on price theory. For example, Robert M. Biggs, *National-Income Analysis and Forecasting* (New York: W. W. Norton and Co., Inc., 1956), pp. 319-20, and Richard H. Leftwich, *The Price System and Resource Allocation* (New York: Holt, Rinehart and Winston, 1961), pp. 83-86.

[15] For a succinct treatment of the natural resource impact, see Harvey S. Perloff and Lowdon Wingo, Jr., "Natural Resource Endowment and Regional Economic Growth," *Natural Resources and Economic Growth,* Papers presented at a conference held at Ann Arbor, Michigan, April 7-9, 1960, under joint sponsorship of Resources for the Future, Inc., and Committee on Economic Growth of the Social Science Research Council (Washington: Resources for the Future, Inc., 1961).

through diverse income elasticities of demand—have always been an important source of change, perhaps now more than ever before. Despite isolated instances of extreme and self-conscious individualism (e.g., "beatniks"), the prevailing opinion seems to be that we are moving toward a mass culture, with our society pursuing security and finding it is increasingly close conformity. The image here is nationwide television networks and Madison Avenue. And by coupling uniform consumption patterns to a high and rising per capita income, an ever greater share of which is "discretionary income," the danger is that capricious shifts in consumption spending may come to dominate the pattern of economic activity.

"Discretionary spending" could come to ebb and flow in massive tides as fads and fashions dictate: from big cars and small boats to small cars and big boats. Manufacturing plants selling in national markets may increasingly find themselves alternately awash with demand, then left stranded on the beach. Even whole industries may rise and fall over very short time periods. The remote small urban economy exporting a single product, probably even a single brand, would run the greatest risks, especially if it is a "luxury" good. Small one-industry towns, long subject to the risk of great cyclical instability, may no longer be a viable long-run form of socioeconomic organization in the Age of Affluence.[16]

. . .

Urban Growth Analysis: The Supply Side

While a demand orientation has been the more fashionable for the past decade, the existence of a supply side to urban-regional economic development has long been recognized, even antedating the demand (export-base) model. A supply orientation is implicit in the typical "inventory" of local resources with which many area development studies begin—and too often end. A supply approach need not be naïve, for its holds considerably greater potential for unraveling the pattern and determinants of urban growth than does the relatively static export-base logic.

We might generalize to the effect that the longer the time period under consideration, the greater the relative importance of supply—local resource endowment and industrial culture. The recent New York study, for example, highlighted the fact that the New York metropolitan area grew by incubating new functions, nurturing them and finally spinning them off to other sections of the country, all the while regenerating this cycle. The flour mills, foundries, meat packing plants, textile mills and tanneries of the post-Civil War period drifted away from New York, their place taken by less transport-sensitive products, such as garments, cigars, and office work. Currently, New

[16] John Kenneth Galbraith in *The Affluent Society* (Boston: Houghton Mifflin, 1958), introduced the first systematic analysis of the economics of affluence; however, he laid siege to orthodox economic theory, and questioned the central concept of *unlimited* human wants as an *inexhaustible* spur to greater production. Here, however, we are concerned less with the rationality or morality of artificially stimulating wants (e.g., advertising, promoting materialistic social values) and more with the destabilizing effect of affluence—a large and growing proportion of income spent for goods which satisfy weakly-felt wants.

York is losing the manufacturing end of many of its most traditional specialties, as garment sewing slips away to low-wage Eastern Pennsylvania leaving only the selling function behind, and as printing splits away from immobile publishing. But New York's growth never seems to falter as the new growth industries are much more than proportionately regenerated in its rich industrial culture.[17]

Further testimony to the fact that the relative proportion of growth industries in the local economic base is a most undependable guide to aggregate area growth can be drawn out of the work of Perloff and associates. They found "no positive correlation between the proportion of workers in 'growth industries' and the relative rates of increases in total economic activity among the many states."[18] A number of possible explanations come to mind: growth industries are (a) quantitatively dwarfed by other activity, or (b) they are based on new products which are most likely to be invented and/or innovated in mature (slow-growing) industrial areas either out of superior know-how, or (c) out of desperation, as suggested above in the challenge-and-response argument. In any event, the industry-mix approach—a demand-side technique which ignores new industry—can only provide a partial basis for a long-run growth theory.[19] We turn, therefore, to a brief survey of the supply side of urban growth, conventionally enough with the economist's classic four factors of production: land, labor, capital, and entrepreneurship.

Labor

The historical pattern of industrial development in an urban area may greatly influence its future pattern of growth, and inherited traits may be especially noteworthy with reference to the local labor force. A farm market town on the verge of its industrial baptism can look to only the most routine kinds of manufacturing operations—a workshoe factory, a textile mill, a food processing plant. After a decade or so of apprenticeship in low-skilled work, the area may be in a position to offer a large supply of semiskilled workers

[17] Raymond Vernon, *Metropolis 1985* (New York: Doubleday and Co., Inc., 1960), pp. 35ff. This historical evidence of New York's vitality as an industrial innovator-promoter is later supplemented with a more analytical exposition attributing New York's growth over the past three decades to its absolute and comparative advantage in the "external-economy industries" (pp. 61–62). Large metropolitan areas, in general, must and can depend on relatively tight-knit industrial complexes for their growth, and on the related group of industries which draw broadly on a well-developed social overhead, ranging from private consultants to public libraries. [18] See footnote 4, above.

[19] Raymond Vernon's New York study moves from historical description to a statistical analysis of industrial change over the past thirty years. The area is characterized as having had an industry mix relatively rich in the fast-growing industries but whose "promise was not realized" as these industries grew locally at rates slower than their national counterparts. While this is a statistically valid explanation of the Region's slower than average total growth, a more revealing formulation might be to see the area as one which grows, despite the fact that it steadily loses share (spins off) in almost every activity it undertakes, by constantly creating some new *raison d'être*. If, indeed, New York is the birthplace of new ideas and new industries, much more than proportionately, and it did not experience a declining market share of these industries as they matured, the New York area would come to embrace most of the nation's economic activity and population. The great value of the New York study is precisely that it demonstrates that giant metropolises grow by serving an entrepreneurial not a caretaker function. This message does come through but only obliquely, probably partly because the historical work showing the long-run industrial sequences and the short-run, industry-mix analyses were performed by different persons. Raymond Vernon, *op. cit.*, Chapter 3.

and perhaps a few highly skilled workers, and ultimately the area will have passed from apprenticeship to journeyman status as a local labor market. Moreover, as skill levels rise, so do wage rates, and the higher local standard of living may automatically evoke a middle-class morality that further spurs growth. Personal achievement—"success"—is not only reasonably attainable now, it is highly emphasized and the financial means are at hand with which the principal instrument toward that end—education—can be applied. Further, personal saving and capital formation become a basic cultural trait, opening the way to entrepreneurship in the form of new small business formation.

Seldom, however, is an appreciation of this process accompanied by a sense of the time dimension of the industrial acculturation process. Do the steps upward in labor skill span a decade? A generation? What is the principal channel for transmitting skills: through the industrial base and personal contact (from father to son) or through earnings and improved public services (from productivity to income to tax base to good schools)? Clearly, a rapidly advancing technology favors the latter.

But "what is past is prologue" may cut both ways. If a strong and aggressive local union presses for wage rate increases in excess of the rate of increase in local labor productivity, and if the local employer is confident that he can easily pass along the increase in labor costs (plus his markup), because his competitors are few and collusive (oligopoly), and similarly circumstanced (nationwide union), the union is likely to find the employer quite accommodating, with only token resistance for the sake of appearance. But a day of retribution arrives when the local economy, affluent beyond its expectation or merit, must face the task of gaining additional employments.

Even if the local export oligopolist survives forever, it is highly unlikely that this firm will add continually to *local* operations, as the typical pattern is for a growing firm to move to multiplant operations and to disperse its plants to minimize transportation costs. But, the natural increase in local population and labor force alone demands expanding employment, and because technological advances ("automation") will probably *reduce* employment in the local plant appreciably, new firms must be acquired and they will probably have to be recruited almost entirely from industries new to the area. But high local wage rates would tend to put most of the low-wage, nondurable goods industries out of reach, as long as large pools of cheap labor exist elsewhere, and high wage rates *relative to local skills* dim the prospects of getting even new durable goods industries. Probably a significant part of the current stagnation and structural unemployment of the Pittsburgh area is traceable to wage rate increases that outran skill and productivity gains during the long, lush periods of the Second World War and its early aftermath. Painful wage rate adjustments under the pressure of protracted unemployment may be an integral part of the industrial redevelopment of heavy-industry towns.[20]

---

[20] Absolute reductions in the local wage rate are rare, especially under trade unionism, but the reluctant acceptance of wage increases of less than average amount is quite common; indeed wage freezes at the current level for a year or two are accepted even under unionism in emergency cases. Thus local wage deflation ordinarily takes the form of a *relative* decrease, as local wages stand still or lag behind national increases.

But the local industrial legacy influences the local labor market in ways other than through labor skills and wage rates; in labor mobility, for example. A growing preference among new entrants to the labor force—the younger generation—for the broad welfare fringe benefits and the prestige of employment in a large corporation is becoming evident. Personnel placement and job recruiting studies have demonstrated that "name" corporations do, in fact, find recruiting easier,[21] as retirement and stock purchase plans attract the young men and glamorous buildings in exciting central locations attract the young women.[22] The security-glamour effects must be separated from the fact that the big corporation also has the added advantage of recruiting with a full-time, professional personnel staff.

Not only does firm size help to augment the local labor force, thereby widening and deepening the selection of human resources available at that location, but the large corporation may also facilitate a more orderly contraction of the local economy under adverse business conditions. Big firms are usually multiproduct operations and are spatially dispersed; therefore when demand or supply conditions change the requisite adjustments in their labor force can often be swiftly and smoothly accomplished within the protective shell of the corporate family. A worker may be shifted from a failing to an expanding line of production within the same plant, assuming the skill level is about the same, or he may be transferred without job change to a distant plant serving a region growing more rapidly than the nearby region, although often not without strong "persuasion." That the new jobs of a firm will be offered first to their own displaced workers seems ever more certain as the courts continually expand their interpretation of property rights to cover jobs,[23] and as the unions win fringe benefits covering this same contingency. In sum, big multiproduct firms probably increase the mobility of labor both in and out of their local labor markets, and thereby both enrich the local supply of labor, and also reduce frictional and structural unemployment in the area. This would seem to be a testable hypothesis.

Finally, *unbalanced* local labor demands have very long-run supply

[21] Henry C. Thole, *Shortages of Skilled Manpower: Implications for Kalamazoo Businessmen* (Kalamazoo: The W. E. Upjohn Institute for Community Research, 1958), especially pp. 26–39.

[22] In a slightly different context, Hoover and Vernon observe that "The young women's preference for a job in the central business district today . . . is based . . . on the increased opportunities for after-hours recreation, lunch-hour shopping (or window-shopping), and the greater opportunities for husband-hunting." Edgar M. Hoover and Raymond Vernon, *Anatomy of a Metropolis* (Cambridge, Mass.: Harvard University Press, 1959), p. 102.

[23] On the Fall 1961 docket of the United States Supreme Court were two cases turning on the question of whether employees of a firm that has relocated its operations have seniority rights to jobs at the new site. One case was filed by Teamster Union Local 852 against the Glidden Company (paints and chemicals) for damages to workers at the old Elmhurst, N.Y., plant who were not offered jobs at the new Bethlehem, Pa., site. In the second case, five employees of the Gemmer Manufacturing Co. (steering gears) of Detroit, Mich., were suing the company for agreeing to hire only local workers at the new Lebanon, Tenn., site, in return for a $2.4 million plant construction loan extended by the community. In both cases, the lower court had ruled in favor of the employees. Reported in *The Evening Star*, Washington, D.C., August 30, 1961, p. B-9.

repercussions which may stimulate local growth. If the local industries hire only males, this creates a shortage of jobs for women, and while temporarily depressing to average family income, the surplus pool of female labor tends to attract industries with complementary labor demands. Hoover cites the classic examples of silk mills being drawn to the Pennsylvania coal towns, and shoe and textile industries to the New England port towns.[24] Clearly, this argument carries more force in a full employment economy than in one with widespread unemployment; moreover, the long experience of Cincinnati, Pittsburgh, and other places with unbalanced labor demands has shown that righting the balance may be greatly delayed—commercial and financial secretarial work does not flow readily into isolated places or gray factory towns. More often the young women leave for the centers of commerce. Still, Boston's industrial resurgence is due in part to a good supply of experienced female workers, highly valued in electronics manufacturing, a legacy of textile-mill days.

. . .

Entrepreneurship

Students of regional economic development are inclined to admit defeat too quickly when faced with the task of quantifying the presumably more qualitative aspects of growth. No one denies that entrepreneurship—inventiveness, promotional artistry, organizational genius, venturesomeness, and so forth—lies at the very heart of industrial development, yet we hurriedly pay our formal respects to this critical factor and then move on in embarrassed haste to surer, more easily chartered grounds, such as the rate of capital formation, capital-to-labor ratios and the like. But this is a mistake; we cannot act so cavalierly toward the entrepreneur, least of all in long-term growth analysis.

A number of naïve but intriguing hypotheses on the role of entrepreneurship in urban-regional growth literally cry out for even the loosest testing, so that we may then strike more sophisticated reformulation. For example, Chinitz offers one that emphasizes risk-taking:

> My feeling is that you do not breed as many entrepreneurs per capita in families allied with steel as you do in families allied with apparel, using these two industries for illustrative purposes only. The son of a salaried executive is less likely to be sensitive to opportunities wholly unrelated to his father's field than the son of an independent entrepreneur. True, the entrepreneur's son is more likely to think of taking over his father's business. My guess is, however, that the tradition of risk-bearing is, on the whole, a more potent influence in broadening one's perspective.[25]

Perhaps one might argue in rebuttal that the relative security of a managerial position in one of the entrenched oligopolies characteristic of heavy industry is somewhat counterbalanced by the cyclical instability also characteristic of

[24] Edgar M. Hoover, *Location of Economic Activity* (New York: McGraw-Hill Book Co., Inc., 1948), pp. 118-19.

[25] Benjamin Chinitz, "Contrasts in Agglomeration: New York and Pittsburgh," *American Economic Review* (May 1961), pp. 284-85.

much of this sector (e.g., steel, metal, fabricating, machinery, automobiles). But violent fluctuations in production and blue-collar employment probably do not pose much personal risk to an entrenched management of these financially secure behemoths, much as they may unsettle corporate earnings and dividends. The steel executive is ordinarily not held accountable for the national business cycle.

A complementary hypothesis offered here is that there are local recurring "cycles" of entrepreneurial vigor. (Perhaps "long waves" of entrepreneurship, more analogous to the Kondratieff long cycles than to the traditional business cycle, would be a more appropriate analogy.) We might argue, again, the dynamics of "challenge and response" at the local level on a more individualized basis. A dynamic entrepreneurial group—even a single outstanding figure—arises in a particular area, perhaps due to mere chance, and this group generates rapid industrial development in that locality. Commercial success and the resultant rise of large local firms produces an environment characterized by complex managerial routines, and administrative talents become both the critical local need and the *sine qua non* of local industrial leadership. The rough and unorthodox inventor-innovator-promoter type is pushed into the background as "scientific management" takes over. The new gods are efficiency and stability and industrial statesmanship.

As the new industry matures, the local giants begin the almost inevitable regional decentralization, as branch plants are spun off into major product markets to minimize transportation costs. This leads inevitably to a slowing rate of *local* employment growth in this industry, and a concomitant growth in local unemployment, as population and labor force grow faster than job opportunities. With local stagnation the dominant concern, necessity becomes the mother of invention, literally, as a frantic search is conducted for unexploited old opportunities and renewed emphasis is placed on concocting new products and processes. Efficiency pales alongside creativity or promotional artistry; the inventor is king again and the unorthodox is welcomed, almost uncritically.

As a corollary to this set of propositions, we might also hypothesize that inventor-innovators tend to bunch in time and space; dynamic persons create an atmosphere that attracts more of the same, to share the fraternity of protest against the old and excitement in the new. The bar-room of the old Pontchatrain Hotel in Detroit is reputed to have been a hot-house of early automotive technology in the early years of this century. Later the burgeoning automobile industry attracted financial wizards (e.g., William Durant who put General Motors together) and finally that host of apt managers who see any rapidly expanding, and therefore mildly chaotic, industry as an escalator to rapid promotion.[26]

---

[26] See Lawrence Seltzer, *A Financial History of the American Automobile Industry* (Boston: Houghton Mifflin Company, 1928), especially Chapter IV, "The General Motors Corporation." Seltzer writes: "William C. Durant was a vigorous promoter and salesman rather than an operating executive; and the career of the General Motors Combination, until very recent years, has largely reflected his personality. His temperament and his unbound confidence in the automobile industry led him to seek rapid growth. . . . He was ready to expand by acquisition . . ." pp. 223–24.

To argue that Henry Ford and some associates and imitators turned Detroit from a middle size regional center into a huge industrial center is not to advance a "great man theory of *economic* history." Certainly, the commercially successful private automobile would have been introduced in the United States by someone else within a few years if Ford had not acted first—but probably not in Detroit. Nor would any other new industry of comparable potential have been developed. Henry Ford, as an individual, was highly substitutable for the nation and probably did not materially alter what would have happened had he never been born, but Detroit today would probably have about one-half of its present population.[27]

The parallel between the challenge-and-response and long-wave hypotheses at the community level, outlined earlier in this chapter, and at the firm level, at issue here, may even be extended to suggest the possibility of some direct linkages between them. For example, the stellar local firm(s) may well catch the brightest young men of the community in its web of glamour, power, and financial security; local public service may have to make do with lesser talent. Both for this reason and because of sheer corporate power, the local legislative and public administrative bodies may be dominated by local big business. In such an event, one would expect the business values to prevail in the community and be reflected in a relatively *efficient* local public economy. But an imaginative and, consequently, unorthodox, local political leadership would hardly be expected, and might not even be tolerated. Thus as the local corporate giant decentralizes and precipitates a local employment crisis, a political revolution may well be a prerequisite to effective community response. That is, political innovators may be—must be—spawned to complement the economic ones generated in the private sector.

· · ·

[27] At the turn of the century, Detroit was about three-quarters the size of Cleveland and the supporting hinterlands of these two regional metropolises were of roughly equal size. (True, the population of Ohio was about two-thirds again as large as Michigan, but this rich base of support was shared with Cincinnati, a city closely pressing Cleveland in population.) Now let us imagine that Henry Ford and R. E. Olds and others had been born in Massachusetts or Illinois and that the automobile industry had never developed in Michigan, except for the occasional assembly plant that has been the lot of nearly every concentration of population the country over. But, instead, suppose that Detroit had garnered a Cleveland-like share of manufacturing—a very handsome industrial fortune, even if not the Arabian wealth of the automobile legacy. With a manufacturing base comparable to that of Cleveland and a hinterland to service of similar size, the population of Detroit metropolitan area in 1950 would probably have been near Cleveland's 1.3 million instead of the actual count of 2.4 million.

Consider, in parallel fashion, Milwaukee, a neighboring lake city somewhat north of the main east-west stream of commerce (like Detroit), a comparable center of heavy industry and endowed with a work force at least as highly skilled as that of Detroit. Even adjusting for the fact that Milwaukee's Wisconsin hinterland is only two-thirds as heavily populated as Michigan, the base of Detroit—raising the expected Detroit population to about one and one-half times that of the Wisconsin regional metropolis—we again arrive at an expected population of one and one-half million persons at most for the Detroit (*sans* auto industry) metropolitan area in 1950. The conclusion is offered that this area is nearly twice as large as the most sophisticated forecaster could have foreseen a half-century ago. Wilbur R. Thompson, "Detroit's Economic Future," *The Michigan Economic Record*, June 1960, p. 7.

Capital

Before becoming deeply enmeshed in the role of local capital supplies in urban-regional growth, one would do well to be sure that a regional context is relevant. Capital more than any other of the four co-ordinate factors of production is highly mobile. The capital market may be almost wholly a national market to which all firms have equal access no matter where located.[28]

The fact of a national capital market would probably make for greater regional growth differentials than would be probable in a set of semiautonomous local capital markets because there would be little or no spatial friction to prevent unlimited amounts of the full national supply of savings from flowing to any given region. In sharp contrast, labor and entrepreneurship move much more sluggishly and the friction of migration dampens the growth of the most buoyant areas and retards contraction and collapse of disadvantaged areas. We have assumed above that a unique local labor market does exist and is highly relevant to much of urban economics, and more hesitantly that a unique local entrepreneurial "market" probably also exists, especially relevant to growth questions. Is there a local capital market of any consequence? Or are interest rates everywhere the same and risk capital everywhere equally available?

The very large, nationally known corporation does operate largely in a national capital market. Its financial needs are such that the urban areas in which it is located could hardly be the dominant sources of funds without precariously concentrating the investment portfolios of local individuals and financial institutions. Besides, commercial banks are prohibited by law from lending to a single borrower sums greater than a specified proportion of their net worth, generally about 10 per cent.[29] Moreover, the larger well-known corporation probably finds that its credit does not suffer appreciably with distance from its physical operations. In short, we may be able to disregard the very large borrowers for our present purposes.

The very small firms, especially the prospective new entrants into business, are usually known only locally (and personally) and can secure outside capital only on the most adverse terms. To them the capital market is predominantly a local market. And we would be surprised if careful study of the medium size firms did not place them firmly in the middle of this spectrum. Less obvious, however, is whether distance makes much difference after the boundaries of the home area have been passed. Can a medium size business in Akron borrow on as good terms in St. Louis as in nearby

[28] Edgar M. Hoover observed some time ago that "capital funds for new investment, however, are highly mobile and show relatively small geographic differentials in price. Interest rates exhibit a tendency to vary with distance from major financial centers but are rarely a significant factor of location within any one country." *The Location of Economic Activity, op. cit.*, p. 70. Hoover cites the empirical work of August Lösch, *The Economics of Location* (New Haven: Yale University Press, 1954), pp. 461, 505. Interestingly, later works have ignored regional aspects of the capital market. Neither the most comprehensive general reference work on location theory, Isard, *op. cit.*, nor that on regional growth, Harvey S. Perloff, *et al., op cit.*, include "interest" in their very detailed subject indexes.

[29] Harry G. Guthmann and Herbert E. Dougall, *Corporate Financial Policy*, Third Edition (Englewood Cliffs, N.J.: Prentice-Hall, Inc., 1955), Chapter 20, especially p. 423.

Cleveland? In general, if we could quantify the degree of a firm's attachment to the local capital market by firm size, size of home area, type of industry or whatever proves to be relevant, subsequent urban-regional growth analyses could move more quickly and surely to those parts of the local capital market that justify studies-in-depth.

When we turn from the users of funds to the sources of funds, we find that it is not so easy to dismiss some sectors to concentrate on others. We must run the gamut from individuals to the largest commercial banks. The widely publicized, purported shortage of risk capital suggests the importance of individual investors, specifically those willing and able to make equity investments. We may care, then, whether a given local economy has more or less than its share of wealthy residents. While the total amount that this group is willing to invest in any given firm may be trivial compared to the needs of a very large corporate business, resident wealth might easily marshal enough capital to build a veritable hot-house for the growth of small firms. Through general and limited partnerships and subscriptions to small local stock offerings, the wealthy residents of an area may serve as financiers and patrons to local inventors and innovators.

The interesting questions concerning local wealth and growth become ones of relative magnitudes. How common is the occurrence of an urban area wherein a small wealthy group could appreciably affect the local supply of risk capital? Are these wealthy groups more inclined toward area industrial development or toward retarding local industrialization and urbanization to keep the area pleasantly rural for residential amenities? These two questions may well be closely interrelated: the smaller urban areas are probably both the places where resident wealth is a more significant component of the local capital supply and where the residential amenity factor is more critical. Which way it goes depends on whether the locality will be deemed by the local rich to be a more pleasant place to live if it remains small and bucolic or grows large and exciting.

Finally, are the local rich venturesome, as those of Houston have often been characterized, or are they inclined toward graceful living, as is often reputed to be the case for most of the Deep South and some of the more idyllic places, such as Denver?[30] At issue here is the kind of capital which is most critical to growth and the source which is most distinctively local. The question is basically one of quantitative significance and therefore demands an empirically based answer.

While the importance of equity capital is universally recognized, the critical role of commercial banks and other suppliers of working capital loans is not so thoroughly appreciated, especially in the case of new and growing businesses. In the early stages of its life cycle, a firm economizes on fixed capital by leasing its plant (an old vacant store or loft spaces in a run-down section of the city)[31] and subcontracts much of its fabricating and sub-assembling to economize on machinery. Often the young firm is most sorely

---

[30] J. Schaefer, "Denver: The Mountain Metropolis," *Holiday* (September 1961), pp. 56–69.

[31] Edgar M. Hoover and Raymond Vernon, *op. cit.*, pp. 49–55.

pressed for working capital to pay wages and buy supplies and to extend credit to customers, and short-term borrowing of working capital can be very expensive for small, unknown firms.[32] The point is that the speed and ease with which new and small firms can gain access to the larger and lower-cost sources of short-term credit (commercial banks, for the most part) is perhaps just as important to local growth as the more dramatic supply of risk capital.[33]

To be quite clear, we do not suggest here that local commercial banks seriously consider increasing their loans to small local firms, with other loans and investments remaining the same. Local banks would lose reserves, on net, if they expanded total loans and investments faster than banks in other areas. We suggest only that local commercial banks might consider lending more to small local firms and less to larger ones. The larger ones are better able to borrow outside anyway. And this could redound to the benefit of local bankers, in the aggregate, if it accelerated local economic development, that is, lending more to riskier small business could be in the *long-run* self-interest of local bankers.

What determines the receptivity of commercial bankers to the needs of smaller, riskier business—how quickly they will pick up the account of a new business? One factor comes easily to mind: alternative opportunities. If local bankers can keep fully loaned-up on prime commercial paper—the business of the bigger and safer local firms—they can minimize administrative costs and maximize safety by ignoring the needs of small business. This may be most likely to occur during periods of rapid local growth, when the local market is a lenders' market. Conversely, when local growth has slowed, excess reserves (unused lending power) pile up and the local commercial banks may begin to take an interest in the more marginal borrowers in the area. At this point, one is tempted to infer that commercial banks, as suppliers of local working capital, act as governors in local economic development by slowing rapid growth and stimulating slow growth. But this sounds much too good to be true and it is much too early in the conceptual stage of so complex a subject to take any purely deductive proposition very seriously.

While no attempt is being made to construct a full-blown model of the local capital market, one further point needs at least a formal acknowledgment. A recurrent theme throughout this section has been that the historical evolution of a local industrial complex leaves a legacy to the present that greatly influences future economic development in that area. We argued

---

[32] A small business that is forced to sell or borrow on its accounts receivable at a discount of face value, to get cash sooner than the normal business sequence would provide, will have to pay interest rates of 12 per cent and over, in most places and at most times. Passing up trade discounts allowed for prompt payment of its own bills is usually even more expensive, for example, one of the more common trade terms ("2/10, net 30") is convertible into an annual interest rate equivalent to about 36 per cent. See Guthmann and Dougall, *op. cit.*, p. 441.

[33] For a most dramatic case of the critical character of working capital in the early years of a new small business, see J. Keith Butters and John Lintner, *Effects of Federal Taxes on Growing Enterprises* (Division of Research, Graduate School of Business Administration, Harvard University, Boston, 1945), Chapter XII, "Lithomat Corporation."

above that aging oligopolies might dampen venturesomeness and even prevent potential entrepreneurs from being "born," as the giant corporations recruit the most talented local graduates. We hypothesize here that aging oligopolies might also, indirectly, lay a heavy hand on local financial practices. Chinitz, reflecting on the state of the stagnant Pittsburgh economy, has guessed that:

> When banks cater to competitively organized industry, they are more likely to accept the insurance principle of making money, not on each customer, but on the average customer. If you have U.S. Steel and Westinghouse on your rolls, you do not have to learn to make money on the insurance principle.[34]

The willingness of Detroit bankers to back the fledgling automobile industry has been cited as an important factor in the rise of that industry in that area.[35] Eastern bankers were reportedly much more reluctant to support the struggling young eastern automobile firms. Has this characteristic of Detroit bankers endured, or did they also become conservative with success and affluence? Perhaps there are "long waves" of local venturesomeness and conservativeness in financing. Are Detroit bankers becoming more inclined toward risk taking now that the automobile industry has matured and growth must be sought elsewhere—among small firms with radical new products and processes?

The Detroit area capital market is, moreover, further complicated by the fact that the now giant automobile firms raise their capital in a national capital market and local bankers are now left with surplus loanable funds which they have had to dispose of in other urban areas. In short, the development of big firms and local maturity would seem to leave the area with the funds for an industrial rebirth, awaiting only entrepreneurial talent and a venturesome spirit among local bankers.

One final caveat lest the unwary be misled by irrelevant relative magnitudes. Since big business accounts for a very large part of total activity and since big business raises new capital largely out of retained earnings and from security sales in a national capital market, one might too quickly conclude that local capital supplies to small business are dust in the balance. But a handful of these small businesses of today are destined to become the industrial giants of tomorrow. Thus the availability of local capital to small business today may be a major determinant of the rate of the area growth a decade hence. The tail does come to wag the dog.

The more one pursues the question of the impact of local capital supplies on regional growth, and, conversely, of growth on regional capital supplies, the more one feels that there is highly useful knowledge to be gained in this direction.

[34] Chinitz, *op. cit.*, p. 286.

[35] Lawrence H. Seltzer, *op. cit.*, pp. 29–30. The author quotes Roy D. Chapin, a man identified with the automobile industry in its early years, as telling him, in a personal interview, that "the banks here played an important part. There was a great deal of prejudice in other parts of the country on the part of bankers, particularly in the east. They lacked the business sense that was needed. The Detroit bankers had it and were not afraid of our sight drafts."

Land

The economist's "land"—natural resources in the broadest sense—would seem to be the least likely of the four classical factors of production to be important in *urban* economic development. But this is not the case. Let us begin by considering the relevance of the rural hinterland of a city to the economic development of that city. The quality of the soils, mineral deposits, and forest resources determine the productivity and income of the surrounding farms, mines, and lumbering operations, and the owners and employees of these facilities are the customers of the trade and service establishments of the central city of the area. Thus the quality and quantity of nearby rural natural resources are important economic factors in urban growth to the degree that the urban economy is a service exporter. While rural area market towns are typically the smaller urban places, even very large cities may depend *indirectly* on rural prosperity by functioning as service centers to middle size cities which serve as service centers to the smaller ones which serve the rural areas directly. The Chicago economy is undoubtedly quite sensitive to changes in the prosperity of the corn-and-hog economy of the Middle West, albeit indirectly.

Further, rural areas are not only important immediate customers of urban areas, they are also suppliers to the cities. A given city may be disadvantaged in interurban competition for industry and share of the national market if the sites of accessible extractive activity are experiencing depleting supplies and/or rising costs relative to the raw material producing areas closer to its manufacturing rivals.

Raw material processing is ordinarily carried on quite close to the source of the material and is therefore ordinarily located in the more remote, small towns. Still, a number of very large urban areas have a very important stake in raw material processing, at an intermediate if not primary stage. For example, the Twin Cities metropolitan area, thirteenth largest in the nation, has more employment in food products manufacturing than any other of the twenty major industry groups in manufacturing, reflecting its rich agricultural hinterland.

Family costs of living also are involved. New York and Buffalo lose ground relative to Chicago and Milwaukee as preferred residential areas when dairying, poultry raising, and truck gardening costs in New York State rise relative to similar costs in Wisconsin. Blending the two concepts together, natural resources developments which favor the Middle West over the East also favor Chicago over New York by enriching the customers of Chicago's service industries—a money income effect—and by lowering food prices in Chicago—a real income effect.

But if reaching into the rural hinterland of a city to relate "land" to urban economic development is regarded as straining a point, we could confine ourselves to the impact of urban land on urban growth. Flat land, for example, promotes urban efficiency by reducing street construction and maintenance costs and by smoothing and speeding traffic flow. Flat land also lowers housing costs by simplifying grading operations and by facilitating mass production building. But hills provide more pleasing housing sites.[36] The net balance of these opposing values of terrain is not so much blurred as variegated. A low-income family would probably choose to have a larger house and lower cost transportation, while the higher-income family might even pay to have the hill built. The half-serious hypothesis is offered that flat terrain raises lower incomes and lowers higher incomes, that is, effects greater income equality, and hilly terrain does the reverse. Further, if the upper-income groups make the basic industrial location decisions that apply at the interurban level, and if they are guided in these business decisions to some appreciable degree by the personal considerations of residential amenities, the hilly, scenic areas might be favored in aggregate growth, or at least suffer a less disadvantage than physical efficiency considerations alone would dictate.

Natural resource endowments other than topography and economic considerations other than construction costs bear heavily of urban growth prospects. What is the net effect on population growth of Los Angeles' sunshine and ocean frontage on the one hand and its smog and water shortage on the other? How does one weigh the rivers of the Washington, D.C., area, rivers which create both traffic congestion and recreational opportunities, with bridges easing the former and pollution burdening the latter?

Practically everyone writing today on industrial location and regional growth hastens to point out the growing role of the natural features that make for pleasant living, especially climate, on locational patterns and trends.[37] With rising productivity, every year more of us can afford the luxuries of living where climates are pleasant, scenery attractive and outdoor recreation facilities convenient—and if the most attractive sites are not also the most efficient ones we do pay a price in foregone production and money income to live there. In addition, that part of our increased productivity which we take in shorter hours of work also operates to move us toward the sites of greatest amenities, as greater leisure may become merely prolonged idleness and weigh heavily unless the environment is enhanced. Exaggerating to illustrate, it may be cheaper to move our cities than to build mountains and lakes. We shall probably do a little of both over the next decade.

To further ensure that the inclusion of "land" as a fourth factor and full partner in this supply approach to urban growth is not regarded as strictly academic, an impressionistic model of the location of economic activity in an Age of Research and Development is offered. Suppose automation reduces the weight of the labor factor in industrial location by reducing the amount of direct labor input and unionization continues to spread its influence equalizing wages everywhere, especially for key skilled labor.

[36] Homer Hoyt long ago called attention to the tendency for the upper income groups to choose the high ground for residential sites, "The Pattern of Movement of Residential Rental Neighborhoods," *The Structure and Growth of Residential Neighborhoods in American Cities* (Washington: Federal Housing Administration, 1939), reprinted in *Readings in Urban Geography, op. cit.,* p. 504.

[37] The best known work here is Edward L. Ullman, "Amenities as a Factor in Regional Growth," *The Geographical Review* (Vol XLIV, 1954), pp. 119–32.

Suppose differentials in capital supply to be of only minor importance, as giant enterprise, omnipresent, creates a national capital market. Entrepreneurship could then become the critical locational factor, especially if inventors and innovators do bunch in time and space, as hypothesized above. But what is more footloose, in aggregate, than an entrepreneurial complex; there is no obvious reason why an exciting and fruitful inventive-innovative environment might not be developed in a pleasant place to live rather than a less pleasant one. What could be more logical than for these intellectual-industrial centers to be consciously implanted in two distinctive environments: places which offer natural beauty and good outdoor recreation, and places which offer the height of urban culture and indoor recreation? The case for Palo Alto and Santa Monica, California, as centers of research and development does not need extended argument; it is hard to argue with success. Similarly, the superb consumer capital (e.g., museums, libraries, theaters, and so forth) in New York and Boston have made it possible for those areas to hold their own in competition for research and development activity with the natural garden spots.

We take limited exception here, then, to the hypothesis above that small towns are not viable in today's economy. Small towns in very *scenic*, *accessible* locations may well be on the verge of a local boom, and become quite viable—as middle size cities, as they attract research, pilot plants, and even full-scale manufacturing operations.

Rules of Play

Two cities will be allowed to develop on the game board in this experiment. City A will be built by three teams and will be contained above line 11 on the playing board. City B will be built by five teams and will be contained below line 11. Each city will have its own accounting and taxing systems kept by an Accountant. The only interaction allowed between cities will be Shopping in LS, CS, and O; residences working for employers, and normal payments for such interactions. Capital may not be exchanged between teams of different cities nor may investments be made in land or buildings in other than a team's own city. The two cities must, however, cycle concurrently at each Step of Play.

The transportation system provided consists of Primary Roads, Major Highways, and Expressways with Mode Weights of 1:½:¼, respectively. The Expressway runs only between the two cities and facilitates inter-city travel. The location of these highways, the Terminal and the utility plants is given in Figure V-2.

Lending and Borrowing

In Basic CLUG the community is allowed to borrow up to ten per cent of the Total Assessed Value of land and buildings at five per cent interest on the Total Cumulative Deficit. In addition, borrowing is always allowed between teams.

Figure V-2. Location of Highways, Terminals, Utility Plants, and City Boundary

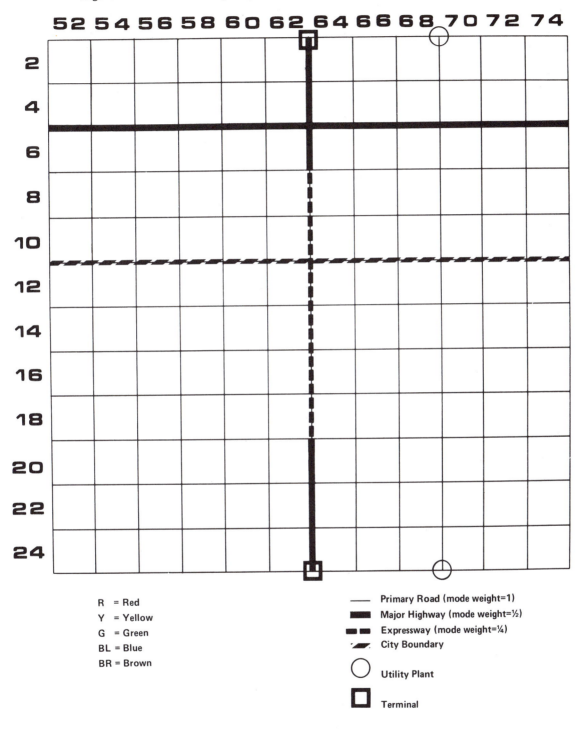

R = Red
Y = Yellow
G = Green
BL = Blue
BR = Brown

——— Primary Road (mode weight=1)
▬▬▬ Major Highway (mode weight=½)
▬ ▬ ▬ Expressway (mode weight=¼)
City Boundary
○ Utility Plant
□ Terminal

In this experiment City A will be very restricted with respect to capital and City B will be allowed a great deal of freedom. Borrowing and lending between teams will be allowed only in City B. City B will be allowed the Basic CLUG provision of borrowing up to ten per cent of its Assessed Value for city expenses, while City A will be on a pay-as-you-go system of community finance. This means that in City A the Accountant will set a Tax Rate each round which, when multiplied times the Total Community Assessed Value, will yield exactly the amount spent that round for Utility Lines and residential units.

Borrowing from the outside world (the instructor) will be allowed in City B, but not in City A. Each round after the first any of the five teams of City B may borrow up to twenty-five per cent of their individual Total Assessed Value minus outstanding loans. This occurs just before Construct Buildings (Step 4). An example of such a loan would be as follows: a team's value of land and buildings in Round 8 is $145,000. Since they had previously borrowed $20,000 in Round 3, they may now borrow up to twenty-five per cent of $145,000 minus $20,000, or $31,250. Alternatively, they may pay off the remainder of the loan outstanding and borrow up to twenty-five per cent of the full $145,000, or $36,250.

Repayment terms are: one-seventh of the principal for each of the ten succeeding rounds, to be collected by the instructor in Step 11 (Pay Taxes). This is approximately five per cent compound interest. If a team cannot make a loan payment, the instructor may seize some of the team's land or buildings or both until the value of seized property equals the amount of the debt outstanding.

Industrial Markets

The basic land use categories in CLUG can be deceptive since they have titles implying certain kinds of activities in the real world. Thus "industry" generally implies manufacturing in everyday terminology. In the game, the land use labeled Industry actually refers to those activities that provide export products for a community, not necessarily factories or manufacturing plants. Thus a printing plant which sold all of its products within the community in which it was located would not be an Industry in terms of the game but a Central Store, or perhaps an Office. Similarly, a large university in a small city which "sold" education to students from other communities is engaged in export activity and would properly be classed as an Industry in the game.

The confusion in these terms is not limited to CLUG but appears throughout the literature of economic base and community commercial activities. It is this kind of consideration that provides the answer to a frequently asked question in the game, "Why doesn't Industry sell some of its products to Stores in CLUG?" By definition, Industry's goods are all exported, since Industry represents all those activities engaged in export production.

In Basic CLUG an unlimited and unresponsive external market is assumed for all the community's exports. All industrial products can be sold at a constant price. In this experiment a variable external market is introduced which will purchase limited amounts of the community's export products with some possible variations in price. In effect, the external economy will begin to have variable demands for industrial products and will always buy those products at the cheapest price possible. To accommodate this process Step 7 (Receive Income) will be broken up into 6 substeps:

A. The instructor gives to each team in each city a marker for each unit of industrial goods it has produced that round. One unit is the amount produced by one worker.
B. The instructor reminds teams of the three possible levels of demand for the round, the maximum allowable price per unit, and then accepts a bid sheet from each team which indicates the number of units being offered at any particular price.
C. The instructor rolls one die to determine the actual demand level in the outside economy for the industrial products of the two cities.
D. The instructor buys the demanded number of units at the lowest Price until his demand is filled, paying the appropriate teams the price per unit they have asked.
E. The instructor announces the three possible levels of demand for the following round.
F. Teams may buy remaining inventory from each other, if they wish or retain it until the next round in hopes of selling it then.

Pennies or paper clips are used to represent units of productivity. The instructor holds a schedule of possible demand levels for twenty rounds of play. However, he only announces the three possible levels one round in advance. Thus, before play begins in Round 1 he will announce that the three possible levels of demand are nine, twelve, and fifteen units, corresponding to rolls of one or two, three or four, and five or six respectively on a single die. In twenty rounds the two cities will have felt the pressures of a normal, a booming, and a depression economy, but they will not know when each will occur. This information will be known only by the instructor.

In Basic CLUG the outside world pays $12,000 for each unit of FI production and $11,000 for each unit of PI production. In this experiment units from either type will be indistinguishable and may be worth as much as $15,000 each (given a high demand period). The owners of FI and PI will submit bids knowing the three possible levels of demand. An example of such a bid sheet for one team appears below:

Blue Team's Bid Sheet

5 units @ $15,000 each
3 units @ $10,000 each
1 unit @ $ 8,000 each

Maximum bids allowed will be $15,000 per unit. The die will then be rolled to determine the actual demand. The Instructor is then required to accept the lowest priced bids fulfilling his demand. This may involve using parts of each bidder's list from each city. In case of ties the instructor will request a re-bid. Thus, he might buy four units from Blue, one from Red, two from Green, and none from any other team. If the instructor cannot fill his demand, this deficiency is not added to demand next round but simply ignored. Inventory remaining at the end of Step 7 (Receive Income) may be traded. Prior to such trading the instructor will announce the three possible levels of demand for the forthcoming Round.

One additional change from Basic CLUG will be made in this experiment. Employer-employee relationships can be terminated at Step 5 (Designate Employment) in *each* round instead of only in rounds divisible by five. Wages are also negotiable each round. None of the other agreements that usually expire in rounds divisible by five can be negotiated every round. Unemployed residential units must continue to pay for both Local and Central Store goods however.

Players should bear in mind the possible effects of the above changes from Basic CLUG. The following points summarize these changes and assist play.

1. In Basic CLUG, a city needs industry to exist, i.e. an export base. This is the only way money is constantly brought into the community.

2. In this experiment there are two cities, and thus economic base can be redefined. For example, a Local Store, if it brings money from one city into another, might be considered economic base.

3. Lowered Transportation Costs make travel between cities relatively inexpensive. This should allow for both cooperation and competition between the two cities.

No special information other than the basic rules changes and modifications in Steps of Play are needed by players for this experiment. This summary of the Steps of Play should serve as an adequate guide while playing the experiment:

1. Purchase Land	Unchanged except that teams may only buy land in their own city.	
2. Provide Utilities	Unchanged except that separate voting and taxing districts are maintained for the two cities.	
[3. Renovate Buildings]	Unchanged.	
4. Construct Buildings	Unchanged except teams in City B may borrow money from each other or Instructor before constructing. No borrowing allowed by teams in City A.	
5. Designate Employment	Unchanged and employment between cities is allowed. All employment agreements are for one round only and wages are negotiable.	
6. Sign Trade Agreements	Unchanged and shopping in other city than residence is allowed.	
7. Receive Income	Occurs in six steps:	

a. Distribute production units.

b. Learn probable demand and submit bids.

c. Die roll determines actual demand.

d. Production units bought to fulfill demand.

e. Three possible demand levels for next round are announced.

f. Teams may purchase excess inventories from each other.

8. Pay Employees   Unchanged except amounts of wages may vary.

9. Pay LS, CS, and O   Unchanged.

10. Pay Transportation   Unchanged. Mode Weights are ¼, ½, and 1 for Expressways, Major Highways, and Primary Roads, respectively.

11. Pay Taxes   Taxes paid separately by each city.
Tax rate for City A determined by Accountant.
Tax rate for City B determined by players.
Instructor collects 1/7 of the principal of any outstanding loans.

Discussion

In this experiment some of the restraints and simplifications of Basic CLUG are removed. The result is a fairly substantial increase in the complexity of the game operation. Most significant among the innovations are an allowance for intercity trade and competition and a variable market for industrial products together with variable wage scales. City A tends to operate at a distinct disadvantage in most runs of the game due both to its smaller size and dependence on City B as well as to the fact that its ability to generate financing is highly restricted. While this condition is somewhat exaggerated in this experiment and is certainly likely to be unwelcome to the players occupying City A, it is not at all unlike some of the economic and political disadvantages encountered by smaller subordinate cities located nearby larger and more dominant metropolises.

Players in both cities also suffer from the vagaries of the market for industrial goods and its impact on employment. If additional variations in the experiment were introduced to provide for both population mobility and for social welfare payments, these effects would become even more pronounced. Unfortunately, however, the game would then become so complex as to become absolutely unworkable without substantial large-scale computer assistance.

Study Questions

A number of topics of interest are usually generated by participation in this experiment. The following questions may serve to help generate discussion and further exploration of some of these topics.

1. The total amount of private capital available in City A was substantially less than that available in City B at the beginning of the game. How great an advantage did this disparity in initial status give to the players in City B over City A? What effect do you think would have been produced if players from City B had been allowed to invest in City A? What effect would the converse policy have had?

2. What were the comparative effects of the pay-as-you-go policy of City A and the free borrowing policy of City B? How much of the relative advantage of one city over the other do you think can be attributed to these two different policies? Does such an advantage appear to be valid with respect to the real world? If the two financial policies were reversed between the two cities, how do you think the final status of the two cities and their development would have been changed?

3. What effect did the addition of fluctuating industrial markets have on play and on planning investments? How severe was the impact of this varying demand on private investors? How severe was the impact on individual members of the labor force represented by the Residential Units? If players had been directly representing these Residential Units and had some voting and striking power within the cities apart from the investment teams, what actions do you think they might have undertaken at various points in the game?

4. Are the base-service ratios the same for each of the cities? Count up the total number of employees in all industries and divide by the total employment in stores and offices for each of the two cities. How different are these two ratios and what information do they convey about the relative economic status of the two? How do you think such ratios might change over time, if City A managed to grow substantially larger?

5. How much intercity commutation existed for employment and shopping for CS, LS, and O goods? As the cities continued to grow, what implications would this have for the future location of new units of LS, CS, and O? If well selected, would these new units have a significant advantage over the older units located nearer the centers of the two cities?

6. What kinds of land uses constitute the economic base of City A and City B? Under what kinds of circumstances can commercial activities be considered a part of the economic base of a city? Think of a half-dozen or more large American cities which have economic bases made up in large part of non-industrial activities. Are these cities significantly different from most other American cities? In what ways?

Experiment VI: Municipal Finance

Introduction

Many central cities in the United States are currently experiencing great difficulty in matching the overwhelming demand for public services with their meager financial resources. Faced with the need for high levels of public spending for health, welfare, and educational services, central cities have found the means for raising such monies becoming eroded.

A number of factors have contributed to this financial crisis. These can be divided into those for which the central city is responsible internally and those for which the central city is not responsible, factors external to its power to alleviate.

External Problems

One major external problem can be traced to the federal government which, historically, has been claiming a growing proportion of all taxes collected, but which has not assumed a proportional responsibility for local service costs. Rather, defense commitments and extra-local projects like the interstate highway system have overshadowed domestic and local needs in our current national priority system. Unable to control federal spending in the short run, citizens have frequently made local taxation and spending the target of their frustrations by attempting to minimize their total tax burden. Generally, they have refused to raise local taxes to provide for additional public services.

A second major external problem is the fragmentation of local governmental structure occurring in most metropolitan areas. As Netzer points out in the reading which follows, such a maze of governmental units has "spillovers" in costs and benefits. Theoretically, in a free economy with a laissez-faire form of government, forces of supply and demand in the market place automatically result in appropriate allocations of society's scarce resources. Economists have found, however, that the market is imperfect and does not automatically result in appropriate balances between needs and resources. What is best for the individual may not be best for his community. Thus, in a society where individuals are free to maximize their own self-interest, the community will probably not be able to maximize its communal interest. These divergencies between individual and societal return are often cited as prime reasons for government intervention and planning.

A concrete example of a cost spillover is encountered in examining the problem of providing welfare to many of the nation's poor. New York State, or more specifically New York City, has been the destination of the migration of poor people from many parts of the United States. This fact has raised the very real problem of determining responsibility for the cost of providing for the welfare of these new urbanites. Current practice places the burden almost entirely on the state and city. Many people have argued, however, that this is a national problem and should be financed by the federal rather than local government. Similarly, it has been argued that suburban residents and visitors should contribute to the cost of operating central city museums, libraries, parks and other facilities used by residents, visitors, and suburbanites alike.

In many cases, the answer lies in charging a fee of the individual who burdens the city with a cost or by making a rebate to one who provides the city with a benefit. In some instances the solution could take the form of charging individuals directly for the goods and services they have consumed. Netzer discusses such "user charges" as a partial solution. However, in many cases, like feeding the poor, user charges are not appropriate. Rather, the answer lies in describing the appropriate governmental unit so that spillovers are minimized—New York, for example, should not be held responsible for the nation's problems.

Why not then assume the largest governmental system, our nation, as the major taxing agent, and pay local as well as national expenditures out of federal monies? This would certainly eliminate all but international spillovers. Two obstacles stand in the way of such a solution.

First, our society places high value on individual freedom to determine place of residence and place of business. As a consequence, individuals tend to group themselves into governmental units which pursue their own notions of taxation and spending for public services. Local control, as a prominent political value to both liberals and conservatives, is an impediment to increasing federal responsibility.

Second, there is a powerful economic argument to prevent such a move. Netzer refers to this as the economizing nature of local government. In essence, this theory states that people attempt to control local budgets much more closely than national budgets. Few Americans are able to comprehend our current national budget, and fewer still have control over its allocation and distribution. Local budgets, however, undergo strict scrutiny by the public.

Until solutions are implemented, the phenomena of people and businesses segregating themselves into high income or high value areas to avoid sharing the burden of supporting services for poorer elements is reaching intolerable proportions. The two most common examples of such segregated communities are 1) middle-income or upper-income residential suburbs and 2) industrial enclaves.

Internal Problems

Problems of equal importance arise when perspective is shifted to the internal financial operations of metropolitan areas. Taxing mechanisms are largely the source of internal fiscal problems. Present taxing structures of most American cities do not begin to account for spillovers between individuals.

Central cities do not match the costs and benefits yielded to the community by individuals and businesses with the costs and benefits charged to these individuals. The result is that individuals in the city often find themselves rewarded for their socially undesirable behavior. Examples are: polluting the air through use of the automobile, permitting apartments to fall into disrepair, and travelling on already congested transportation systems at peak traffic hours. Conversely, those persons benefiting the city by not owning an auto, maintaining their apartments, and commuting at nonpeak traffic hours often find themselves penalized for their pro-social behavior by outmoded revenue collection mechanisms. Consequently, individuals are discouraged from socially desirable behavior. In either case, the central city suffers an economic loss.

These problems of inappropriate tax charges and benefits have increased substantially in recent years. Most American cities use the property tax (a tax on land and real property) to finance city services. This tax was begun when the ownership of real property served as a good indicator of personal wealth. Today, however, the insensitivity of the property tax to the degree to which real property actually yields income has made it outmoded. In America today, wealth is more accurately judged by less visible factors such as savings, stocks, bonds, and other "intangible property."

Very often the property tax works perversely on cost and benefit spillovers. A good example of this phenomenon is the way the property tax affects apartment landlords. A landlord who invests money in improving his buildings is taxed on the increased value of them, whereas a landlord who does not invest saves through lowered assessments due to depreciation. Thus, the property tax may discourage housing maintenance. This example is only one from a long list of negative effects which can be traced to reliance on a tax on real property for financing public services. As Netzer points out, despite these problems, the property tax accounted for over thirty-nine per cent of the revenues spent for public services in 1962.

Several strong alternative solutions exist to the internal problem of financing public services: the application of "user charges;" taxes on intangible property like sales and income; and conversion to a tax based solely on the value of land. Solutions to external problems could include more reliance on federal and state taxes with commensurate rebates and grants, and the "metropolitanization" of local governments to include both central city and suburbs.

The Readings and Experiment

These problems and some potential solutions are explored in the reading by Netzer. This is followed by a brief discussion by Thompson of a tax based purely on land and the consequences of such a tax for the housing market. The experiment following the readings is divided into two parts. Variation I underlines several of the existing fiscal problems in large cities today: the relative poverty of the central city vis-à-vis the suburbs, the emphasis of federal monies on other than local projects, and the perverse nature of the property tax on the housing market, allowing great tax savings to slum building owners. Variation II explores three possible solutions to these problems: changing from a property to a land tax, annexation of the suburbs by the central city, and a reversal of federal spending priorities toward central city problems.

FEDERAL, STATE, AND LOCAL FINANCE
IN A METROPOLITAN CONTEXT

Dick Netzer

Effects of Financing Arrangements on the Output of Services

Local Tax Sources

As Table 1 indicates, local taxes finance slightly less than half of the cost of public services in metropolitan areas.[1] And when we speak of "local taxes," we mean the property tax and little else, except for the small number of large central cities (like New York, Philadelphia, St. Louis, and a number of Ohio cities) which obtain significant revenues from non-property tax sources. Moreover, at least some of the intra-metropolitan consequences of the property tax are common to other locally imposed tax devices.

The usual conclusion is that the fragmented governmental structure with its attendant spillovers of costs and benefits leads to: ". . . an allocation of resources to collective consumption that is below the optimum level that would be indicated if all benefits of such consumption were appropriable in the spending community. . . . The inefficiencies, in terms of under-allocation

Table 1. Sources of Funds For Public Services in Metropolitan Areas, Per Cent Distribution, 1962[a]

Source		Per cent of total
Federal and state governments		32.3
Federal aid	1.7	
State aid	19.4	
Other state government funds[b]	11.2	
Local taxes		45.7
Property	39.3	
Other	6.5	
General sales	2.6	
Income	0.8	
User-charge-type revenues		17.4
Charges and special assessments	9.1	
Utility revenue	8.3	
Other local sources[c]		4.5
Total[b]		100.00

[a]Based on data in U.S. Bureau of the Census, *Census of Governments, 1962,* especially Vol. V.

[b]Includes direct state government expenditure for highways and public assistance, and estimated state government contributions to retirement systems for metropolitan area local government employees.

[c]Includes employee contributions for retirement, liquor store revenue, sale of property, interest earnings, and other and unallocable.

Note: Because of rounding, detail may not add to totals and subtotals.

From Harvey Perloff and Lowdon Wingo (eds.), *Issues in Urban Economics* (Baltimore: Johns Hopkins, 1968), pp. 440-457. Reprinted by permission of the publishers. Published by the Johns Hopkins Press, for Resources for the Future, Inc.

[1] Table 1 includes, as revenue, direct state government outlays for highways and public assistance and estimated state contributions for employee retirement; this was done to adjust for differences in the distribution of functional responsibilities among the states.

of resources to the public sector, and the accompanying inequities, go a long way toward providing some understanding, if not explanation, of the major problems confronting metropolitan America."[2]

In concept, the coexistence of a large number of small governmental units within a single urban area need not lead to undernourishment of public services or other suboptimal results. Tiebout has provided a model, at a fairly high level of abstraction, in which individuals reveal their preferences for public goods much as they do in the course of voluntary exchange in the private sector.[3] Under a set of restrictive assumptions, he views suburban communities as competing for residents by offering differing packages of public services combined with the tax rates required to finance the services; consumers choose among the communities on the basis of their relative preferences for collectively provided vis-à-vis privately provided goods and services. Obviously, to the extent that this abstraction is applicable to the world we live in, it offers an attractive means of arriving at an optimal solution to local finance problems, a solution which reflects consumer choice.

Unfortunately, Tiebout's restrictive assumptions usually do not apply: mobility and knowledge is restricted; externalities exist; and actual fiscal flows are complex and often unrelated to decisions of individual consumer-voters. Therefore, it is not surprising that the pattern of tax rates and expenditure levels the Tiebout thesis would lead one to expect—a high and positive correlation—is seldom observed in metropolitan areas.[4] In fact, the most common pattern is the opposite one: tax rates and expenditure levels are *negatively* associated. At least, this has been the finding in most reported studies.[5]

The explanation for this appears to lie in the enormous disparities in taxable capacity among the political jurisdictions in the larger metropolitan areas. There is a strong positive correlation between tax base and expenditure levels. The richer communities—those with extensive concentrations of business property (or non-property tax bases) and those dominated by high-value residential property—do spend a good deal more than the poorer communities, by and large. But they do not spend as much more as their superior tax bases would permit. Therefore, tax rates and tax base tend to be

---

[2] Brazer, "Some Fiscal Implications of Metropolitanism," *op. cit.*, pp. 144, 145. See also Lyle C. Fitch, "Metropolitan Fiscal Problems," in Chinitz (ed.), *City and Suburb*, for a good exposition of the undernourishment hypothesis.

[3] Charles M. Tiebout, "A Pure Theory of Local Expenditure," *Journal of Political Economy*, Vol. 64 (October 1956).

[4] Indeed, the surprising thing is that this pattern is *ever* observed. But it is, for example, in regard to non-school expenditures and taxes in upper-income Chicago suburbs (the presumed laboratory for Tiebout's observations). See Netzer, *Economics of the Property Tax*, pp. 125–31.

[5] See, for example, *ibid.*, pp. 125–31; Julius Margolis, "Municipal Fiscal Structure in a Metropolitan Region," *Journal of Political Economy*, Vol. 65 (June 1957); and "The Variation of Property Tax Rates within a Metropolitan Region," *National Tax Journal*, Vol. 9 (December 1956); Donald J. Curran, S.J., "The Metropolitan Problem: Solution from Within?" *National Tax Journal*, Vol. 16 (September 1963).

negatively correlated; the richer communities provide superior services at lower tax rates.

This is a general description of the pattern of variation among jurisdictions outside the central cities. The central city-suburb comparison presents a somewhat different, but analogous, pattern. Generally, central cities spend significantly more, on a per capita basis, than suburban communities which are, on balance, richer. This is mainly (but not entirely) a consequence of the concentration of poverty-linked public service needs and outlays in the central cities. However, the per capita property tax base in most large central cities is well below that of their surrounding areas.

This has not always been the case. At one time, the central cities had a near-monopoly on non-residential property which offset their parallel near-monopoly on low-value housing. But they have lost the former near-monopoly, with the dispersal of industry away from central locations, while retaining the latter. The upshot is that effective property tax rates in most large central cities exceed those outside the central cities. In most other places the effective rates are roughly equivalent. This is usually explained by existence of important non-property taxes utilized mainly by central cities. On the whole, therefore, tax levels in central cities are significantly higher than in suburbs (as a group). Moreover, these higher tax levels buy services which are inferior in a number of important respects, notably in regard to schools.[6]

Some observers have argued that there is a pronounced observable trend toward reduction in intrametropolitan fiscal disparities—a trend toward uniformity accompanying increased economic specialization within metropolitan areas.[7] To a considerable extent, such observations have been a result of rising expenditures, values, and tax rates on the newly urbanized, formerly rural fringes of metropolitan areas: they have become more like the already developed sections. It is by no means certain that disparities are disappearing within the already urbanized sections of metropolitan areas, and it may be that central city-suburban disparities are *increasing*.

However this may be, the existing disparities afford a rational explanation of the notorious resistance of suburban communities to metropolitan-area-wide solutions to governmental problems, and also an explanation of the observed tendency to control land use for maximum fiscal advantage: the fortunate low-tax, high-expenditure communities seek to preserve their favored positions, a natural response.[8] One result is to insulate part of the

[6] For discussion of city-suburbs disparities, see Netzer, *Economics of the Property Tax*, pp. 117–24; Curran, *op. cit.*; Margolis, *op. cit.*; Brazer, *Some Fiscal Implications*; Advisory Commission on Intergovernmental Relations, *Metropolitan Social and Economic Disparities* (1965); Mordecai S. Feinberg, "The Implications of Core-City Decline for the Fiscal Structure of the Core-City," *National Tax Journal*, Vol. 17 (September 1964).

[7] See Jesse Burkhead, "Uniformity in Governmental Expenditures and Resources in a Metropolitan Area," *National Tax Journal*, Vol. 14 (December 1961); Netzer, *Economics of the Property Tax*, pp. 132–35

[8] On the land use effects, see Dick Netzer, "The Property Tax and Alternatives in Urban Development," *Regional Science Association Papers and Proceedings*, Vol. 9 (1962); and Lynn A. Stiles, "Financing Government in the Suburbs—The Role of the Property Tax," *National Tax Association Proceedings, 1960.*

metropolitan area's economy from local taxation. The extreme cases are the industrial enclaves with few residents and fewer school children; in effect, industrial property in such enclaves is exempt from school taxation.

These are obvious and special cases of the undernourishment hypothesis. The more general cases fall into two classes. First, given the fragmentation and the disparities, local tax support of redistributive services is likely to be restrained. If the poor are concentrated in already high-tax communities, redistributive services can be more amply supported only by taxing the poor more heavily, a self-defeating proposition; the resources of the rich are not available, since these resources belong to other jurisdictions, those with minor needs for redistributive services. Second, non-redistributive services with heavy benefit spillovers are likely to be undernourished simply because, as noted earlier, the benefits cannot be appropriated by the communities which individually tax themselves for the service. And although all would benefit from a broader base for financing such services, the well-off communities resist nonetheless, since they cannot be sure that a breach in the existing pattern, for financing services affected with major externalities, will not become a much wider assault on their advantageous positions.

Intrametropolitan fiscal disparities thus have both equity and efficiency consequences. Moreover, the efficiency consequences include effects on the location of activity as well as the effects on the level of output of public services. What has been called "fiscal zoning" presumably has some effect on locational patterns; the direction of the effect must be assumed to be suboptimal, away from the pattern which would prevail in the absence of land use controls. There is also likely to be a more direct cause-and-effect relationship: differentials in tax rates within urban areas no doubt have some bearing on location decisions of firms and individuals, and presumably the results are often suboptimal.

The extent of the actual influence of taxes on location is open to question (see below). However, there is no doubt that *fear* of potentially adverse tax influences is a critical factor in state and local tax policy decision-making. It is almost certain that these competitive fears have restrained the increase in local taxes and thus have had feedback effects on the output of public services; this, of course, is not susceptible to quantification.

Anxiety about the competitive effects of tax differentials has given rise to a fairly extensive literature on the subject.[9] Most studies take a whole state as the unit of observation. They generally conclude that "relatively high business tax levels do not have the disastrous effects often claimed for them,"[10] mostly because state-local taxes are so small an element in business

[9] Examples are Wilbur R. Thompson, "Importance of State and Local Taxes as Business Costs," *National Tax Association Proceedings, 1957;* Reuben A. Zubrow, "Some Difficulties with the Measurement of Comparative Tax Burdens," *National Tax Association Proceedings, 1961;* and the studies cited in John F. Due, "Studies of State-Local Tax Influences on Location of Industry," *National Tax Journal,* Vol. 14 (June 1961); and Netzer, *Economics of the Property Tax,* pp. 109–10. Perhaps the best analytical pieces are Harvey E. Brazer, "The Value of Industrial Property as a Subject of Taxation," *Canadian Public Administration,* Vol. 55 (June 1961); and Wolfgang F. Stolper, "Economic Development, Taxation, and Industrial Location in Michigan," in *Michigan Tax Study Staff Papers* (1958).

[10] Due, *op. cit.,* p. 171.

costs, even in business cost differentials at alternative locations. This conclusion must be accepted with some reservations. For one thing, the usual studies are too aggregative to uncover the marginal cases in which tax differentials are in fact the only significant cost differentials. Such marginal cases surely exist, and as local tax levels rise relative to total income and output, these cases will become more frequent.

Moreover, tax differentials may reinforce, rather than offset, other cost differentials. This is the prevailing situation with regard to manufacturing activities and the central cities. The dispersive tendencies are powerful, even without tax differentials which work in the same direction. Finally, there is the distinction between *inter*regional and *intra*regional locational effects. Tax rate differentials may not be important enough to offset the major interregional factor cost differentials but can easily be far more significant within a single metropolitan area where other cost differentials are relatively minor.

And tax levels within metropolitan areas do vary considerably among alternative locations. The Campbell study of the New York area, for example, showed a three-to-one range for a sample of twenty-five manufacturing firms among sixty-four locations in the region, a range which surely must affect locational decisions.[11] A more recent study of New York City's finances provides fairly clear evidence that the major business tax differentials which have existed in the area actually have stimulated decentralization of economic activity away from New York City.[12] Indeed, the evidence is so clear that is has had a major effect on recent tax policy decisions in both New York City and its periphery.

Local business tax differentials will affect locational decisions only to the extent that the tax differentials are in excess of the location rents for a given activity at a particular site and of the value of public services provided to firms in return for the tax payment.[13] Ordinarily, the user-charge component of local tax payments is small indeed for business but it is by no means small for individuals, especially in dormitory suburbs which perhaps partly explains the apparent insensitivity of residential location decisions to local tax rate differentials.[14] There have been few studies of this, but one survey of high-income individuals suggests almost complete insensitivity.[15]

[11] Alan K. Campbell, "Taxes and Industrial Location in the New York Metropolitan Region." *National Tax Journal*, Vol. 11 (September 1958).

[12] See the papers by Leslie E. Carbert, James A. Papke, William Hamovitch, and Henry M. Levin, in *Financing Government in New York City*.

[13] See the exposition in Brazer, *The Value of Industrial Property*.

[14] Another explanation may be found in the federal individual income tax offsets to local taxes. See Benjamin Bridges, "Deductibility of State and Local Nonbusiness Taxes under the Federal Individual Income Tax," *National Tax Journal*, Vol. 19 (March 1966); "Allowances for State and Local Nonbusiness Taxes," in Musgrave (ed.), *Essays in Fiscal Federalism*.

[15] James N. Morgan, Robin Barlow, and Harvey E. Brazer, "A Survey of Investment Management and Working Behavior Among High-Income Individuals," *American Economic Review*, Vol. 55 (May 1965), p. 259; this is more fully developed by the same authors in *Economic Behavior of the Affluent* (Brookings, 1966), pp. 169–70.

However, because the tax-service nexus is far from clear to individuals within central cities, it is reasonable to suppose that high property taxes on housing in the cities are a serious deterrent to central city housing consumption. The consumer perceives only the annual or monthly cost of housing, 25 per cent or more of which reflects property tax payments in most large central cities; he sees little connection between this cost and the quality of public services offered. He therefore is presumably less willing to pay a high price for the housing-cum-taxes package than in a suburban location, where the connection with public services is far more obvious. To the extent that this is true and that its truth is appreciated, however incoherently, by public officials it may explain, indeed justify, the common big-city policy of taxing housing much more favorably than other types of real property. [16] But this, too, is a circular process, with feedbacks on the output of public services: keeping tax rates low on a large fraction of the tax base restrains the ability of central cities to increase the output of public services.

In summary, then, the prevailing metropolitan area local tax structure—heavy reliance on the property tax by a large number of taxing jurisdictions—appears to restrict the output of public services to a level below that which might obtain under other institutional arrangements. The existing structure also has suboptimal effects on location decisions and land use patterns, and these effects in turn probably further restrict the output of public services. What other institutional arrangements (confining the discussion here to locally imposed taxes) might there be?

For the central cities, at least, a partial solution is to be found in non-property taxes, on personal income and/or consumption (non-property business taxes levied by local governments have no obvious advantages, on any score, over business property taxes). Personal taxes of a general nature avoid the serious deterrence to increased housing consumption (which is a goal most large older cities actively pursue with a variety of policy devices) inherent in the property tax. They also afford a means of moderately extending the geographic scope of central city taxing powers, by a form of reverse-suburban-exploitation, that is, taxing those suburbanites who happen to work or shop in the central city to defray part of the "excess burden" or redistributive central city services. But presumably the scope for central city non-property taxation is limited by the locational impact; very large differentials will not work. [17] Perhaps the greatest potential is in central city personal income taxation, partly because so few state governments rely heavily on income taxation. [18] In any event, those large cities which impose some type of income tax do appear able to reduce their reliance on the

[16] For an extended discussion of this, see my *Economics of the Property Tax*, pp. 74–85, and *Financing Government in New York City*, pp. 58–61, 710–15.

[17] It is estimated that, when New York City's sales tax rate was 4 per cent and there was no sales tax in surrounding areas, the tax differential reduced retail sales in New York City—of the types sensitive to and covered by the tax—by close to 25 per cent. See the papers by Hamovitch and Levin in *Financing Government in New York City*.

[18] See Advisory Commission on Intergovernmental Relations, *Federal-State Coordination of Personal Income Taxes* (1965), p. 11.

property tax by more than do the sales tax cities in places like Illinois and California.

De-emphasis of the property tax would tend to reduce the land use and location effects of local tax structures. The process could also be helped by radical reform of the property tax, into a tax based largely on land values (or land value increments). The potential of land value taxation has recently gained new and well-deserved attention.[19]

But the essential need appears to be some mechanism for levying local taxes on a broader geographic base, that is, converting some portion of local taxation into area-wide taxes. The objective here would be to provide for more satisfactory financing of both redistributive services and non-redistributive services affected with major externalities. A corollary advantage of area-wide taxation is that the metropolitan area affords a more satisfactory basis for application of the superior forms of taxation—on income and consumption rather than property—than does a large collection of separate small taxing units. But one cannot be sanguine about the possibilities here. Indeed, one can argue that resort to increased grants from the state and federal governments has been, and will continue to be, the most likely and popular means of spreading the tax burden geographically.

Table 2. Financing of Public Services in Metropolitan Areas, by Major Function, 1962[a]

Function	Expenditures ($ billion)[b]	Sources of funds (per cent distribution)		
		Federal and state governments[c]	User-charge-type revenues[d]	Other local sources[e]
Education	12.4	33	6	61
Highways	4.9	68	5	27
Welfare	2.8	75	—	25
Health and hospitals	1.6	10	25	65
Housing and renewal	1.1	26	30	44
Local utilities	3.2	—	89	11
Other and unallocable[f]	10.1	10	14	76
Total[g]	36.1	31	16	53

[a]Based on data in U.S. Bureau of the Census, *Census of Governments, 1962,* especially Vol. V.

[b]Includes direct state government expenditures for highways and public assistance, estimated state government expenditure for retirement systems for metropolitan area local government employees, and estimated local government contributions to their own retirement systems. Interest allocated crudely by function and, where possible, retirement system amounts also allocated.

[c]Includes, in addition to aids, the state government expenditure described in the preceding note. Functional distribution estimated.

[d]Functional distribution partly estimated.

[e]Computed as residual; includes taxes, miscellaneous revenues, employee contributions to retirement systems, liquor store revenues, borrowing and net use of cash balances. Net borrowing amounted to $2.8 billion in 1962, about one-seventh of the total in this column.

[f]Includes employee retirement system amounts not allocated by function and liquor store finances, as well as other and unallocable general expenditure and its financing.

[g]The percentages differ slightly from those in Table 1; that table compares revenue amounts to total *revenues,* while in this table the revenue amounts are compared to total *expenditure.*

[19] See Netzer, *Economics of the Property Tax*, Chap. 8; Clyde E. Browning, "Land Value Taxation: Promises and Problems." *Journal of the American Institute of Planners*, Vol. 29 (November 1963); James Heilbrun, *Real Estate Taxes and Urban Housing* (Columbia, 1966).

Federal and State Financing

As Tables 1 and 2 indicate, federal and state funds finance somewhat more than 30 per cent of the cost of the public services provided in metropolitan areas. This is on the basis of a broad definition of federal and state financing, to comprehend identifiable direct state government provision of public services in metropolitan areas, as well as the intergovernmental payments through which the external governments help support locally provided services. The most important of such identifiable direct state services are highways and public assistance.

The states differ considerably in their distributions of responsibilities among the state government and the local units.[20] On the average, state governments directly account for about one-third of combined state-local expenditure, but state participation is substantially lower in states like New York, New Jersey, and California and substantially higher in places like Pennsylvania and Connecticut, among the more urbanized states. Greater state aid may or may not offset lower direct state participation, but both factors must be considered in appraising the state role. In some states, like New York, the major intergovernmental problem is in fact the distribution of functional responsibilities, and not state aid formulas and the like.[21]

Federal and state funds, using this broader definition, finance one-third of local education costs (and, of course, nearly all the *public* costs of higher education), over two-thirds of highway and welfare costs, and much smaller, almost nominal, proportions of the costs of other public services in metropolitan areas. It is clear that local revenue sources bear a substantial residual burden in connection with redistributive services (about $2 billion for health and welfare purposes, as of 1962) and that external financing is not of major consequence in connection with other services with major spillovers.

These are 1962 proportions, and the percentages have risen somewhat since then. However, the role of external financing has changed relatively little during the past fifteen years; the really revolutionary expansion of the roles of the state and federal government occurred in the 1930's. This is evident from the following tabulation of the percentages of combined state-local expenditures met from state and federal sources:[22]

Year	Per cent	Year	Per cent
1964—65	54	1940	49
1960	53	1927	26
1955	51	1902	18
1950	54		

[20] See the paper by Morris Beck in *Financing Government in New York City*. Mushkin points out that differences in the assignment of the welfare function are the most important consideration. See Selma J. Mushkin, "Intergovernmental Aspects of Local Expenditure Decisions," in Howard G. Schaller (ed.), *Public Expenditure Decisions in the Urban Community* (Resources for the Future, 1963).

[21] *Financing Government in New York City*, pp. 29–31, 36–40.

[22] Calculated from U.S. Bureau of the Census, *Census of Governments, 1962,* and *Governmental Finances in 1964–65* (1966).

Financing from taxes levied by higher levels of government tends to overcome spillover problems, disparities in local tax bases and disparities in the concentration of the poor within metropolitan areas; it can also result in greater reliance on taxes with more appropriate distributive effects than usually result from metropolitan area local tax structures. It *can* do these things, although these are not necessarily the explicit reasons for intervention by higher levels of government. More commonly, the motivation for federal action is to encourage the provision of *additional* public services; equalization features are designed to effect this expansion with minimum burdens on taxpayers in the poorer states. In contrast, state government action is usually often justified as a *substitute* for local tax support of a given level of services (notably in connection with state school aid), although some programs give priority to stimulation of local action.

. . .

User Charges

As Tables 1 and 2 show, user-charge-type devices finance about one-sixth of public services in metropolitan areas; if state and federal highway-user taxes are classified as user charges, the proportion rises to one-fourth. Relatively heavy reliance on price-like devices to finance urban services seems appropriate. True, user charges are highly inappropriate for redistributive services but, as we have seen, the allocation branch appears dominant in metropolitan finance.

Moreover, within the metropolitan area allocation branch, a significant portion of the output of public services consists of services of an essentially private character, for which the exclusion principle applies: the consumer can be, or actually is, excluded from enjoyment of the service unless he is willing to pay its price.[23] Some of these are affected with no greater externalities than are most privately produced goods and services (water supply, most transportation services, many recreational activities). In such cases, individuals can vary their consumption (within limits) on the basis of price without efficiency losses, indeed with significant efficiency gains. For other services, where major external *diseconomies* are involved (e.g., air and water pollution, traffic congestion), there is an argument for user charges as "social economy" reimbursements or to induce consumers to eliminate the diseconomies their actions produce.

Intuitively, it seems obvious that financing from user charges, rather than from general taxes, should affect the level of output of public services. If the general thesis, that existing institutional arrangements produce under-nourishment of urban public services, applies to services that are amenable to user charges but are not presently financed by them, the effect should be a substantial increase in the output of such services. One reason for this is that user charges can overcome the political fragmentation problem. The charge, presumably, is based on actual use of services or facilities, not the domicile of the taxpaper; the demand of "foreign" as well as "domestic" users can be satisfied, on a compensatory basis, by the managers of the enterprise.

[23] See Musgrave, *The Theory of Public Finance*, p. 9.

There has been surprisingly little systematic empirical investigation of the effect of user charge financing on the output of services. Casual empiricism suggests that there are in fact higher standards of service where user charge financing is employed. For example, the essence of the frequent criticisms of the operations of public authorities is that they produce their own "private opulence amidst public squalor." That is, they utilize their command over user charges to produce unusually high-grade services within their spheres of operation.[24]

Rigorous analysis has been applied to one aspect of this question—the effects of earmarking taxes for specific purposes. Buchanan has developed a model, based on individual fiscal choice, which suggests that earmarking will lead to an efficient solution in which expenditures are higher than would otherwise be the case.[25] An empirical effort to test the Buchanan hypothesis produced negative results—the extent of or change in earmarking seemed to have little effect on expenditure levels.[26] In an earlier paper, Margolis found that earmarking, in the form of school districts independent of general government, tended to reduce school expenditure.[27] He explained this on the basis of a log-rolling theory of voting behavior—the multipurpose expenditure package combines the consumer's surplus for specific projects so that voters accept the entire package rather than lose the specific project. His discussants, however, suggested that "backward log-rolling" is possible as well and that the empirical evidence is far from conclusive.[28] The case, then, must be regarded as not proved, although the Buchanan model is most attractive.

The potential for user charges in metropolitan finance can perhaps be illuminated by a brief review of the extent of user charge financing in metropolitan areas currently, that is, as of the 1962 Census of Governments. As we would expect, charges are of minor significance for services with a major redistributive aspect. *Education* charges amount to about 7 per cent of current operating expenditure, and these are largely school lunch fees, which are far below the full costs of the resources devoted to the program; the subsidy here, of course, is a federal one. *Hospital* charges equal about 35 per cent of current expenditure. The bulk of the revenue is collected outside the largest cities and largest metropolitan areas, where the hospitals serve the general population and not just the indigent as in the bigger cities. Small-city public hospitals in effect are substitutes for the big-city voluntary hospital.

[24] For a more sophisticated view of authorities, see Robert C. Wood, *1400 Governments* (Harvard University Press, 1961), Chap. 4.

[25] James M. Buchanan, "The Economics of Earmarked Taxes," *Journal of Political Economy*, Vol. 71 (October 1963).

[26] Elizabeth Deran, "Earmarking and Expenditures: A Survey and A New Test," *National Tax Journal*, Vol. 18 (December 1965).

[27] Julius Margolis, "Metropolitan Finance Problems: Territories, Functions and Growth," in Universities—National Bureau of Economic Research, *Public Finances: Needs, Sources and Utilization* (Princeton University Press, 1961).

[28] Lyle C. Fitch, pp. 272–73, and William F. Hellmuth, pp. 276–80, in *Public Finances . . . Utilization*.

Public housing charges (rents) amount to about 90 per cent of current expenditure and in-lieu-of-tax payments; the redistribution occurs here because the federal (and any other public) subsidy is designed to cover all, or nearly all, of the capital costs of public housing.

Turning to allocation branch expenditures, *sewerage* charges are about equal to current expenditure, in the aggregate. But annual economic costs for this heavily capital intensive service are far above current expenditure. Special assessments probably cover about one-fifth of capital outlays. In regard to other *sanitation* services (mainly refuse removal), charges are only about 15 per cent of expenditure. Charges are more commonly utilized in smaller cities and suburbs than in the big cities. Local *parks and recreation*, probably the most rapidly growing urban expenditure, generate charges equal to about 20 per cent of current expenditure. *Fire protection* can be viewed as very much a private good, [29] one which could readily be provided by a privately owned public utility company, but charges are negligible and the service is financed from general taxes.

Transportation services, other than streets and highways, are largely financed from charges. Charges for airports and water terminals substantially exceed current expenditure and probably largely cover debt service costs as well. Public transit systems come close to breaking even in regard to current expenditure; the very large deficits on capital account are concentrated in a very few places, notably New York. Local government parking operations generate large surpluses, in the form of net parking meter revenues, only a small part of which is used to subsidize off-street parking.

Highways are a rather different matter. In 1962, highway expenditure in metropolitan areas totalled $4.9 billion, of which $3.3 billion was financed from federal and state funds. The bulk of these funds were derived from earmarked highway-user taxes, which can be considered as user charges in a very aggregative sense. Users provide the funds, and no doubt at a more ample level than might be the case without earmarking, but there is little connection between user tax payments and specific uses of the roads. Of the locally financed $1.6 billion, about 20 per cent came from user sources, equally divided among local highway-user taxes (mostly licenses and often not earmarked), special assessments for street improvements, and more specific types of charges (mostly tolls). These figures relate to a fairly narrow definition of highway expenditure. Associated street functions and police traffic control activities probably involve at least $400 million more in expenditure, and generate only minor user charges.

This review suggests significant potential for greater and more sophisticated application of user-charge-type financing. One of the most serious obstacles to effective utilization of pricing devices in financing public services can be traced to the traditional justification for user charges (and analogous taxes) on the basis of benefits received. The benefit principle, however, is concerned with equity, not allocation: how can we equitably

---

[29] Ignoring the tiny fraction of fire losses due to fires originating on adjacent properties.

spread the costs of public goods among individuals? But this principle is inappropriate for allocation branch decisions on the financing and provision of services with a substantial private character. Efficiency in allocation requires that prices (or other types of charges) and the level of services provided be determined on the basis of the marginal *costs* of the services. More often than not, there is little correspondence between benefit-determined charges and cost-determined charges.

Vickrey had done extensive work on this. In a major paper, he contrasts benefit and cost solutions for a number of urban services, and advances imaginative (and reasonably workable) cost-based charging schemes.[30] A number of these schemes involve charges based on site characteristics, such as land area and frontage; in effect, these are offered as substitutes for the existing benefit-justified taxation of the value of land and improvements, that is, the property tax. The pricing of urban transportation services, on a cost basis, has received more attention than anything else, by Vickrey and by others, especially in Britain.[31] Fairly elaborate and detailed pricing schemes have been advanced, schemes which radically depart from the conventional benefit approach to highway financing.[32] Such proposals have met with a rather negative response in this country, but seem to be on the verge of acceptance in conservative Britain.

[30] William Vickrey, "General and Specific Financing of Urban Services," in Schaller (ed.), *Public Expenditure Decisions in the Urban Community.*

[31] See, for example, William S. Vickrey, *The Revision of the Rapid Transit Fare Structure of the City of New York*, Finance Project, Mayor's Committee on Management Survey of the City of New York (1952); Lyle C. Fitch and associates, *Urban Transportation and Public Policy* (Chandler, 1964), Chap. 4; U.K. Ministry of Transport, *Road Pricing: The Economic and Technical Possibilities* (1964).

[32] For a good exposition of this approach, see A. D. Le Baron, "The 'Theory' of Highway Finance: Roots, Aims, and Accomplishments," *National Tax Journal*, Vol. 16 (1963).

PROPERTY TAXES AND HOUSING CONSERVATION

Wilbur R. Thompson

Good urban public management would use relative prices of various kinds to reward behavior which favors property conservation and to penalize that which accelerates depreciation. Especially at issue is the local property tax. A long line of thought, dating back to Henry George's *Progress and Poverty*, has pressed for taxing land values ("rent") very heavily because land is a gift of nature and yields its owners an "unearned income." Since, moreover, the supply of land is fixed, no level of taxation up to its full earnings would reduce the supply of land available to society. Heavy land taxes have, therefore, been championed on the grounds of ability to pay.

On the other hand, handsome buildings in good repair are not at all fixed in supply and depend on the profitability of investment in such capital. The local property tax, the "land-taxers" (intellectual heirs of Henry George) argue, acts in a most perverse fashion, by rewarding those who permit their property to depreciate into slums and penalizing with higher tax assessments those who improve their property. The "land-taxers" would eliminate or at least greatly reduce taxes on property improvements, and some have gone to the extreme to argue that our present heavy property taxes have almost single-handedly created our slums.

Without trying to assess the relative share that the local property tax has had in creating our slums, we can approach this subject constructively and programmatically by asking what our tax strategy should be. We quickly recognize that the local property tax cannot be rationalized on a benefit theory basis; it is clearly not a *quid pro quo* for public service benefits received. An old, dilapidated firetrap should pay more, not less, in benefit-type taxes than should a modern, fireproof building of higher value. Similarly, when a property owner puts in a new safer furnace or a garbage-disposal unit or paints the exterior of his building, he is causing the city less cost and creating social benefits—in return for which, perversely, his property is assessed at a higher value and his tax liability increased.

With respect to *rental* properties, one might make a strong case for a true benefit theory local property tax on buildings, distinct from but consistent with and even complementary to a heavy ability-to-pay land tax, to conserve and enhance urban capital. Such a tax package would not, moreover, impose any difficult income distribution problems or serious ability-to-pay questions; old, run-down *rental* properties do *not* imply poor owners. But when we turn to owner-occupied property, we need a fresh approach.

Deteriorating owner-occupied property poses a problem not unlike that of devising a way to make public assistance payments in a constructive way. One cannot realistically contemplate raising property taxes on rundown, owner-occupied dwellings—taxing the poor—no matter how much they may

From Wilbur R. Thompson, *A Preface to Urban Economics* (Baltimore: Johns Hopkins 1965), pp. 318–320. Reprinted by permission of the publisher. Published by The Johns Hopkins Press, for Resources for the Future, Inc.

cost society in police and fire protection and public health services. But in discussing public assistance we argued there that rewards for socially beneficial behavior could be paid even if penalties for recalcitrant behavior could not be levied. A similar case can be made here for rewarding renovations on deteriorating residences by taxing them less heavily. Municipalities in New York State may now, in fact, grant property tax exemptions of up to twelve years on increased residential valuation created by installing hot water and central heating systems.

To sum up this section, the scope of public policy that bears on efficiency in urban blight and renewal clearly includes housing policies which provide for the orderly filtering down of aging housing in the great gray area. Considerable consensus exists that only by greatly retarding the rate of structural deterioration and slum formation can we even begin to solve the urban blight problem. Thus neighborhood conservation programs are central to urban renewal efforts and racial problems in housing and property tax policy are central to neighborhood conservation.

Rules of Play

Variation I of this experiment will attempt to describe, in game terms, the fiscal situation existing in many metropolitan areas today. This city will use the Property Tax for the major portion of its revenue generation and share a part of a Federal—State Income Tax. There will be an urban and a suburban taxing district.

Variation II will explore, in game terms, some suggested solutions to the central city's financial crisis. A straight Land Value Tax will be substituted for the Property Tax, the central city will annex the suburbs, and the Federal government will begin spending more on domestic problems.

General Rules Applicable to Both Variations

For both variations several of the rules of the Basic CLUG model will be altered. First, in order to simulate city growth in an environment where Transportation Costs are less restrictive, Mode Weights will be reduced from a ratio of 2:1 (Secondary Roads to Primary Roads) to 1:½ (Primary Roads to Major Highways). The Association Weights will be multiplied by one for Primary Roads and one-half for Major Highways. Therefore a greater proportion of monies will be available for investment.

Second, savings on Construction Costs will be introduced through specialization in type of construction. The following table expresses these costs. There are two main changes shown by this chart. First, higher density Residences (R4, R3, and R2) no longer cost more per unit than low density Residences (R1). Each residential unit, whether stacked up or spread out, costs the same. Second, each team can save money on construction by specializing in one kind of land use. For example, a team building its fourth Full Industry saves $16,000—the difference between $96,000 and $80,000.

For purposes of renovation, an R4 will use the schedule of Partial Industry (original value $48,000), R3 will use the schedule of Office (original value $36,000), R2 will use the schedule of Local Store (original value $24,000) and R1 will use its own schedule. No matter what the cost paid to

Table VI-1. Reduced Construction Costs Due to Specialization*

Unit To Be Built	Type of Unit								
	FI	PI	O	CS	LS	R4	R3	R2	R1
1st	$96	$48	$36	$24	$24	$48	$36	$24	$12
2nd	90	48	36	24	20	48	36	24	12
3rd	85	48	36	20	18	48	36	24	12
4th	80	48	36	18	18	44	33	22	11
5th	80	48	36	18	18	44	33	22	11
6th	80	48	36	16	16	44	33	22	11
7th	75	48	36	16	16	40	30	20	10
8th	75	48	36	15	15	40	30	20	10
9th	75	48	36	15	15	40	30	20	10
10th or more	75	48	36	15	15	36	27	18	9

*In thousands of dollars.

construct an R3, for example, its original Assessed Value will be $36,000 and its depreciation rate $1,800, just like an Office.

As indicated previously, the first variation will use a property tax and the second a land tax. Both, however, will use a Federal-State Income Tax which will be applied to all land uses according to the following schedule:

Table VI-2. Federal-State Tax Schedule

Full Industry	$1200 per round
Partial Industry	500 per round
Residential Units	200 per round
R1	200 per round
R2	400 per round
R3	600 per round
R4	800 per round

Local Store, Central Store, and Office Formula:

$$\left[\frac{Price \times Number\ of\ Customers}{10} \right] - \$1,000 = Federal\text{-}State\ Tax$$

In the case of industries operating below capacity, a prorated tax will be paid. Unemployed residents, any buildings lost on the roll of the dice, and Stores and Offices with an income loss or an income less than $50 will pay no Federal-State Tax. Stores and Offices must include customers from their own team in computing this tax. In both experiments, the instructor will be responsible for collecting and dispersing Federal-State monies.

The Basic CLUG model has three types of public expenditures each round: $1,000 for each residential unit (e.g., R4 costs $4,000 per round); $2,000 for each new service line, $1,000 to maintain old service lines; and ten per cent interest on the outstanding Deficit. These are all paid out of community Property Taxes on land and buildings.

In this experiment Utility Lines continue to cost the community the same amounts: $2,000 to install and $1,000 per round to maintain. Interest on the community's Deficit will also be ten per cent.

The charge to the community for residential units will be changed from $1,000 per unit to the following schedule:

Table VI-3. Residential Service Charges

R1	$1,000 per round
R2	$2,300 per round
R3	$3,600 per round
R4	$5,200 per round

These charges shall be doubled if the building should become older than five rounds. For example, if an R4 is built in Round 1 and not renovated in Round 5, then it would begin in Round 7 (six rounds old) to cost the community $10,400 per round. Buildings older than five rounds should be coded on the playing board. The instructor will check these ages in each round at the Construction Step.

The player should weigh each of these changes from Basic CLUG rules very carefully before play begins. The following effects should be considered:

1. Because of the change in Mode Weights, it becomes economical to locate many uses much further from their destinations. For example, in Variation I a Full Industry may now locate in some parts of the suburbs at no increase in Transportation Cost above that paid in Basic CLUG.

2. Because of Specialization Benefits, a team can save substantial money by constructing only one type of land use.

3. Because high density residential unit costs have been reduced substantially, a team may save money and land by constructing R4's, R3's and R2's as opposed to R1's. However, the community pays a substantial cost for high density residential units and will probably exert pressure on the owners of residences to avoid higher densities, and especially seek to avoid allowing such buildings to become over six rounds old.

4. In addition to savings due to higher densities, a team constructing residential units will find major savings accruing to it through reduced Assessed Values (and therefore reduced Property Taxes) when units are allowed to depreciate and age.

Variation I

In this variation, the Property Tax as used in Basic CLUG and the Federal-State Tax described above will be in effect. Play begins in Step 5 (Employment) of Round 10. Figure VI-1 depicts the Playing Board at this point.

There will be two taxing authorities for the Property Tax. They will be administered separately and be kept in totally separate records. One is the central city, the area shown inside the boundaries in Figure VI-1, and the other the suburbs, shown outside the boundary. Tables VI-4, -5, -6, and -7 should also be consulted for the initial set-up of this variation. Each team will pay Taxes (since each owns property) to each governmental unit. However, a team will not have a vote in either the city or the suburbs unless

Figure VI-1. Central City and Suburban Land Holdings

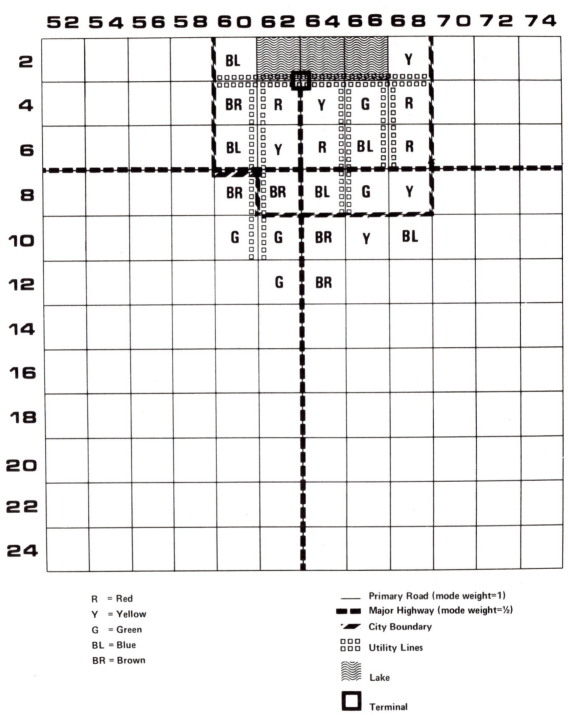

it owns a parcel with a building on it in that area. As in Basic CLUG, a team's Tax will be determined by a rate set by the teams, times its Assessed Value of land and buildings.

Table VI-4. Team Holdings for Variations I and II — Round 10, Step 5

Coordinates	Team	Land		Building		
		Purchase Price	Assessed Value	Type	Round Built	Assessed Value
2–60	BL	$4,000	$3,500	R4	2	$28,800
4–60	BR	3,000	3,600	PI	10	48,000
6–60	BL	2,400	2,600	CS	8	21,600
8–60	BR	2,200	2,600	R2	7	20,400
10–60	G	1,800	3,000	R1	8	10,800
4–62	R	5,000	4,200	FI	2	57,600
6–62	Y	3,000	3,800	O	7	30,600
8–62	BR	4,200	4,100	PI	7	40,800
10–62	G	5,000	4,100	—	—	—
12–62	G	5,000	5,100	—	—	—
4–64	Y	6,000	4,800	FI	3	62,400
6–64	R	4,200	5,700	PI	7	40,800
8–64	BL	6,000	5,200	R2	7	20,400
10–64	BR	4,200	4,500	—	—	—
12–64	BR	5,400	4,900	—	—	—
4–66	G	4,000	3,800	R4	8	43,200
6–66	BL	3,200	3,400	LS	3	15,600
8–66	G	3,400	3,600	R4	7	40,800
10–66	Y	2,000	3,000	—	—	—
2–68	Y	1,600	1,800	—	—	—
4–68	R	2,000	2,400	—	—	—
6–68	R	2,000	2,600	—	—	—
8–68	Y	3,200	2,700	—	—	—
10–68	BL	2,200	2,500	—	—	—

Table VI-5. Team Standings: Variation One (Game Starts in Round 10, Step 5)

	Red Team	Yellow Team	Blue Team	Green Team	Brown Team	Total
Property Assessed Value						
City	$113,300	$106,100	$101,100	$95,500	$101,000	$517,000
Suburban	—	3,000	2,500	18,900	27,900	52,300
Total	113,300	109,100	103,600	114,400	128,900	569,300
Cash on Hand	16,700	20,900	26,400	15,600	1,100	—
Property Taxes @ 5%						
City	5,700	5,300	5,100	4,800	5,100	26,000
Suburbs	—	200	100	900	1,400	2,600
Federal Taxes*	1,700	2,800	6,300	1,800	1,400	14,000

*Assuming full employment and all shopping on the board at instructor's prices. If either employment is not full, prices are not the same as the instructor's, and/or all shopping is not done on the board, then Taxes should be revised for Round 10 according to the instruction given earlier.

Table VI-6. City Financial Standings (Round 10)

1 new service line @ $2,000	$ 2,000
11 old service lines @ $1,000	11,000
5% interest on Outstanding Deficit	1,300
Residential Units	
Over six years old	
1 R4 @ $10,400	10,400
Under six years old	
2 R4's @ 5,200	10,400
1 R2 @ $2,300	2,300
Total Expenditures	$37,400
Outstanding Deficit in round 9	$26,000
Allowable Deficit (10%) in round 10	$56,900
Property Taxes ($26,000)	
minus Expenditures ($37,400)	
equals Round Deficit (−$11,400)	

Table VI-7. Suburban Financial Standings (Round 10)

0 new service lines @ $2,000	0
1 old service line @ $1,000	$1,000
5% interest on Outstanding Deficit	0
Residential Units	
Over six years old	
None	
Under six years old	
1 R2 @ $2,300	2,300
1 R1 @ $1,000	1,000
Total Expenditures	$4,300
Outstanding Deficit in round 9	0
Allowable Deficit (10%) in round 10	$5,200
Property Taxes ($2,600)	
minus Expenditures ($4,300)	
equals Round Deficit (−$1,700)	

Step 11 will now be altered to include six substeps:

A. Instructor collects the Federal-State Tax.

B. Instructor rolls the "National-Local" die.

C. Instructor rolls the "City-Suburban" die.

D. Instructor gives proportionate refunds to city and to suburban coffers which then get added to their round Surplus or subtracted from their round Deficit.

E. The instructor collects the Property Tax for the city and makes a financial report; appropriate teams set a Tax Rate for the next round.

F. The instructor collects the Property Tax for the suburbs and makes a financial report; appropriate teams set a Tax Rate for the next round.

In Substep B, the instructor rolls one die. The resulting number is the number of tenths of the total Federal Tax collected that is refunded to the local community for domestic spending. In Substep C, the instructor again rolls one die and the result is the number of tenths of the total refund that goes to the city. The rest goes to the suburbs. An example follows:

> $10,000 is collected jointly from city and suburbs in Federal-State Taxes. The instructor rolls a four, so $4,000 is refunded locally. He then rolls a two, indicating two-tenths of that $4,000, or $800, is given to city coffers, while the rest, $3,200, is awarded to the suburbs.

The Property Taxes collected in each district go to pay for each district's Utility Lines, residential units, and interest on Total Deficit.

In Step 2, a majority of the teams eligible to vote in each district vote on Utility Line placement in that district. If any Utility Line abuts the city boundary or is inside it, the Line is constructed and maintained by city funds.

Play should continue through Round 20 or beyond, having started in Step 5 of Round 10.

To summarize the steps of play:

1. Purchase Land	Basic CLUG rules apply.
2. Provide Utilities	Utilities paid by the appropriate community, city or suburb. Same prices as Basic CLUG.
[3. Renovate Buildings]	By renovating old residential units a team gets charged more in Taxes for higher assessed valuation, as in Basic CLUG. Unlike Basic CLUG the community is charged a high cost for buildings over six years old.
4. Construct Buildings	There are now reduced costs for specialization. R2's, R3's and R4's cost the team no more per unit to build now than R1's. However, they cost the city substantially more to service. The instructor will check the Age of each residential building at this point in the game each round and code those over six years old.
5. Designate Employment; 6. Sign Trade Agreements; 7. Receive Income; 8. Pay Employees; 9. Pay Local Store, Central Store, and Office	There may be interchanges between all land uses in the city and all land uses in the suburbs.
10. Pay Transportation Cost	Transportation Costs have been reduced, making many more locations accessible even for industry.

11. Pay Taxes

The city and the suburb keep completely separate Tax and Expenditure records. A team must own a developed parcel in an area in order to vote on Tax rates.

A summary of the new information and changes needed to play this variation is provided on a tear-out sheet at the back of this manual. It is entitled "Summary of Changes for Municipal Finance Experiment." Initial set-up conditions are not included since they are needed only once and are readily available in the text.

Variation II

In this variation the Land Tax is used in addition to the Federal–State Tax. There will be only one governmental unit and thus only one taxing authority, just as in Basic CLUG. This change can be thought of as the city of Variation I after annexing the suburbs. The Playing Board is the same as in Variation I (Figure VI-I) except that the city Boundary is deleted. Tables VI-8 and -9 should be consulted for initial data. Thus, for the entire board each team's Assessed Value of Land will be multiplied by a Tax Rate set by the teams. The new allowable debt limit will be seventy per cent of the entire community's Assessed Value of Land.

In order to help administer the Land Tax equitably, an Assessor will be elected whose job it will be to assess land throughout play. Unlike Basic CLUG, assessment will not simply be the average of the Purchase Prices of

Table VI-8. Team Standings: Variation Two (Game Starts in Round 10, Step 5)

	Red Team	Yellow Team	Blue Team	Green Team	Brown Team	Total
Total Assessed Value	$113,300	$109,100	$103,600	$114,400	$128,900	$569,300
Cash on Hand	16,700	20,900	26,400	15,600	1,100	—
Assessed Value of Land	14,900	16,100	17,200	19,600	19,700	87,500
Land Taxes @ 40%	6,000	6,400	6,900	7,800	7,900	35,000
Federal Taxes*	1,700	2,800	6,300	1,800	1,400	14,000

*Assuming full employment and all shopping on the board at the instructor's prices. These Taxes should be revised for Round 10 Taxes when employment is not full, Prices not the same as the instructor's Prices, and/or all shopping is not on the board.

Table VI-9. Community Financial Standing (Round 10)

Same Expenditures Total as Variation I	$41,700
Outstanding Deficit in Round 9	26,000
Allowable Deficit in Round 10	56,900
Land Tax ($35,000)	
minus Expenditures ($41,700)	
equals Round Deficit (–$ 6,700)	

adjacent parcels. This is a rather static method of assessing since few changes come about unless land is exchanged between teams. Instead, the Assessor will try to judge, as does an assessor in the real world, what price a particular parcel would bring if it were to be sold on the open market. This will then be the parcel's Assessed Valuation. The Assessor will be elected from the teams before Step 1 of every round divisible by *three*. He must relinquish his team status for these three rounds.

The instructor and Assessor should work closely in setting the criteria for assessment; these criteria should be made clear to the players. It will be most important for players to be familiar with the assessment procedures and also the price and location of other teams' land. They may get this information at any time from the Assessor's record sheets.

In rolling the "National–Local" die in Step 11, the instructor will retain the tenths of the total showing on the die for national programs and give the remainder to the local community to help pay expenditures. In effect, this represents a reversal of national priorities from Variation I.

Thus the Substeps of Step 11 are:

A. Instructor collects the Federal–State Tax.
B. Instructor rolls the "National–Local" die.
C. Instructor refunds the appropriate amount to community coffers.
D. Instructor collects the Land Tax, makes a financial report, and teams set a new Land Tax Rate.

Play should continue through at least Round 20 having started in Step 5, Round 10. A summary of reminders for each Step of Play follows.

1. Purchase Land	Election of assessor in rounds divisible by 3. Community Taxes are now based solely on Land Values. Therefore, extreme sensitivity to land prices and holdings will be necessary for each team.
2. Provide Utilities	Service lines are voted and paid for by the single community as in Basic CLUG.

[3. Renovate Buildings]
 4. Construct Buildings;
 5. Designate Employment;
 6. Sign Trade Agreements;   } Same as Variation One.
 7. Receive Income;
 8. Pay Employees;
 9. Pay Local Store, Central Store and Office;
10. Pay Transportation Cost

11. Pay Taxes	Taxes on land are computed in only one voting district — the entire community.

Except for the change in taxation system and the combination of the city and suburbs, this variation operates in almost the same fashion as Variation I. No new summary page is necessary, therefore, and the summary page provided for Variation I can be used again.

Discussion

The experiment as a whole seeks to emphasize three important problems in municipal finance and management and three of the types of solutions which have been proposed for one or another of these problems.

Variation I provides the problem-setting covering (1) fragmentation of metropolitan governments and the resulting fiscally impoverished central city as opposed to fairly affluent suburbs, and (2) the existence of a national system of priorities that emphasizes national spending over local spending and then redistributes what little money is available away from central cities to suburban areas, and (3) reliance on the property tax as a major revenue source with its perverse effect on the city's housing market.

Variation II deals with the nature of three of the proposed solutions and their possible impact: annexation or combination of suburbs with the city as a single taxing and voting district; a reversal of national priorities toward greater local spending with more attention to central city areas; and conversion of the property tax to a tax on land alone, thereby seeking to eliminate the perverse effects of the property tax on the housing market.

Study Questions

1. What new kinds of problems arose in this experiment due to the existence of two nearby competing governing bodies, that of the central city and that of the immediate suburbs? How much worse might these problems have become if different players had consistently been representing one or another of the two jurisdictions?

2. How did the financial status of these two jurisdictions compare with respect to total indebtedness and current tax rates? If you were a new arrival in the area do you think you would be more likely to invest in property in the suburbs or in the central city? Why?

3. Does the relative allocation of national funding to local problems with an emphasis on suburban spending seem unrealistic to you? How do you think state and federal funds are currently distributed between local and national problems and between central city and suburban locations?

4. If annexation of suburbs to the central city is a proposed solution to some of these problems, what effect is it likely to have on current efforts towards self-governance among urban minority groups? Is such self-governance fiscally possible without some form of consolidation or annexation of suburban areas?

5. If property taxes were based only upon the value of land without respect to the buildings placed upon the land, how high would tax rates have to be in order to provide appropriate revenue sources for cities? What effect

do you think this would have upon the kinds of buildings constructed on expensive central city properties? What effect do you think it would have upon real estate speculation?

6. If the property tax in itself is not sufficient to provide revenues for local government finance, what other practical sources of local revenue might be found? How great a portion of local property tax revenues are currently consumed by local school districts? Is this proportion increasing or decreasing over the past several decades? How difficult would an income tax or a sales tax be to establish and administer under the forms of government found in Variation I? In Variation II?

Experiment VII: Environmental Pollution

Introduction

Pollution of the environment has recently become a topic of great concern to citizens and governments alike. Increases in the number and frequency of major cases of air and water pollution in particular have drawn attention to the catastrophic consequences of an uninformed and short-sighted view of the environment. Though these instances of major problems have yielded many specific lessons, they must be viewed as examples of the more general problem of man's role in the eco-system. In this way, lessons derived from one type of environmental problem may shed light on others yet to develop which might be avoided. In order to deal with its problems, the eco-system must first be understood.

Environment and System

When the environment is viewed in an eco-system perspective, several important principles emerge.

Inherent in a systems perspective is the axiom that any system is made up of a set of interdependent or mutually influencing parts. When the interrelations of these parts are relatively stable over time, the system can be said to be in a state of equilibrium. On the other hand, changes in any part produce changes in other parts of the system.

For purposes of explication, these system parts can be conceived of as technology, population, and environment. In Experiment III, system interdependencies were observed when technological innovations in transportation and energy made it possible for population to increase and to extend into previously unsettled territory. Through the three stages of that experiment, dependence on the environment for energy and transport was gradually decreased, though the environment itself was unaltered as far as the game was concerned. While developments such as these are often evaluated as progress, system change can also be linked to noxious consequences.

While technology may make new levels of economic activity and population possible in a given locale, these developments may themselves lead to partial, or even complete, exhaustion of environmental resources. An undesirable chain of events may be set off, the consequences of which may not be apparent initially. This is the type of situation that players will attempt to avoid in Experiment VII.

Though systems exhibit properties of persistence and self-restoration, these processes may not be capable of overcoming disequilibrating influences. A new set of interrelations and balances would then evolve. Depletion of the environment, for instance, might prohibit future population increases or negate the benefits of new technologies by limiting cities to current (or even past) levels of development.

From an eco-system perspective such as that outlined very briefly above, it is possible to understand that both progress and retreat are different consequences resulting from a common underlying cycle of balance, change and rebalance. Understanding on this abstract level can now be applied to a more realistic problem.

Environmental Responsibility

The existence of environmental pollution as a definite social problem is well documented elsewhere and need not be repeated here. Instead, attention is focused on the question of who is or should be responsible for remedy of the problem and what that treatment should be. Two broad positions exist on these issues.

On the one hand, it is argued that those who pollute should be held responsible since they are the immediate cause of the problem. They should pay the cost of environmental renewal. Industry, for instance, should provide its own waste treatment facilities instead of pumping sewage into public waterways.

On the other hand, it is pointed out that since pollution is a problem of imbalance in the eco-system and since we are all members of that system, we are all responsible for eliminating pollution. For example, while industry may be a prime contributor to pollution, households and businesses both benefit from the employment opportunities and the sale or use of the goods that industry produces. According to this argument, pollution should be paid for by all out of taxes or in the form of higher costs of living.

No final resolution exists between these two contradictory positions. Self-interest, along with financial and political power, will ultimately resolve the issue. In the interval pollution may well increase.

The Reading and Experiment

This experiment involves a case study approach to the general arguments above. Water pollution is the specific instance of the problem in which players will resolve the issue of responsibility and the burden of remedy. The reading by Goldman first presents a general discussion of the history, causes, and consequences of pollution.

POLLUTION: THE MESS AROUND US

Marshall I. Goldman

1. Introduction

Today's news media devote almost as much attention to air and water pollution as to the problems of poverty. Virtually overnight pollution seems to have become one of America's major issues. To the economist the problem provides a unique opportunity to see the result of the divergence of social and private benefits from social and private costs, or what economists call external diseconomies. The destruction of natural resources occurs largely because of the difficulty of imposing direct costs or monetary responsibility on the polluters. Attempts to prevent pollution illustrate how economics along with politics and science can be utilized to cope with an increasingly dangerous situation.

Until recently few individuals or organizations were concerned with the problems of pollution. The only previously interested ones were a few conservationists and hikers and mountain climbers. Why, then, is there this sudden clamor about pollution?

A. Pollution Through the Years

Pollution has plagued mankind for centuries. There is virtually no naturally pure water and air. The mere presence of humans and animals is enough to alter whatever conditions existed before. Such changes, however, are not serious unless they radically affect the existing balance or make the environment unfit for other organisms. It is necessary to distinguish between *impurities*, which make water and air economically or aesthetically undesirable—and may also destroy some forms of flora or fauna—and *contaminating substances*, which endanger the health of human beings.

That undesired changes were taking place in the water supply was recognized by the Romans before the first century B.C. Because the sewage generated by a city of about one million people endangered the drinking water, the Romans built one of the first major municipal sewers in history, the Cloaca Maxima. Venice disposed of its sewage effortlessly into the sea twice a day by using the natural flow of the tides. Subsequent generations in northern Europe, however, were ignorant of such necessities and dumped their sewage whenever and wherever convenient. The result was dysentery and periodic epidemics of such diseases as cholera and typhoid.

Smog has also annoyed man for centuries. Although smog in Los Angeles did not reach dangerous proportions until 1943, in the mid sixteenth century Spanish explorers landing at Los Angeles noted layers of smoke from Indian fires hanging above the area. In the scientific terminology of today, this is called an inversion layer. For centuries England has been similarly plagued by polluted air. As early as the thirteenth century, English

From *Controlling Pollution* Marshall I. Goldman, Ed. (Englewood Cliffs: Prentice-Hall, Inc., 1967), pp. 3–39. Reprinted by permission of the publisher.

authorities complained about smoke from coal and charcoal fires. By the sixteenth century attempts were initiated to pass laws restricting such fires. These laws were not too successful. Charles Dickens' England continued to suffer from sunless skies and smoky moors. Ironically, the English government during World War II, encouraged smoke emission in order to obscure bombing targets from the Germans.

Still, despite isolated examples, until the beginning of the twentieth century, man has been able to coexist with his wastes. There was little or no interference with nature's self-regenerating system. Generally harmonious proportions were kept among such living organisms as human beings, vegetation, and animals. Moreover, since there had been little experimentation with the earth's minerals, almost all waste decomposed rapidly or served as nutrient or raw material for other forms of life. For example, kitchen garbage was nicely disposed of by the livestock, usually kept for human consumption. The circle seemed to be perfect.

By the late nineteenth century, however, the careful observer could find some disproportion in the circle. Pollution which for centuries had not been especially offensive, gradually became intolerable in a growing number of places. In the years following World War II, there was no longer any doubt that the circle had popped and left gaping holes out of which an increasingly alarmed population gasped for fresh air and water.

B. An Annoyance Becomes a Crisis

The emergence of concern about pollution among Americans was caused by a combination of developments. First and most important, the population after World War II began to grow at an annual rate of almost two per cent. To escape the thickening crowds in the cities, a mass exodus to the suburbs ensued. Green spaces began to disappear; before long airline pilots and geographers found themselves unable to distinguish where one town ended and another began. "Megalopolis" was how Jean Gottman described this growth phenomenon stretching from New Hampshire to Virginia.

Factories and stores, moving out to be near workers and customers, brought with them wastes, highways, asphalt parking lots, and demands for water and air. In many areas it became harder and harder to find natural preserves still capable of processing smoke and liquid wastes. As the population grew and increased its quantities of refuse, the natural facilities for treating waste began to shrink.

Secondly, not only did the population grow in size, but it also grew in wealth. With per capita income reaching historic heights, production rose to satisfy growing demands. This increased consumption of natural resources for industrial purposes and in turn generated greater waste. In some circles, it came to be called the "effluent society."

It was not only with the production of goods that wastes were multiplied; it was also in their consumption. For example, as annual automobile production rose from three and a half million in 1947 to eight million by the mid 1960's, the fumes produced by the almost ninety million combustion engines of American automobiles threw off an estimated ninety-two million tons of carbon monoxide a year. This is enough to poison the combined air space over Massachusetts, Connecticut and New Jersey. Even though the automobile is the king of American consumer goods, it is also a complete portable factory. Each one generates power, on a smaller scale, as do thermal electric power plants.

Some cities have been particularly hard hit by automobile pollution. Because of Los Angeles' topography, even the slightest gas or smoke has a severe effect on the purity of the air. The prevailing winds are not very strong, and those that come from the ocean are unable to carry the smoke over the hills surrounding the city. As a result, Los Angeles has passed exceptionally rigid laws that have limited and almost stopped smoke from factories and municipal incinerators. Unfortunately, Los Angeles has had much less success controlling automobile exhaust. Vehicular exhaust is now the main cause of Californian smog. Automobiles are responsible for approximately 80 per cent of the city's air pollution as compared to New York, where automobiles are responsible for only about one third of it. Los Angeles is said to be the only city in the country where you wake up in the morning and hear the birds coughing.

Of almost equal importance, automobile junking, like the disposal of other consumer goods, has become a serious problem. As homes and highways have grabbed up larger and larger quantities of land, less room remains for disposal areas. As people spread out and increase mobility, it becomes harder to find dumping grounds that are obscure. Moreover, our national wealth has made it possible to keep reconstructing and enlarging our cities. With increasing urban renewal, there is a desperate need for space to dump and burn our demolished buildings and other civic refuse.

The introduction of the oxygen process of steelmaking has compounded the difficulty. The traditional open hearth system consumed large quantities of scrap iron and steel in the production of steel. Accordingly, used automobiles were sought after by junk dealers because of the value of scrap metal. It was necessary to sort out the nonferrous metals and other nonmetallic scrap from the autos, but the price of iron scrap was high enough to provide a profit margin and incentive for the scrap dealers. Smoke control laws were not rigid, and it was still possible in many areas to burn away most of the waste. This simplified and cheapened the scrapping process. With the increased use of the oxygen system in America in the last decade, however, came the reduction in demand for scrap metal since the oxygen system primarily uses iron ore and taconite pellets. As the price of scrap fell, scrap dealers found it less profitable to buy up used cars. In addition, new prohibitions on the open burning of junked automobiles made it still less profitable for many junk dealers to continue stripping junked cars for use in the open hearth furnaces that remained. Some dealers even began demanding fees for hauling away scrapped cars. Predictably, this led to the widespread practice of abandoning cars in countless unexpected places. In New York City alone, hundreds of cars a month are left abandoned in the city. It then becomes the city's task to haul them away to the automobile graveyard.

The increase in national wealth produced a keener awareness of pollution for yet another reason. More wealth brought with it not only more products but also more leisure making it possible for people to become aware of and to explore the countryside. More and more they found that what was left was becoming polluted. Invariably, this made an indelible imprint. A famous Michigan labor leader unexpectedly asked to testify before antipollution hearings conducted in Detroit. Since this particular leader had never taken much interest in pollution control before, he was asked to account for his sudden enthusiasm. He sadly explained that after years of hard work, he finally managed to buy a summer retreat. To his dismay, within a few years, the lake adjacent to his cottage had become polluted; from Shangri-la to a cesspool. As one government official explained it, "This is how we win our most ardent supporters."

A third factor influencing the serious pollution problem has been the rapid advance in industrial technology. Every day new and exotic products are placed on store counters. Some, like aluminum tin cans, are virtually indestructible. The old steel tin cans would at least rust after a time. Unfortunately manufacturers are moving further and further away from containers like the ice cream cone, ideal from the point of view of pollution control, and more in the direction of permanent plastic cups and cones and nonreturnable bottles. The nonreturnable bottle means more convenience for the consumer but more litter along the picnic grounds and roadside. There is no longer monetary compensation for bottle returns. The withdrawal of the economic incentive, small as it was, made clutter an inevitable result.

The effects of technology have been even more serious in other fields. Deadly pesticides and insecticides are now composed of chemical derivatives which do not always break down easily. Such compounds have accidentally entered the water stream and become ruthless killers of the fish population. The soap industry switched from a fat to a detergent base which did not readily dissolve (was not biodegradable) in the normal course of sanitary treatment. Consequently pools of froth began to cover drinking water reservoirs. Frequently floods of suds would return to the household through the kitchen faucet.

Finally public attention was directed to pollution for an unusual reason. By the mid 1960's our government had almost run out of domestic crusades to conduct. After years of battle, legislation had been adopted to contend with most of the major challenges: mèdicare had been approved, as well as programs in highway expansion, poverty control, urban renewal and education improvement. Pollution control was something that could evoke a similar missionary spirit among voters and politicians alike. There could be no Great Society if the water, air and dumps were dirty.

The need for a crusade gained additional support after a series of serious incidents. Because medical science has found more and more cures for our more traditional disease-causing enemies, we have become subject to different disease causes. Not surprisingly therefore, many people, especially the elderly, find themselves becoming affected more and more by pollution in the environment, especially the air. Thus poor air has been blamed for cancer, pneumonia, bronchitis, emphysema and tuberculosis. Scientists point out that by breathing the air in New York City, one inhales an amount of cancer-producing benzyprene equivalent to smoking two packs of cigarettes a day. It is further claimed that air pollution is responsible for the 80 per cent rise in deaths from respiratory diseases from 1930 to 1960.

Clearly delineated surges in the death rate have been traced directly to air pollution. Such incidents have occurred in Donora, Pennsylvania, in October 1948 when the death of nineteen and the illness of 6,000 of the town's 13,800 citizens were blamed on smog. Smog was also blamed in London when the normal death rate rose by 4,000 in December 1952, and when 8,000 died prematurely in January and February 1953. Similarly air pollution was considered a major cause of death in New York City in January and February 1963 when there were 647 more deaths than normal. Some scientists also cite air pollution as a factor contributing to streets riots in Los Angeles and other large cities. In addition to the normally expected discomfort, pollution is said to generate depression and melancholia. As for water pollution, in 1965 at Riverside, California, 18,000 people were afflicted with gastroenteritis from the town's water wells, and, apparently, three died. Such tragedies more than anything else naturally heighten people's awareness of the problem.

C. Pollution and Industrialization

It is worth repeating, however, that despite the immense concern we in the United States now have, "effluence" is not just a byproduct of the modern affluent society. For that matter pollution is not a problem peculiar to only certain locations or types of societies. [As indicated elsewhere], pollution is not restricted to developed capitalist countries. The Soviet Union, like other countries, has its pollution difficulties. There is reason to believe that it is only the very wealthy countries, able to afford the luxury of clean water and air, that can make a fuss about it. It is expensive for industry, whether it be state or privately owned, to control pollution. Usually pollution prevention is regarded as a nonproductive expense not very much different from charity. Both expenditures are characteristic of civilized living, but expendable luxuries nonetheless which have the effect of reducing the manager's net profit. Despite the logic of economic theory which teaches that only privately owned factories pollute at the expense of the general public, state enterprises in Eastern Europe pollute with generally less restraint than private enterprises in the United States. In communist society, the factory manager is usually just as eager as his American counterpart to show as high a net profit as possible and so he too tends to neglect pollution control. But in the United States, the government frequently interposes itself in the problem of pollution because its interests are not always the same as the polluters'. In the Soviet Union, the government is generally an economic partner of the state-owned factory and therefore not as much of an external agent as government is in the United States. Any expense that detracts from the performance of the Soviet factory in the region similarly detracts from the economic performance of the overall region. Therefore political and party officials frequently find themselves more in agreement with the polluters than with the conservationists.

There is good reason to believe that pollution control is more a function of income per capita than of socialist ownership of the means of production since the problem also confronts countries which are just beginning to industrialize. Valuable resources which should be used to control pollution are used more profitably in the increase of production. Since production processes in the developing countries are usually less sophisticated, they usually spew out more waste per unit of product and are therefore more of a menace. Municipal water treatment in Africa and Asia and parts of Latin America is particularly deficient. However, in most industrially developing countries, the problem does not seem to be as serious and does not provoke an outcry. This may be due to the still limited stage of industrial development, at which stage industrial wastes are not by themselves enough to cause concern. In addition, no one wants to frustrate industrial production any more than is already the case. But precedents are being set which become difficult to alter. Manufacturers who begin production at a later time will expect the same kind of concessions since the diverting of resources for pollution abatement would put them at a competitive disadvantage. Consequently only when the state decides it is rich enough to afford some production sacrifices for cleaner air and water, can there be any initiative for pollution control from the state or from industry itself.

II. Why Do Polluters Pollute?

It is not difficult to understand why there is pollution of the air and water and even the land. Moreover it is not just industries and municipalities that are contibutors. Some of your best friends use septic tanks or cesspools instead of a public sewer system for the disposal of household wastes. How many of them also burn trash in a home incinerator? Does anyone you know burn leaves in the backyard or in the street? When did you have your last cookout or throw a beer can on the beach or highway? Did you ever leave the car motor on while running an errand?

Few people stop to consider that they are polluters when they do such things. And if they recognize that they are creating some form of air, water or solid litter, they always say to themselves that their little bit of waste will not make much difference. In addition it would cost more to have someone haul the trash and leaves away; it might be prohibitively expensive to link up a house with a sewer system. Similarly, industries and municipalities follow the same reasoning: it is cheaper, it is more convenient. To the polluter, there never seems to be great harm in just his little pollution, but there may be great expense involved in trying to clean it up.

The waters are usually so plentiful and the sky is so vast that it is hard to believe that one person can cause pollution. In fact, one person usually cannot cause pollution; it is when there are numerous "one persons" who all think the same way that pollution results. Moreover when one person pollutes, he himself is not usually the one to suffer or bear the expense. In fact the private cost to the individual is most often cheaper if he does pollute than if he has to use expensive disposal equipment. If the water is polluted, it is the people downstream who are affected. If the air is polluted, it is the people in the direction of the wind. This is an instance where the private costs of pollution are almost always less than the costs to the rest of society. Pollution is a way of relinquishing what should be your responsibility to someone else who is usually anonymous. Thus pollution is one of those rare situations where social costs exceed private costs.

In many cases it was indeed perfectly proper for a city or factory to reason that its wastes were not a problem for anyone else. Moreover, as indicated in Part I, the rivers and the air can cleanse themselves if not overburdened; the air can be used to dilute fumes and absorb other wastes. In fact industries are often specifically located just because there is a body of water or air nearby which can be used for waste disposal. Wastes have to be deposited somewhere. But if we permit each firm to throw off a little pollution, as the number of polluters grows, the wastes become harder to absorb. Eventually there is a pollution threshold beyond which what had been trouble-free becomes troublesome. Furthermore once that threshold is crossed, it becomes all but impossible to place responsibility.

Economists call the pollution which arises from such a situation an external diseconomy. It becomes necessary to spend money to clean the air and water before anyone else can use it. These are the costs that arise from having a concentration of industry in a given area. Alone, one factory does not normally create a problem because its water and air wastes are sent off downstream and downair. But as more and more factories locate in a given region, what is released externally by one factory enters into the internal operations of another and creates an expense, a diseconomy. Yet if several polluters are located along a lake or are affected by one another's smoke when the wind shifts, who should bear the responsibility? Was it the most recently completed factory? It may have been its smoke or water which caused the ecological system to break down, but is it ultimately to blame? In all likelihood if one of the older and probably dirtier factories were to be closed down, the new firm could pollute in peace. Therefore should the older firms be penalized as well? Clearly it would be unfair to compel the new firm to purchase expensive pollution control equipment and allow the older firms to produce waste as freely as before. This would put the new firm at a competitive disadvantage and would also discourage the location of new industry in the neighborhood. Yet if the old firms were required to buy pollution control devices, they might move out to other areas which were more permissive. Similarly, factory management could argue very persuasively that even if hundreds of thousands of dollars were spent to clean up wastes, the pollution problem might still exist unless the other firms and towns in the area were also forced to clean up their waste. Management would have to justify such expenditures to stockholders who might wonder if such expenses are warranted when they add absolutely nothing to sales revenues. Viewed from the perspective of the industrial unit such expenses are nonproductive and, if anything, benefit primarily the downstream or downwind company or town.

Obviously in such circumstances the traditional price mechanism which we rely on to guide us in the production and distribution of most of our natural wealth can do nothing to solve the problem. Normally through the market system, prices are used to balance off the demand pressure for a product with all the production costs involved. In this way goods can be purchased by those who are willing and able to pay a high enough price for them. This, we say, shows that private costs equal private benefits. The price one is willing to pay usually indicates that one expects to receive at least that much benefit from the product. Each productive resource is used until the cost of an additional unit is just equal to the extra revenue that resource will bring to the producer. When all producers react in the same way, then the price that must be paid for the productive resource will tend to equal the value of the product which is produced.

If demand for a good increases, the price will be increased. This in turn should induce an increase in production. Prices will rise also if the raw materials used in the production process become harder to find, or if workers suddenly decide they would rather work elsewhere. When the costs of production factor inputs are increased, the manufacturer tries to pass this on to the consumer by raising the sale price. It also happens in most instances that when the cost of production rises, it is necessary to cut back production to make sure that there is no overproduction. Higher prices usually mean fewer purchasers.

It is also essential, if the price system is to function properly, that someone or some group control and sell or otherwise allocate all the factors of production. Thus, whether they be landlords, bankers, laborers or managers, fees are collected for the use of an input which presumably provide proper compensation for the cost of reproducing the article or for the revenues foregone by not taking advantage of opportunities available elsewhere. In this way, the cost of all inputs used in the production process are properly identified. Thus we can say that private benefits and costs equal social benefits and costs since no resource is utilized unless someone is compensated for it at a rate which normally will reflect the demand and supply pressure for the good.

One of the reasons that air and water pollution is hard to control is that no person or organization is normally considered to be the owner of the air and water. With few exceptions such resources are considered to be readily available to those who want to use them. It is difficult to attach a value to either clean or dirty air and water. They are treated as if they were free goods.

The price system cannot be expected to function properly, however, if the factor inputs are priced improperly or are not priced at all. If a factor is overpriced, this will lead to the increased price of the final product and a reduction in the amount sold. Conversely, if the factor is underpriced, then the selling price will not reflect the full cost to society of all the inputs that are involved, and more of the good will be sold than should be. At the same time, more of the resource will be used in production than if only the price of the factor properly reflected the alternative uses to which it might be put.

Abuse of water and air resources comes about largely because air and water are undervalued. Air and water are regarded as free goods. For example, officials in New York City have long resisted the plea of economists and conservationists that meters be installed to measure all household use of water. Since there is no economic incentive to conserve water, there is great waste. All too frequently we have failed to distinguish between rain and readily available drinking water and between air and fresh air. As one critic said, it is as if there had been no differentiation between grass and milk.

Until recently, there has always been enough drinking water and fresh air available in the United States. There are usually alternative sources available even with water except perhaps in the West. Accordingly, in almost all other areas of the country, water and air have had no value which could be translated into dollars and cents. Hence in many areas of the United States, there is an economic rationalization and even a stimulus for pollution. Many tend to treat water and air as if they are free goods. Input costs are understated and more air and water are used for production than necessary. Because water and air resources are underpriced, private costs are less than social costs. Under the circumstances, as even the conservative economist Milton Friedman points out in Part II, unless additional steps are taken, there will be inevitably be a misallocation of society's resources and more pollution than society would otherwise deem desirable.

III. The Social Costs of Pollution

Because they are generally considered to be nonmarketable products, it is difficult to evaluate the costs of polluting water and air. Yet before there can ever be a workable solution to the pollution problem, some estimates of the costs of pollution must be made so that proper values can be assigned to air and water. The task is made even more complex because so many things affected by pollution—swimming in a river or smelling clean air—are also nonmarketable and impossible to price. Also it is not always easy to ascribe correctly an economic loss to pollution. A house in a factory district may be priced low, but how much of this is due to pollution and how much of it is due to environmental factors which might also exist in the area. Finally, how much crime and other abuses are due to pollution which hastens the exit of more socially responsible elements of the population.

There are countless illustrations of the difficulty of providing a measure of the cost of pollution damage. Because of emissions of industrial waste into Lake Michigan from Chicago's South Side, it was necessary to close several beaches on the lake in 1965 and 1966. It turned out that Negroes were the predominant users of two or three of these beaches. When the industrial and municipal polluters complained about the cost of an accelerated cleanup schedule, federal authorities replied that failure to reopen the beaches might touch off race riots. Such riots would be directly attributable to the withdrawal of recreation facilities because of the pollution and the blame would rest squarely on the shoulders of the polluters. Whatever the material costs which might have resulted from the damage and the additional costs necessitated by travel expenditures to other swimming sites, the polluters apparently agreed that there were also political and public relations costs involved which more than justified expensive remedies. The accelerated cleanup program was accepted. Yet is this also the appropriate measure to apply to the estimate for cleaning up Lake Erie? Cleveland's civil rights problems may not be as directly affected by pollution in Lake Erie, but certainly there is something equally tragic in watching the death of the fish industry and the cessation of recreational swimming in one of the Great Lakes most accessible to large numbers of people.

Air pollution controls are even more difficult to measure. If a factory installs air pollution controls, it is unlikely that the whole expense should be charged to pollution. Some changes would probably provide for increased productive efficiency as well as pollution abatement. Electrical utilities are consistently making improvements for the sake of increasing combustion efficiency and lowering operating costs. In the process, air pollution is reduced. Joint costs like these are particularly difficult to allocate so that usually double counting takes place.

Many other estimates of cost must be handled in an equally arbitrary fashion. What value should be placed on the premature death of an engineer from asthma induced by polluted air? Is a retired engineer worth as much? What is the cost to society of "blue babies" who suffer from methemoglobinemia? This results when oxygen is boiled off from polluted water used to make baby formulas so that what remains contains increased quantities of nitrogen having an adverse effect on the stomachs and bladders. In addition to the charges for medical care, should there also be a calculation to determine how much discounted earning power will be lost by pollution patients in the years to come?

Somewhat less tenuous but still arbitrary are the estimates of the losses due to plant closings or relocations because of pollution. Even more questionable are the estimates of the losses from industries which decide not to locate in an area because of pollution. For places like New York City, these are vital but obviously difficult questions to evaluate. As indicated in Part III, estimates of this nature were made to show that the benefit to Pittsburgh of clean air would offset the costs involved in trying to clean it. Whatever losses due to industries that left Pittsburgh because they could no longer use the skies as sewers were more than offset by other industries and institutions newly attracted to or contented to remain in a cleaner Pittsburgh. Today Pittsburgh is a city with a revitalized economy. Moreover as shown in Table 1, what was once America's smokiest city now has a record of air cleanness exceeded by few cities its size.

In the same category of cost estimates is the loss to the optical industry that comes from being unable to sell contact lenses in a city like New York City. Doctors there have found that it is extremely dangerous for their patients to wear contact lenses for any length of time because of the possibility of lacerations to the eye. Specks of dirt and ash are periodically caught between the retina and the lens. Presumably the loss entailed from this could be calculated by determining the per capita use of contact lenses in other less polluted cities and then comparing this with similar ratios in New York City. To this should also be added the cost of eye surgery necessitated by pollution.

Attempts have also been made to evaluate any additional living costs for a family in an air polluted area. Irving T. Michelson of Consumer's Union in New York City estimates that a family which owns its own home in New York pays over $800 (or $200 per person) more a year than a family located in a less polluted area. He estimates that families living in apartments pay on

Table 1. Air Pollution Levels in 13 Major Cities in 1965

	Sulfur Dioxide	Nitrogen Dioxide	Suspended Particulates
Baltimore	0.04	0.06	125–132
Boston	0.03	0.05	108–131
Chicago	0.10	0.06	115–179
Cleveland	0.04	0.06	112–162
Denver	0.01	0.04	97–118
Detroit	0.01	0.05	106–140
Los Angeles	under 0.01	0.11	114–151
New York	0.16	0.08	151–189
Philadelphia	0.08	0.08	147–160
Pittsburgh	0.03	0.06	126–164
San Francisco	0.01	0.05	57–64
Seattle	0.02	0.04	58–76
Washington	0.03	0.06	88–126

NOTE: Sulfur and nitrogen dioxide given in parts per million parts of air. Suspended particulates in micrograms per cubic meter as range of annual geometric means. All on 24-hour averages.
Source: U.S. Public Health Service. *The New York Times,* May 11, 1966.

the average of over $400 more. This includes added expenditures for household maintenance—extra painting, cleaning and washing, extra laundry bills—and extra expenses on personal cleanliness. It does not include an estimate for extra medical expense, replacement of clothing, fewer sunlight hours, and lower real estate values. Even so, Michelson's figures may be a little high. Nevertheless his calculations clearly indicate that the usual estimate of $65 per person is too low an estimate of the cost of air pollution in certain areas of America. It is entirely possible however that the $65 figure is correct when applied to the country as a whole. This would mean that air pollution costs the country the fantastic sum of $11 billion a year in extra charges. Other authorities estimate that the figure is lower, close to one billion dollars.

It should also be possible to measure the cost of air pollution to companies in New York City that fill air tanks for scuba divers. Public health officials suddenly realized that the air tank companies were compressing polluted New York City air into their tanks. It was bad enough for those who have to breathe New York air in more relaxed circumstances, but to have to breathe it in concentrated form several feet under water was obviously dangerous. Accordingly, the New York City Air Pollution Control Act of May, 1966, prohibits the sale or distribution of compressed air tanks for underwater breathing use without special permits. The cost of air pollution in this case could be measured by ascertaining how many compressed air companies have been forced to close their doors and how much existing firms have had to spend in new equipment necessitated by the new law.

The costs of water pollution and purification of water are difficult to measure accurately, but there are losses or remedial efforts which can be measured with more certainty. The shellfish industry estimates it suffered a $45 million loss because water pollution in tideland areas led to the spread of hepatitis through the clam and oyster beds. It is calculated that the shift to soft or biodegradable detergents cost the chemical and soap industry over

$100 million. Such a move was ordered in Germany in October 1964, and later adopted by individual American states like Wisconsin because more and more sewage plants found they could not eliminate the growing sea of suds in their sewage. Finally in July 1965, the whole American chemical industry started to make detergents out of linear alkylate sulfonite instead of the hard alkyl benzine sulfonite, that could not be decomposed easily in most sewage treatment plants.

Another way to approximate the cost of water pollution is to see how much it would cost to manufacture fresh water. In some areas, reprocessed water is the only alternative source available. Therefore the cost of such reprocessing might serve at least as the upper limit for the value of water, even though such estimates do not measure the cost of pollution directly. This may be a fairer estimate of the cost of polluting the water, since the practice otherwise is to set the price of fresh water at the amount necessary to cover only the operating costs of the well. Such a system fails to make allowance for the fact that the well may be slowly going dry as is often the case in the West.

Traditionally attention has been focused on the cost of refining sea water. Given present technology, this is quite expensive. The best desaliniza-tion plants can almost produce drinking water at a cost of one dollar per thousand gallons. The facility at the United States Naval Base in Guantan-amo, Cuba, produces one thousand gallons for $1.16. This is a considerable improvement over the fourteen dollars per thousand gallons that existed in 1952. With the aid of special subsidies, it is hoped that by 1971 Los Angeles will have an atomic powered desalinization plant. The subsidies combined with the revenue from the sale of electric power will make it possible to price water at about twenty-seven cents per thousand gallons. Still, unless special subsidies are provided as in Los Angeles, desalinizated water is unlikely to be cheap enough to compete with the normal cost of well or reservoir water, about fifteen cents per thousand gallons. Some authorities have argued that this cost disparity will always exist because scientists are misdirecting their attention toward desalinization. Instead such critics urge that more effort be devoted to reusing sewage water. Sewage is often only 1 per cent polluted while sea water has 3 per cent pollution and therefore is harder to clean.

There have been two or three experiments with reprocessing sewage water. At Lebanon, Ohio, a treatment plant operated in conjunction with the Taft Center of the United States Public Health Service has been able to reprocess drinking water at a cost of fifty-four cents per thousand gallons. This is one half the price of similarly treated salt water and could be very promising for the future provided that engineers can overcome the aesthetic resistance that people have toward drinking reprocessed sewage.

A related problem is the disposal of sewage water. In some areas there is no convenient body of water that can be used as a city sewer. This is the problem at Lake Tahoe. If the lake, one of nature's purest, is not to be used as a sewer itself, some other repository must be found. Unfortunately there are no other outlets available unless the sewage is pumped over the moun-tains. Santee, California, also had a disposal problem. They decided to experiment and a treatment plant was built. Then the water was further purified by running it over a dried-up riverbed. After a mile of this natural filtration, the water was stored in small artificial lakes stocked with fish and opened to boating. Although unfit for drinking, some of the water is being sold to golf courses for watering the grass. The price is twelve cents per thousand gallons, which is cheaper than fresh water. Since some nutrients are probably still left in the water, this may actually turn out to be a bargain since the water can also be used as a fertilizer.

Finally it is necessary to take account of the costs of modernizing the present sewage facilities. Again estimates vary, but it is frequently reported that it would cost $10 billion to provide adequate sewers throughout the country. In 1963, 12 million people had untreated water, 18.6 million had inadequate sewers and 5.2 million had no sewers. Some authorities insist that it would cost another $20 billion to separate storm and waste sewers as must be done ultimately.

By this time it should be clear that the exact cost of air and water pollution is uncertain, but whatever it is, it is large. Undoubtedly some of the estimates are exaggerated by those who feel that the only way to obtain action is to create a crisis atmosphere. Unfortunately only too often it takes a scandal or a crisis to win public support for a meaningful program.* But exaggeration does not necessarily advance the cause of those who seek reliable economic data. One of the greatest challenges open to an economist today is to make a careful cost study of the effects of pollution. Until there are reliable estimates of damage, no appropriate value can be attributed to clean air and water. And, as long as the cost of clean air and water is undervalued, it will be used wastefully and irrationally.

Walter Heller, a former chairman of the Council of Economic Advisers, argues that we overestimate our country's productive capacity when we ignore pollution. In one of his Godkin lectures at Harvard in 1966, he suggested that the country's gross national product be calculated only after deductions are made for the waste that pollution causes. As he sees it, it is deceptive to consider only the value of what a factory produces if in the process it pollutes water so that a lake can no longer be used for swimming. A resource has been consumed in the process of production and this should be recognized by subtracting the loss due to pollution from the value of the company's output.

· · ·

V. Conclusion

By this time it should be clear how complex are the problems of pollution. As our society continues to grow and expand, the control of pollution will become even more complicated. It is fortunate therefore that

*Harold Wolozin, ed., *The Economics of Air Pollution* (New York: Norton, 1966), p.127.

responsible citizens are becoming aware of the difficulties involved. Unless we have a running start, we may never catch up with the solutions that will be required. Some authorities argue that it may already be too late and that places like Lake Erie may be lost beyond hope.

Some biologists have suggested that we would have no problem today if our population had only stopped growing in 1850. If our population were only 23 million and it was sprawled out across the whole continent, they feel there would be so much water and air per capita that all of our wastes could be easily absorbed and diluted. At the same time there would be fewer wastes to contend with since not only would there be fewer people, but presumably there would be less need for some of the more hazardous products which have been necessitated by the increasing crush of population. Thus it is argued that there would be no need for insecticides, fertilizers and pesticides since we would use a much more land-intensive form of farming and let nature do its own fertilizing.

Such thoughts are intriguing. To the economist, however, it does not appear that simple. Acknowledging that it is just as hard to prove, it nevertheless would seem that not only would the population have to stand still at the 1850 level, but so would technological and sociological change. If there were a smaller population in the United States, would it necessarily follow that the newer plastics and nonreturnable aluminum cans would not have been invented? Would we or the rest of the world have bypassed the discovery of atomic energy with its radioactive wastes? Would the country's population have remained predominantly rural or with time would there have been a desire to cluster in the cities? Assuming that people would eventually prefer to live in metropolitan areas, there would still be urban pollution (though perhaps on a smaller scale) and farmers would probably still want to use pesticides, herbicides and fertilizers.

Perhaps it is idle to conjecture about what could have been. Yet there are lessons to be learned from such speculation. As long as our technology and population continue to grow, the problems of pollution are likely to become more and more serious. It is more essential than ever that the population be alerted and that technology be harnessed for the prevention and treatment of pollution. Hopefully this can and must be done if the affluent are not to choke on their effluent.

Rules of Play

This experiment alters the Basic CLUG rules so as to introduce water resources and the subsequent possibility of pollution. Play will begin with a community already existing on the playing board. Figure VII-1 illustrates the layout of the road and utility systems and land holdings. Tables VII-1, VII-2, and VII-3, respectively, itemize Team Holdings, Team Standings and Community Financial Standing. Play is initiated in Round 4, Step 1.

Other than the fact that play begins with an existing set of land holdings, Step 1 (Purchase Land) is carried out in the same manner as in Basic CLUG.

Figure VII-1. Location of Roads, Utility Systems, and Land Holdings

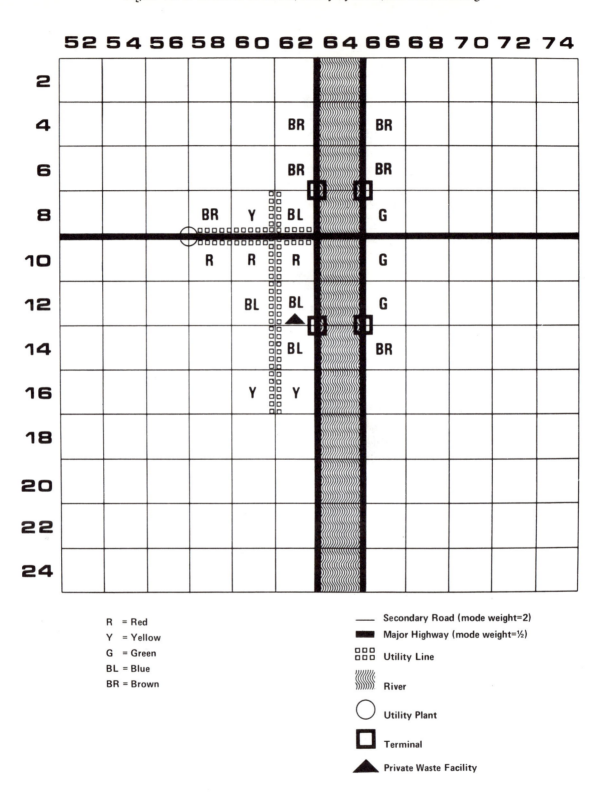

R = Red
Y = Yellow
G = Green
BL = Blue
BR = Brown

— Secondary Road (mode weight=2)
■■■ Major Highway (mode weight=½)
□□□ Utility Line
〰〰 River
○ Utility Plant
□ Terminal
▲ Private Waste Facility

Table VII-1. Team Holdings (in Round 3)

	Land			Buildings		
Coordinates	Team	Purchase Price	Assessed Value	Type	Round Built	Assessed* Value
8–58	Br	$1,500	$1,400	R1	2	$12,000
10–58	R	1,600	1,700	R2	3	30,000
8–60	Y	2,000	2,200	R3	3	48,000
10–60	R	1,900	2,200	R4	1	72,000
12–60	Bl	1,600	2,100	LS	2	24,000
4–62	Br	1,100	1,500	R1	3	12,000
8–62	Bl	3,300	2,800	FI	1	96,000
12–62	Bl	3,000	3,100	PI	1	48,000
16–62	Y	2,000	2,400	R2	1	30,000
6–66	Br	2,800	2,400	PI	3	48,000
8–66	G	3,100	2,400	FI	3	96,000
16–60	Y	1,000	1,500			
6–62	Br	1,800	2,700			
10–62	R	4,000	3,100			
14–62	Bl	3,800	2,900			
4–66	Br	1,400	2,100			
10–66	G	1,200	2,000			
12–66	G	1,600	1,600			
14–66	Br	1,900	1,800			

*Before renovation which occurs in Round 5.

Table VII-2. Team Standings (in Round 3)

	Red Team	Yellow Team	Blue Team	Green Team	Brown Team
Property Assessed Value	$109,000	$84,100	$178,900	$99,600	$83,900
Cash	300	58,200	200	38,400	59,600
Taxes and Rate @ 4%	4,400	3,400	7,200	4,000	3,400

Loans — Blue owes Red $40,000 or $8,000 plus 5% interest for 5 rounds (4 through 8)

Table VII-3. Community Financial Standing (in Round 3)

Total Assessed Value	$555,500
Tax Rate	4%
Total Taxes	22,200
Utility Lines (6 old and 2 new)	10,000
Residences	13,000
Interest @ 5%	900
Total Expenditures	23,900
Round Surplus or Deficit	(− 1,700)
Total Surplus or Deficit	(−19,700 or 35% of Limit)
Debt Limit	(−55,600)
Tax Rate for Round 4	5%

In Step 2 (Provide Utilities) a number of major alterations of the Basic rules are made. Utility Plants, in this experiment, have a maximum capacity of ten Utility Lines. At the beginning of Round 4, the existing Plant is serving eight Lines. New Utility Plants can be constructed at any location by the community for a total cost of $100,000, of which $50,000 must be paid out of taxes in the round of construction, with the balance being paid in $10,000 installments over the next five rounds. In order for Residences, Local Stores, Central Stores, or Offices to be constructed, the parcel of land must either be served by one Utility Line or be adjacent to the River. Construction and maintenance costs for a Utility Line are the same as in Basic CLUG: $2,000 for construction and $1,000 for maintenance in each subsequent round. Full and Partial Industry, on the other hand, must either be served by two Utility Lines, be adjacent to the River, or provide their own Private Waste Facility at a cost of $20,000 (to be paid at the time of construction, with $2,000 paid in Step 11 in each subsequent round for maintenance). The construction cost of a Private Waste Facility is not added to a team's Total Assessed Value. While Utility Lines may be abandoned (i.e., removed from the playing board) at no cost, it costs the community an extra $20,000 to run a Utility Line under the River. In other respects, Step 2 is conducted in the usual manner.

Step 3 (Renovate Buildings) is carried out in rounds divisible by five as in Basic CLUG. For the purpose of determining the probability of loss on the dice roll, the usual procedure is followed with one exception. In the case of Residences located adjacent to the River, an additional one per cent chance of loss is added for each Waste Unit (FI=4; PI=2; R4=4; LS, CS and 0=1; etc.) pumped into the River upstream from the parcel in question. Flow is north to south. Odds of loss not given in the Basic CLUG table should be rounded to the next highest unit given.

Construct Buildings (Step 4) is treated the same as in Basic CLUG except for those changes already discussed relating to Utility Lines, the River, and Private Waste Facilities.

Steps 5 and 6 (Designate Employment and Sign Trade Agreements) are carried out simultaneously in this experiment because industrial wages as well as wages and prices for LS, CS, and 0 are negotiable. Agreements on these items are valid until the next round divisible by two. In Round 4 wages are set at $7,000 for all employers. In subsequent rounds divisible by two, each employer may negotiate his own wage. New employers make wage offerings during the round in which their buildings are constructed. Central Store goods and Office services are available from the instructor at $1,000 for CS goods; and $4,000 to FI, $2,000 to PI, and $1,000 each to LS and CS for Office services. These CS and 0 instructor Prices do not vary for the entire experiment and will serve as a benchmark for setting prices within the game.

The Local Store pricing mechanism is a bit more complicated. In this experiment, Local Stores buy Wholesale Commodities from sources located outside the game (i.e., the instructor). The price of Wholesale Commodities is a function of the extent to which the River is polluted. The same is true of Local Store Retail Goods available directly to Residences from the instructor. These increases represent increased costs to downstream producers as a result of the necessity of using polluted water for production. Table VII-4 gives the schedule of these two sets of prices. In Round 4, when play begins, the price of Local Store Retail goods available directly to Residences from the instructor is $3,000. The price of Wholesale Commodities is $1,000 per customer to Local Stores. The Local Store at 12–60 on the board, for example, must set his price to compete with Retail outlets selling at $3,000, as well as to cover Wholesale Commodity costs of $1,000 per customer. While Local Stores on the board may alter their price only in rounds divisible by two, the instructor's prices can vary in any round as a result of pollution.

Table VII-4. Instructor's Prices

Total Net Pollution	Local Store Retail	Local Store Wholesale to Local Store per Customer
0 to 5	$3,000	$1,000
6,7	3,200	1,200
8,9	3,400	1,400
10,11	3,800	1,800
12,13	4,200	2,200
14,15	4,600	2,600
16,17	5,000	3,000
18,19	5,500	3,500
20 and above	6,500	4,500

The Accountant will monitor the pollution level of the River each round and announce the level which determines prices. Pollution is calculated in the Pollution Control Chart (Table VII-5) as the sum of the Waste Units pumped into the River minus 3 Units (representing self-restoration) accumulated over the number of rounds played. The effect of the level of pollution on the instructor's Prices is lagged by two rounds. At the beginning of play in Round 4, the number of Waste Units in the river is 7 (4 from the Full Industry plus 2 from the Partial Industry plus 1 from the R1 unit). The Net Pollution for Round 3 is 4, giving a Cumulative Pollution of 4 to have an effect in Round 5. These initial entries are given in the first two lines of Table VII-5, with subsequent entries to be calculated and entered by the Accountant.

In the Round of Consequence, 4, Cumulative Pollution equals 0 so that the instructor's Prices from Table VII-4 are $3,000 and $1,000 as noted previously. After price and wage negotiations have gone on for a short time the instructor may wish to impose time restrictions on further discussion in order that the next Step of Play may Begin.

In Step 7, each fully employed Full Industry receives $52,000 income while each Partial Industry is paid $24,000. Gross Industrial income does not vary in this experiment.

Employees are paid in Step 8 according to the agreed upon wage.

During Step 9, LS, CS and O are paid at the predetermined price and

Table VII-5. Pollution Control Chart

Round of Play	(a) Waste Units In	(b) Waste Units Out	(c)=(a)−(b) Net Pollution* for Round	Cumulative* Pollution	Round of Consequence
2	0	−3	0	0	4
3	7	−3	+4	+4(=4+0)	5
4		−3			6
5		−3			7
6		−3			8
7		−3			9
8		−3			10
9		−3			11
10		−3			12
11		−3			13
12		−3			14
13		−3			15
14		−3			16
15		−3			17
16		−3			18
17		−3			19
18		−3			20
19		−3			21
20		−3			22

*May not be negative.

Local Stores pay the instructor for Wholesale Commodities at the price per customer in effect for that round.

Transportation Costs are paid in Step 10 using Mode Weights of ½ for the Major Highway and 2 for Secondary Roads. The River may be crossed at any point and does not impede travel other than by increasing distance by one square. Industry to Terminal Association Weights in this experiment are $8,000 for Full Industry and $4,000 for Partial Industry.

Taxes are paid in Step 11. A Tax Rate of five per cent has been set for Round 4. Private Waste Facility maintenance should also be paid at this time.

If, in future rounds of play, the pollution level reaches 15 or more, an interest-free federal loan of up to $80,000 is available to the community for the purpose of pollution abatement. Repayment is made at a rate of $5,000 per round. In order to obtain this loan, application must be made to the instructor and include a description of the community pollution problem, an assessment of its history and causes, and specific proposals to remedy the problem within five rounds.

Steps of Play are as follows:

1.) Purchase Land	Unchanged from Basic CLUG.
2.) Provide Utilities	Utility Plant capacity = 10 Lines. R, LS, CS or O need either: one Utility Line or River. FI and PI need either: two Utility Lines, Private Waste Facility, or River.

[3.) Renovate Buildings]	Residences increase odds of loss due to pollution. Dice rolled in rounds divisible by five.
4.) Construct Buildings	See 2.) above.
5.) Designate Employment	Employment, wages and prices are all
6.) Sign Trade Agreements	negotiable. Agreements are renegotiated in rounds divisible by two. Accountant announces LS Wholesale and Retail Prices from the Operator.
7.) Receive Income	FI=$52,000; PI=$24,000.
8.) Pay Employees	As agreed upon in 5.) above.
9.) Pay LS, CS, and O	As agreed upon in 6.) above. LS pays for Wholesale Commodities.
10.) Pay Transportation Cost	Mode Weight of 2 and ½ are assigned to Secondary Roads and Major Highways respectively. Industry to Terminal Association Weights are: FI=$8,000 and PI=$4,000.
11.) Pay Taxes	Instructor collects Private Waste Facility maintenance cost of $2,000.

A summary of the basic information and changes needed for this experiment is provided as a tear-out form at the back of this manual. It is entitled "Summary of Changes for Environmental Pollution Experiment."

Discussion

While this experiment does not seek to in any way realistically approach the basic elements of environmental pollution, it does provide a very strong vehicle for considering the relative impact of pollution on the community and the question of which parties bear the responsibility for pollution and cleaning up pollution. Reconsideration of the elements of individual and community self-interest which usually arise in this experiment serve to point out the difficulties of resolving responsibility for pollution, its prevention, and its correction. Players should discover that all pollution cannot be blamed simply upon greedy industrialists while at the same time those operating as industrialists will also discover that localized effects of a deteriorating environment eventually erode their own operating position in terms of higher wages for dissatisfied and environmentally deprived workers.

While the elements producing these effects in the experiment are somewhat contrived, they serve to point up the major features of this critical controversy regarding current efforts in pollution abatement. Since the experiment is relatively easy to run, it might be worthwhile running it through twice, with one run focussing responsibility for pollution abatement on industry and the second focussing the responsibility on the community as a whole. Comparisons of community development under these two conditions may provide surprising contrasts.

Study Questions

1. How much pollution occurred in your community? If you had not been concentrating on pollution as a problem but had been simply playing a game of Basic CLUG under these conditions would the problem have been more severe?

2. Which kind of players in the game seemed to be most responsible for creating pollution in your community? Were these players willing to accept the responsibility for their actions or did they leave the problem for the community as a whole to solve? Did this attitude continue throughout the game?

3. The fact that the river cleansed itself at the rate of minus 3 units of pollution each round indicates a relatively fast moving stream with good cleansing possibilities. How much more severe would the problem have been if the rate of cleansing had been at minus 1 unit of pollution per round? What additional problems would your community have faced if another game playing upstream from you had delivered water to your stream which was already highly polluted at arrival? To what authority or jurisdiction would you appeal to seek to control their behavior, particularly if they were represented by some other Instructor or State government?

4. If the river in this game had been called an airstream rather than a water stream, would the results and problems be significantly different from those you encountered? Once again, who should bear the responsibility for pollution abatement: the community or the polluter? In what proportions?

Appendix I: CLUG in Action

After covering the details of operating a CLUG game, some consideration of the way players behave with this model may be worthwhile. As with almost all operational games, it is very difficult to understand what happens with this kind of device until one has participated in a "run" of the game. We face the same problem with this game but a brief attempt at a partial solution will be offered by providing a few brief "scenes" from a typical Round One of CLUG.

Cast of Characters:

Fifteen students on five teams, designated by team color and member number.

A game manager — usually the instructor, an experienced assistant, or a knowledgeable student.

An Accountant — a lab assistant or a student volunteer.

Scene One

The manager has completed his briefing on the basic components of the game and has answered a few of the players' questions. Some questions have been put aside for better explanation at the appropriate point during play. The group is seated around a large table with the manager at one side and the Accountant seated at a separate small table behind him. The manager has just announced the beginning of Round 1 with Purchase Land. The individual team members are consulting with each other.

BLUE ONE *(whispering to another Blue Team member)*: Listen, I think we ought to get into industry. I think we can make a killing if we get land right next to the terminal. Let's bid high on this parcel. *(Points to Board.)*

BLUE TWO: Good idea. Do you think $6,000 is too high a bid?

BLUE ONE: No. That's probably not enough. If we were one square away on the main road it would cost us $4,000 per round for transportation. Let's bid $9,000 on 4–64. It'll pay for itself in a couple of rounds.

RED ONE *(whispering to team mates)*: I think we should get into housing. How about buying some land near the edge of the city cheaply and providing housing for these other guys?

RED TWO: Sounds good. *(To the other teams.)* Is anyone interested in getting workers? We'd like to provide housing if anybody is going to need any.

BLUE ONE: Yeh, we're thinking of putting up industry and we'd like some workers. How about keeping your bids away from the industrial sites, then?

RED ONE: Look, why don't we all just pick a square and bid the minimum? *(To the manager.)* Can we do that? All of us cooperate and bid the minimum amount?

MANAGER: Sure, you can do anything you want within the basic rules you've read. You can collude with each other, bribe each other, cheat each other, anything you like. Remember, though, that your own reputation among other teams is a factor in how well you're able to play, just as much as the play money or the buildings. The idea of cooperating on land purchase to keep the price low is a good one. It doesn't usually work, though.

GREEN ONE: Come on, let's everyone just submit a bid and see what the prices are going to be. You'll take all day trying to figure out who gets what.

BROWN ONE: Yeh, let Blue and Red cooperate if they want to. We're going to submit our own bid.

MANAGER: Come on you guys, its time to submit your first bid. Let's go, I'll give you thirty seconds to get them in. *(After a pause and accepting the bids.)* Blue gets 4-64 for $9,000, Red gets 8-64 for $1,000, and Yellow gets 4-66 for $2,500. Green and Brown have tied bids at $2,000 for 4-62 and will have to resubmit bids on that parcel. *(After taking the rebids, calling the winners, accepting two additional bids from each team, and allocating the land, the manager announces the next step of play, Provide Utilities.)*

Scene Two

BLUE TWO: Listen, we'd like to build an industry, so we'd like utility lines running along these squares here. *(Pointing to Board.)*

GREEN TWO: You paid a hell of a lot for land. Can you afford to put up an industry?

BLUE ONE (counting money hurriedly): No, I guess we can't afford a full industry, but since we have the best site, we ought to provide some industry. Maybe we'll build a Partial. Anyways, we still need a utility line.

RED THREE: We'll vote for those two lines over there if you'll vote for these three here. How's that?

YELLOW ONE: Hey, we'll go along with that if you'll add on this one more line, here. No, these two lines, here. We'll need one more to make it connect up.

MANAGER: That's seven lines proposed. Do you have three votes for that? *(Counting show of hands.)* OK, that passes. Now, any more utility lines?

GREEN ONE: Yes, we'd like two over here by our property, or else we won't have a chance to use our capital this round. You need our investment to make the community grow.

BLUE ONE: I think we could find a way to use your capital without building utility lines. We need $30,000 to put up a full industry and we'll give you fifteen per cent interest on a loan. How about it?

GREEN ONE: No, we want to do our own constructing.

MANAGER: Can I get three votes for Green's proposal to add these two lines? *(Counting show of hands.)* Sorry about that, Green. I'm afraid you won't get the lines and that means you can't build this round. If you're done then we'll move on to the next step. Accountant, they built seven lines in total. Now, the next step on your sheet, Renovate Buildings, only comes up on the fifth round. So we pass on to Construct Buildings. Red, you're first one this round.

Scene Three

RED ONE: Blue, is it agreed that we'll provide you three of the residences for your full industry?

BLUE TWO: What say, Green, how about that loan? $30,000, and I figure we can pay it all back in a couple of rounds at ten per cent interest.

GREEN ONE: OK, but we'll want to build ourselves next round so we'll also need your commitment to vote on any utility lines we want.

BLUE TWO: It's a deal. We'll put up a full industry on 4-64.

RED ONE: Then we'll provide Blue with residences to work in his factory. How about an R-4 on 8-64?

MANAGER: That will cost $72,000.

RED ONE: Man, that's expensive. *(To other team members.)* How about spreading them out some?

RED TWO: Yeh, let's put an R2 here, and R1's here and here.

RED ONE: Right on! That'll cost a lot less.

MANAGER: That will be $54,000. Accountant, Red built one R2 and two R1's. The locations are . . . *(calling off coordinates to the Accountant).*

BROWN ONE: Listen, we want to provide the commercial activities in this town, but nothing seems to be likely to pay much at this point. It'll keep capital in the town if we build them. We wouldn't have to pay money to the outside world for our goods and services and all that. So how about us building the stores and everybody agreeing to pay full prices to us for the first five rounds?

YELLOW ONE: You mean you want us to support your businesses by paying more than we'd have to pay the manager? No deal. I think its more important to have another industry and we'll build it on 4-66 if Brown will provide housing.

BROWN ONE: We want to put up a local store and a central store.

MANAGER: Yellow, its your turn. What will it be?

YELLOW ONE: Brown, will you provide us with residences or has anyone else got the money to do it?

GREEN TWO: We've got the money but since you guys wouldn't come across with utility lines, we can't use it.

BROWN ONE: We're going to build our stores, and we'll provide our own workers, if we have to.

YELLOW ONE: OK, then we'll check.

BROWN ONE: We'll build a local store on 6-64 and a central store on 6-66. Yellow, how about those workers?

YELLOW TWO: All right, but I think it's a mistake.

BROWN ONE: Then that's all for us.

MANAGER: That will be $48,000 for the two stores. Green, you don't have any improved land so you can't build. Back to Yellow, then. What will you have?

YELLOW ONE: We'll put an R2 on 4-66.

MANAGER: That will be $30,000. Next step is Designate Employment. *(All teams mutually adjust who works for whom. Yellow and Red decide to switch employers in one case in order to save themselves some transportation costs.)*

Scene Four

MANAGER: Brown, what are your prices going to be in the Local and Central Stores? My prices are $2,000 for the Local Store and $1,000 for Central Store. Since there is no Office on the board, the industry and stores will have to buy these services from me.

BROWN ONE: What if we charge full prices for the first five rounds?

RED ONE: What if you had no customers the first five rounds? We'll lose money shopping with you because the transportation costs will be high. You'd better cut your prices by at least twenty per cent below the manager's prices.

YELLOW ONE: I told you, fella. It was too early for those stores. You should have gone along with my idea. We'll pay no more than $1,000 for Local Store and $500 for Central Store.

BROWN TWO: That's not even reasonable. You're just bitter because we wouldn't give you housing. Red, will you pay $1,600 for LS and $800 for CS?

RED TWO: Agreed, if you vote with us on Utilities next time.

BROWN TWO: Agreed. Yellow?

YELLOW ONE: Nope. We're shopping with the manager.

BROWN One: I hope everybody notices the great community spirit Yellow is showing. He's sending $6,000 out of the economy just for spite. Let's all remember that on the next vote.

MANAGER: If you've got agreements on those prices, Brown make sure you keep track of your customers and what they owe you. Yellow you're shopping with me, right? All industries and stores are shopping in my Office. O.K., now it's time for income.

Scene Five

MANAGER: Blue, you get $48,000 for a fully employed full industry. Now the next step is Pay Employees.

YELLOW ONE: Notice that if I had been able to build another industry we would have another $48,000 entering the community. Brown saved us about $7,000 with his stores and cost us $48,000. We're just taking in each other's washing so far.

MANAGER: That's about right. You can save some money by providing services locally but you're not going to provide a lot of growth without establishing a strong economic base; that means more industries. O.K., pay your employees. *(Blue pays $6,000 to Yellow and $18,000 to Red. Brown Pays $6,000 to Red and $6,000 to Yellow.)* O.K., now it's Step 9, Pay Stores and Office. For Office charges I'll take $4,000 from Blue and $2,000 from Brown. Yellow owes me $6,000 for local and central stores charges for his two residences. Red, take care of your payments to Brown.

BROWN ONE: Everybody see that money go by from Yellow? He's really helping the local economy.

Scene Six

MANAGER: Let's pay for transportation now. Blue, you owe nothing because you're adjacent to the terminal. Red, you owe $900 for journey to work for your residences, $600 for journey to local store, and $300 for journey to central store. Yellow, you owe nothing because you're adjacent to your place of work and you're shopping with me. Green owes nothing and neither does Brown. Do you all see how I calculated those costs? *(Manager points out some typical calculations.)* We have set your tax rate at five per cent for the first round and your taxes are as follows.

ACCOUNTANT: Multiplying five per cent times each of your total assessed value, I get the following taxes due. Red — $3,200, Yellow — $2,100, Blue — $6,500, Green — $300, and Brown — $2,900. Pay the manager. *(Money is passed in to manager.)* Now pay attention please. The following is your community financial situation. You collected a total of $15,000 in taxes this round. Your expenses were $14,000 for utilities, and $6,000 for social services to six residences. That's a total expense of $20,000 against $15,000 raised in taxes; leaves you with a deficit of $5,000 for this round. The interest on that debt will cost you $300 next round at ten per cent. Your debt limit is $30,000 so you're at about sixteen per cent of your debt limit. What tax rate do you want to set for the next round?

GREEN ONE: We'd better raise it to about ten per cent or we'll run another deficit.

BLUE TWO: So what? A deficit only costs us ten per cent a round. How much do we make on investments in the game?

BROWN TWO: I figure that I'm losing about five hundred a round. . . .

MANAGER: If you make reasonably good decisions, you ought to be able to make from five per cent to twenty per cent on your investments, at least in the long run. I think it would be a good idea for each of you to make some calculations on your expected and actual rate of return from the two or three rounds we'll get in today. You can bring them in when we meet again next week.

BLUE TWO: So, let's assume that at least most of us have made pretty good decisions this round. Except Brown, of course. Then running a deficit means we are borrowing money for local investment at ten per cent. In the long run we ought to do all right with that.

GREEN TWO: No. I think we should keep the taxes high and pay for services as we use them. A pay-as-you-go policy.

YELLOW ONE: Look, you guys. Don't listen to Green. He's not interested in pay-as-you-go. He has almost no assessed value right now and he wants us to pay a lot in taxes now so he won't have to help pay off the debt when his assessments go up.

BLUE ONE: What happens to us if we exceed our debt limit?

MANAGER: Essentially you will lose your credit rating and you will then have to pay cash for everything. You'll lose all financial flexibility. If you get up near eighty per cent of your debt limit, I'll warn you of the possible consequences in more detail. It's covered in the rules if you want to look it up.

BLUE ONE: But how high should we set the tax rate in order to be safe?

MANAGER: I really can't tell you. How much money you'll need will depend on how many utilities and residences you have to service in the next round. How much money you'll raise at a given tax rate depends on how much building you do and how high your assessments are. If you can answer that, you know what to do. Since you probably can't, I would suggest that you avoid doing anything too dramatic with the tax rate until you begin to get a better feel for how it affects the game.

BLUE ONE: O.K. We're all going to construct some more buildings and we'll be sure to give Green some utilities so he can add to the tax base. I think we can afford to cut the tax rate. How about four per cent?

GREEN ONE: Oh no. You're trying the same thing I did in the opposite direction. You want a low tax rate for now because you have the highest assessed value. I think we should set it at five per cent for now and see what happens.

ALL TEAMS: O.K. Let's leave it at five per cent.

MANAGER: Well, that's the first round. We're now ready to begin land buying in Round Two. Get your bids ready, all three at once.

Appendix II: Notes for Conducting the Special Experiments

Experiment I: Urban Politics

The political modification of CLUG can be used independently or in conjunction with one or another of the other experiments. Care should be taken not to superimpose it on too complex an experiment in the first attempt, however, since players will tend to become lost in a maze of new rules and modifications and fail to understand the important points of this experiment alone. It can be most easily added to Experiments II or VII.

In running this experiment, it may be necessary to provide some basis of appeal to higher authority such as the instructor in the event of a particularly aggressive or venal Mayor. Insofar as possible, however, the players should be left to their own devices in removing a difficult or dishonest Mayor through the election process.

It is important for the instructor or some other player such as a game manager to make some notes of political actions occuring during play in order to provide a written record of events as they occur. These can serve both to verify agreements and actions which have been taken as well as to provide some basis for later discussion and recapitulation of the way in which the various players behaved during the experiment. Such records need only be in the form of a rough diary or set of minutes of significant events occuring during play.

Experiment II: Rural–Urban Interdependence

Aside from the fact that most players have probably come from an urban background and may consider this experiment to be dealing with unimportant phenomena, no particularly difficult operational problems usually arise during this experiment. The first ten rounds are generally highly uneventful until enough capital accumulates to allow the first stages of urban development. This period will probably seem boring to the players and they should be encouraged to move through it as quickly as possible. Impress upon them the importance of accumulating capital for an urban development. A number of important moves can be made during this period in terms of acquiring land and borrowing money, with that player who sells off his agricultural holdings often becoming the person first able to undertake urban development. Nevertheless, relatively little can happen for several rounds and players should be discouraged from engaging in pointless debates on unimportant issues until growth can actually occur.

Another tendency often noted is for all players to sell off their farm holdings as quickly as possible in order to get into more urban types of businesses. The game is far more meaningful if at least some of the teams retain and expand their farm holdings. They can become quite profitable if well managed. Teams rarely recognize the potential advantages of farms until they have sold their own holdings. Hence, it is sometimes necessary to suggest the advantages of staying in farming to some of the players in order to ensure the continuance of some farming activity for the purposes to be illustrated by the experiment.

It might be helpful to remind players in Round 10 that R1's may now be built without Utility Lines. Construction of such R1's will mean greater use of land by urban uses, thus producing greater pressure on teams retaining farms. This pressure often results in teams having to make choices between agricultural and urban land uses.

Also helpful is the reminder that when players construct any building other than an FM unit on a piece of property, such parcel immediately goes out of all farm use. If a team should choose to build on one of the pieces which connects two major portions of their farm, they may no longer cultivate the severed portion of their farm. When a team has only twenty-four parcels in agricultural land use, their income is taken from a different column of the income table and is significantly less. When a farm drops below twenty parcels in Stage I or twenty-five parcels in Stage II (including the parcel the FM unit is built on), it goes out of farming altogether.

The accounting procedure in this experiment is fundamentally the same as in Basic CLUG, except that virtually all the land is owned by the teams as the game begins. Each team should have an Assessed Value of $32,500 entered on the assessment record sheet as the game commences. Twenty thousand of this Assessed Value represents the team's FM unit already placed on the board as play begins. The other $12,500 represents the value of twenty-five parcels of land assessed at the base price of $500 each.

A suggested board layout is shown in Figure II-1. Several items on the board are worth noting. First, remove twelve parcels from play by designating them as hills, i.e., terrain unavailable for either building or farming. This is done to reduce the supply of available land and to confront the players with the choice between farming and urban development early in the game. (These areas may also be designated as water, desert, or such.) Second, place the terminal in the center of the board to encourage equal competition for land in all four quadrants around the terminal. Third, lay out farms so that team holdings are somewhat mingled. Otherwise, teams will tend to build in only the single area of the city in which they own land. Such segregation of team construction results in many inefficient land uses, as will be evidenced primarily in high Transportation Costs.

In Round 9, after setting the Tax Rate, Primary Roads become Major Highways at a mode weight of ½ and Secondary Roads become Primary Roads at a mode weight of 1. An additional Major Highway is added along line 13 so as to intersect the original Major Highway at the terminal.

Any FM units lost on the roll of the dice are inoperable for any other use. If the parcel they are located on is to be employed in any other use, they must be demolished. A team cannot build on top of an FM unit, i.e., they cannot add a residential unit on top of an FM unit.

Important points to remember include:

1. Collect the Private Service Plant charges, and note that they change from Stage I to Stage II.

2. The base price for land is now $500.

3. FM units must buy from LS and CS also.

4. FM units do not have to buy from the Office until Stage II.

5. Only FM units may be built with Private Service Plants in Stage I whereas both FM and R1 units may be built with these Plants in Stage II.

6. Before teams undertake a large amount of public utility construction, encourage them to consider the amount of urban development which they can accomplish at that stage. Overambitious utility development in early stages is often a cultural carryover from having played more urban-oriented versions of CLUG such as the Basic game.

Experiment III: Transportation and Technology

The intent of this experiment, as well as Experiments II and V, is to provide an understanding of some of the factors frequently cited in the literature as responsible for patterns of urban growth and development. None of these factors alone is viewed as sufficient to explain urbanization, yet all are necessary. Many variables, in addition to those in the experiments, are no doubt of equal significance. Some of these are contained in the Basic CLUG model but not highlighted in an experiment, while others are totally excluded from consideration. Partial views of the world, such as this game and experiment, enhance comprehension by reducing the task to manageable size. Encourage players to realize the limits of the arguments presented and to think beyond the familiar condition of "all other things being equal."

Two levels of understanding can be identified and discussed in this experiment. On the one hand, it is intended that players develop an understanding of the concept of technology as a critical link between populations and their environment. On this level of understanding players should be encouraged to think of the world from a systemic point of view by searching for instances of equilibrium, change, adaptation, and structural rigidity within the evolving urban system. On the other hand, it is intended that players become familiar with aspects of the historical evolution of city growth in the United States. Such historical awareness may prove useful for creating an ability to view current city problems dealt with in later experiments with some historical perspective. While this experiment in no way claims to be an exact historical reconstruction, it does depict three historically significant types of events: changes in transportation technology, improvements in energy production, and rapid urban expansion.

Specifically, this experiment depicts the relative characteristics of water-transport as having high loading and port costs, relatively little increase in shipping cost with increased distance, and particular appropriateness for heavy shipment to distant markets. Rail transport exhibits approximately the same traits as water transport. In the case of highway transport though, the inverse is true: low loading facility costs, great cost sensitivity to increased distance, and particular orientation to less distant markets.

The main characteristic of the technology of energy production treated in this experiment is the limitations of water power to locations immediately adjacent to naturally favorable sites. Contrasted slightly with this is the relative transportability of fuels for the production of steam power. In contrast, electrical energy is virtually free of locational constraints and available equally to most sites. With each of these advances unit energy costs have decreased.

The third and most easily observable factor dealt with in this experiment is the rate and pattern of urban development resulting from changes in transport or energy. In Stages I and II a generally tight and compact city should develop. In Stage III, on the other hand, growth should accelerate precipitously and extend linearly out from the previous compact city.

These comments are intended to aid in drawing player attention to the major features of this experiment. Some specific changes in the rules of Basic CLUG are called for in each experiment. In the present case, three major changes should be remembered:

1. Payments to Full and Partial Industries are increased to $65,000 and to $32,000 respectively.

2. Industries must pay Energy Costs in addition to other costs found in Basic CLUG.

3. Computation of Industrial Transportation Costs now requires the consideration of four elements: Cost to Terminal, Terminal Fee, Shipping Costs to external market, and Energy Transportation Cost. Industry-to-Office Cost is, of course, a normal additional expense.

Experiment IV: Land Use Regulation

The general intent of this experiment and its two variations is to acquaint players with two mechanisms of public land-regulation and to suggest some of the potential benefits and problems resulting from such efforts. Several difficulties exist in designing game versions of these highly specific real-world phenomena; they are particularly apparent in Variation I, which deals with zoning.

In devising land-use regulation systems in game terms, a number of abstractions and simplifications have been necessary which reduce the direct correspondence between the game world and the real world. These reductions have been necessitated principally by the scale of CLUG and its specific view of the world.

This scale problem is evident in the variance-granting rationale employed in Variation I. In the real world, a variance would be granted only if the applicant could show that non-conformity with the ordinance would not alter the character of the neighborhood where he desired to develop. In the game, where parcels represent an area of approximately one square mile, neighborhood scale does not exist. Each game parcel, in fact, could be a neighborhood in itself. A compromise solution was necessary, therefore, in order to introduce variances into play. The scheme devised and contained in Table IV-4 (in this *Player's Manual*) is based simply on the extent to which the desired use departs from the zoned use. At best, neighborhood considerations are modelled in a macroscopic fashion.

Other simplifications and compromises were necessary in order to introduce non-economic variables into the game. Plans and ordinances are frequently based on either positive esthetic values or their opposites in the forms of noise, smoke, or traffic hazards. In order to devise a zoning map and plan for the game, these non-CLUG values appear as "irrationalities" in the sense that they decrease profitability of a land use. (Profitability, it should be recalled, is the prime criterion of value in CLUG.) The park specified in the plan is one example of such an "irrationality." This is intended to imply not that parks lack economic benefits, but rather that these benefits are not represented in CLUG.

The mechanics of play are sufficiently clear to require no specific comment here. General advice, however, can be given as to the selection and motivation of the Corporation Administrator.

Either the players or the instructor may select the person to fill the Administrator role. The latter alternative is preferable because it assures that the person selected has a fairly good understanding of the game. Personality is also an important factor to be considered because success of the corporation may frequently be determined by the ability of the Administrator both to make his position known and to withstand probable disagreement and criticism from his peers. In order to assist the Administrator in withstanding occasional social pressures, the instructor should provide moral support and verbal encouragement for the Administrator's actions. Since the Metropolitan Plan is not obviously desirable in terms of game parameters, the Administrator should be provided with incentive to ultimately guide development into the specified pattern by verbal encouragement. The instructor may wish to remind the Administrator of the Penalty Points assigned for long term deviations from the Metropolitan Plan. Standards of conformance, land value and community growth have been suggested; a good basis of comparison and assessment can be derived from applying these same criteria to the zoned community and its developments. Deviations from the zoning ordinance are assigned Penalty Points in the same manner as was discussed in the experiment itself. For purposes of comparison, the Total Penalty Points in each game should be divided by the number of parcels developed to yield an average per-parcel value. The suggested standards should be used when only Variation II has been played.

Zoning can be expected to allow for more deviations from the ordinance because it is adopted in Round 5 after development has taken place, whereas the Municipal Land Corporation acquires land in advance of development and therefore should be able to better restrict deviations. While the Corporation is not hampered by political boundaries, zoning is municipal. In the zoned community it could be expected that early development would leap political boundaries in order to avoid regulation. Zoning tends to be inflexible and not sensitive to developmental processes, whereas the Corporation Administrator is allowed short-run discretionary power as a step toward ultimate compliance. The time horizons of the two schemes are thus somewhat different. The Zoning Ordinance looks to approximately Round 8 whereas the Metropolitan Plan represents development in approximately Round 15. It could be anticipated, then, that Zoning would prove more stifling to growth than would the Metropolitan Plan.

These statements simply represent expectations which may not in fact always materialize; they may also occur but go unnoticed. Hence it is the instructor's job to raise the above points and to direct discussion toward comparing the game, the readings, and the real world.

Experiment V: Inter-Regional Relations

In this experiment two communities are developed simultaneously on the board instead of running two separate parts to the experiment. In this fashion comparison is far more dramatic, although operation of the game is made somewhat more difficult. Supervising eight teams of players, maintaining the separate and cooperative aspects of the two cities, and managing the substeps in Step 7 require additional effort on the part of the game manager or instructor.

Some possible points of difficulty are discussed in detail here to assist the game manager or instructor. Because it is important to keep players from learning the nature of the variable external market demand function, all information needed to administer Step 7 is provided only in the *Instructor's Manual.*

The Steps of Play must be carried out simultaneously in the two cities, with separate tax and expenditure records being kept for each. The three-team community will experience far less growth and action so that players will probably find themselves with extra time during play. This time can be used in several ways. First, they will be in a dependent position to the larger city, so they can spend time formulating strategies as a city on how to extricate themselves from their position of economic dependency. Second, they can become involved in the particular problems of the larger city through the instructor's offering advice and drawing lessons from play. Finally, the small city should be able to keep its own taxing and expenditure records, provided the players receive some initial instruction from the Accountant.

Since wages are negotiable and employment and wage agreements are valid for only one round, the instructor should set a reasonable time limit on these discussions in order to keep the game moving.

In signing trade agreements the instructor can encourage cooperation between the two cities by reminding players of the cheaper transportation costs in effect, especially between the two cities.

There will be additional tasks for the Accountant in keeping records of loans to teams in City B and in setting the round-by-round tax rate for City A. This may be mitigated by encouraging players from City A to assist the Accountant in some of his tasks.

Since the ability to borrow money is one of the major variables in this experiment, the instructor must be certain that the following rules are carefully observed:

1. All forms of borrowing in City A are strictly prohibited, including borrowing between teams, borrowing from the instructor, incurring any community deficits, or borrowing from teams in the other city.

2. Most forms of borrowing money in City B are allowed, including borrowing from each other or from the instructor, and incurring community deficits within the normal debt limits established in Basic CLUG. Only borrowing from teams in City A is prohibited.

Experiment VI: Municipal Finance

The aim of this experiment is to allow experience with both some of the problems and some of the possible solutions encountered in discussing the fiscal crisis confronting American central cities in the 1970's.

Variation I

Separate tax and expenditure records will be kept for the city and the suburbs. The intent at the start of the game (Step 5, Round 10) is to describe a situation in which the combination of old and high-density buildings with a high outstanding deficit and operating costs are creating a crisis situation in revenue-raising for the central city. Meanwhile, the suburbs start with no outstanding deficit and no problems in financing their expenditures. Many of the lessons provided in this variation as well as the next are subtle and should be constantly emphasized by the instructor. For example, the shift of extra costs for high-density residential construction from the team building them to the community tax burden should be pointed out. In addition, the savings in taxes to those teams allowing great depreciation of their buildings should be pointed out often, and those buildings over six years old should be announced frequently. In most runs the setup of the team holdings and the ability to specialize, coupled with the profit motive, will create conflicts between city and suburban interests, "slumlords" versus other property holders, and other competing interest groups. Such conflicts are not necessarily undesirable and tend to reflect the simulation of real inequalities in the system.

Variation II

Tax and expenditure records in this variation will be kept for only one body—the entire community, as in Basic CLUG. However, taxes will be computed on each team's Assessed Value of Land only. Land will be assessed by an Assessor chosen by the teams. The criterion used for assessment is the market value of a land parcel—what a parcel would bring if it were to be sold on the open market. Since few of the more central, older parcels change hands during play and sell at free market prices, the Assessor (in cooperation with the instructor) must estimate what such prices might be. Of course, these potential market prices vary from round to round and generally rise as the game proceeds.

A possible assessment map is provided in Figure A-VI-1. It is important to stress the relationship of a team's tax burden to the location, price, and number of its land holdings. Also worth noting is the fact that slum landlords can no longer get tax breaks for holding aged residential units. Landlords would probably be penalized for using expensive land parcels to carry out less economically viable activities under the Land Tax of Variation II.

Figure A-VI-1. Suggested Land Assessments in Thousands of Dollars for Variation II of Municipal Finance

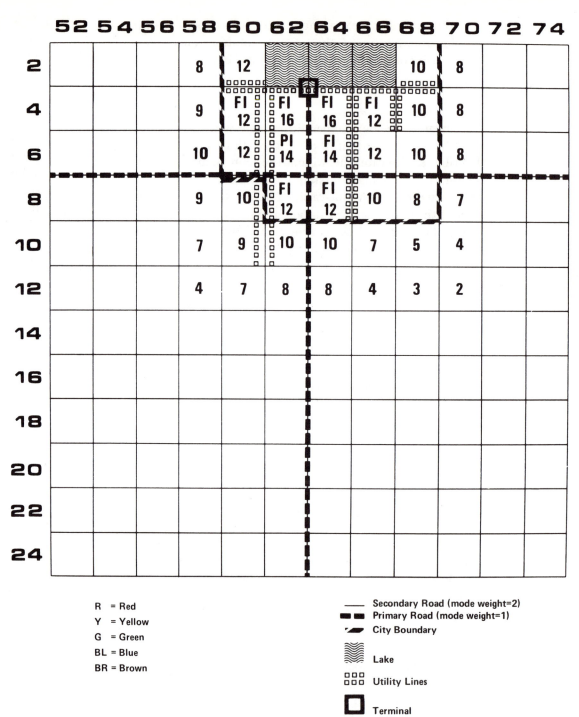

R = Red
Y = Yellow
G = Green
BL = Blue
BR = Brown

—— Secondary Road (mode weight=2)
▬▬ Primary Road (mode weight=1)
◣ City Boundary
〰 Lake
▫▫▫ Utility Lines
■ Terminal

Experiment VII: Environmental Pollution

This experiment models a situation in which water pollution may develop as a community problem. Water pollution itself, however, is not so much the topic of this experiment as is pollution in general. The actual focus of this experiment is on properties of the ecosystem and on the roles of various parts of that system in altering it. The issue of responsibility for environmental damage is therefore raised. Discussion should be directed to these considerations and away from specific talk about water pollution.

The rules of this experiment were devised to make it likely that after a few rounds of play, water pollution will become a local problem. Since the fate of the game rests in the hands of the players, this result cannot be assured. Players may successfully avoid pollution, in which case the instructor must direct attention to the hypothetical question of what would have happened if pollution had occurred. Such an event, however, is probably less likely than its opposite: the creation of a pollution catastrophe. While such a situation would surely bring home the lessons of this experiment, some persons feel it undesirable to leave an experience on a bad note. It was for this reason that the federal loan mechanism was set up (see p.   of this manual). This safety valve can be used or not at the instructor's discretion.

The course of events in the game will also influence the decision to terminate play. It is best to play long enough to create a pollution problem and then solve it. Ten to fifteen rounds of play should be adequate; if it appears that players have successfully avoided pollution, further play is probably less useful than post-game discussion. The same comment could be made about situations in which the pollution problem appears insoluble.

Finally, it may be instructive to ask players to compare their opinion about technology and urban growth after Experiment VII with their opinion after Experiment III. This comparison should contrast optimistic views of technological "progress" with pessimistic views now current. The result should be a more balanced view of the processes of urbanization.

Appendix III: A Glossary of CLUG Terms

Accountant—A student or teaching assistant helping in running the game by keeping accounts of land ownership, building construction, assessed values, taxes due, the financial status of the community, etc.

Age of Buildings—An indicator of how old a building is, based upon the difference between the current round number and the recorded round in which the building was first built.

Assessed Value of Land or Buildings—An estimate of the current market value of land or buildings. Land value is assessed upon the basis of its purchase price and the purchase price of adjacent properties. Building value is assessed based upon its initial construction cost less five per cent depreciation for each round.

Association Weight—A measure reflecting the volume of interaction necessary between any two land uses in a single round; reflects the volume and frequency of movements over a unit time period.

Central Store—The CLUG land use representing more specialized kinds of shopping facilities generally found in larger population centers and requiring a larger population base for support than a Local Store.

Check—The term used by a player to indicate that he wishes to defer his turn to construct a building until after another team or player has made a decision. If no other player undertakes construction following a check, the player checking loses his turn for that round.

Community Deficit or Surplus—The financial status of the CLUG community at the end of any given round. A surplus results when the taxes collected for that round exceed the community expenditures; a deficit results when expenditures exceed the taxes collected. Current surplus or deficit is added to the cumulative surplus or deficit from the previous round to provide the current round cumulative surplus or deficit.

Debt Limit—The maximum amount of debt which a community may incur in terms of its cumulative deficit. The limit is usually set by state governments as some percentage of the total assessed value of the community over the past several years. In CLUG the limit is ten per cent of the previous round's total assessed value for the community.

Designate Employment—That step of play during which players owning factories or stores seeking employees and other players owning residences seeking employment, agree to cooperate by providing employment until the next round divisible by five. The length of an employment contract is shorter in some experiments.

External Markets—Places outside the CLUG community and outside the game board which purchase manufactured products from the industries built during the game. In all but one experiment, these markets are considered to be unlimited and inelastic and not to respond to the actions of CLUG players.

Full Industry—A land use in CLUG which represents economically basic forms of commercial activity through local production and external sales.

Game Manager—An instructor, teaching assistant or selected student who acts as director of game activities, by, e.g., announcing the steps of play and the community financial status.

Local Store—The CLUG land use representing nonspecialized retailing activities for local convenience shopping and requiring a smaller supporting population than a Central Store.

Major Highways—A high-quality highway usually having limited access at points designated by the game manager or in instructions for an experiment and normally counted at a Mode Weight of ½. Only used in some of the experiments.

Mode Weight—A figure representing the relative efficiency and cost of movement along a particular form of highway, expressed as a number in relation to other values for differing types of highways. Thus, numbers 1 and 2 are given as the ratio of Mode Weights for Primary and Secondary Roads in most of the experiments. The Mode Weight multiplied by the appropriate Association Weight gives the cost of moving along a single unit distance of the CLUG board on the particular type of highway present there.

Office—The CLUG land use representing provision of administrative, accounting, and management services which are consumed by other businesses.

Parcel—A term sometimes used to refer to a unit segment of land in CLUG which is always the amount of land contained within a single grid square.

Partial Industry—A CLUG land use which represents a smaller, less expensive, and slightly less efficient form of Full Industry.

Pass—The declaration made by a player or team not wishing to construct or demolish any buildings on a particular round.

Primary Roads—Highways which have general access to all parcels touched but which are located only on particularly designated lines on the board. Usually counted at a Mode Weight of 1.

Renovation—Renewing a building built in an earlier round by paying to the bank or game manager an amount equal to its state of deterioration, thereby reducing the chances of loss of the building through the dice roll.

Residential Unit—A CLUG land use representing both housing, and population including labor force. Residential units may be built in densities ranging from R1 to R4 representing simple multiples of housing and population units located in a single parcel.

Secondary Roads—The equivalent in CLUG play to minor local streets and roads serving primarily local residential and shopping purposes. Usually counted at a Mode Weight of 2, 3, or 4, depending upon the purpose of the experiment.

Set Prices—That step of play at which owners of newly constructed Stores or

Offices announce the prices they will charge until the next round divisible by five; usually based upon an estimate of existing or potential competition and the size of the potential market area which might be attracted at a given price.

Steps of Play—The uniform sequence of events occurring within a given round of CLUG; all activities within a round must occur within the appropriate Step of Play.

Team—One or more players operating in conjunction who represent a single economic and political interest within the community.

Terminal—The point to which all manufactured products from Full and Partial Industries are shipped for transportation and sale to external markets. A single board may have more than one terminal for some of the experiments.

Transportation Cost—The cost of moving people or goods between required interdependent land uses during a period of time represented by a round. Computed on the basis of the type of movement required of particular land uses and the corresponding Association Weight, computed over the number of unit distances traversed, mulriplied by the appropriate Mode Weights for the kinds of highways available.

Tax Rate—That figure which, multiplied by a team's assessed value, determines the amount they will have to pay in taxes in a given round; usually expressed as a percentage figure or in terms of dollars of taxes due per one thousand dollars of assessed value. For example, a tax rate of five per cent is equivalent to a tax rate of $50 payable per one thousand dollars of assessed value.

Unit Distance—The distance from one corner of a parcel to the next corner of the same parcel, moving along a grid line.

Utility Lines—Service lines, usually provided by the community at public expense, which represent the provision of the full range of public services necessary for urban development, including water, sewers, police and fire protection, etc. All Utility Lines must be linked to a Utility Plant.

Utility Plant—A publicly-owned land use which provides the full range of urban services along Utility Lines. In a few of the experiments, utility plants may be privately constructed.

Player's Information Form

Table 1. Unit Characteristics (in $1000's)

	Construction	Income	Employment	Payroll	LS* Cost	CS* Cost	0* Cost
FI	$96	$48	4	$24	—	—	$4
PI	$48	$22	2	$12	—	—	$2
LS	$24	**	1	$ 6	—	—	$1
CS	$24	**	1	$ 6	—	—	$1
0	$36	**	1	$ 6	—	—	—
R1	$12	$ 6	—	—	$2	$1	—
R2	$30	$12	—	—	$4	$2	—
R3	$48	$18	—	—	$6	$3	—
R4	$72	$24	—	—	$8	$4	—

*These are the charges for such goods provided by the Operator. Teams may set their prices above or below these.

**Income equals price times number of customers.

Table 2. Association Weights*

From	To	
FI	Term. $4,000	0 $400
PI	Term. $2,000	0 $200
CS and LS	— — —	0 $100
R (per unit)	Emp. $ 300	LS $200
		CS $100

*To determine transportation cost for any land use multiply weight by the appropriate Mode Weight for type of highway and sum over number of unit distances traveled.

Steps of Play

1. Purchase Land
2. Provide Utilities
[3. Renovate Buildings]
4. Construct Buildings
5. Designate Employment
6. Sign Trade Agreements
7. Receive Income
8. Pay Employees
9. Pay LS, CS, and 0
10. Pay Transportation
11. Pay Taxes

Table 3. Probability of Building Loss

Age	Probability	Losing No's.
0	.056	3
1	.111	5
2	.167	7
3	.195	2,7
4	.250	2,7,11
5	.306	2,7,9
6	.362	3,7,8
7	.417	5,7,8
8	.445	6,7,8
9	.500	3,6,7,8
10	.556	5,6,7,8
11-20	See Player's Manual, p. 20	

Player's Information Form

Table 1. Unit Characteristics (in $1000's)

	Construction	Income	Employment	Payroll	LS* Cost	CS* Cost	0* Cost
FI	$96	$48	4	$24	—	—	$4
PI	$48	$22	2	$12	—	—	$2
LS	$24	**	1	$ 6	—	—	$1
CS	$24	**	1	$ 6	—	—	$1
0	$36	**	1	$ 6	—	—	—
R1	$12	$ 6	—	—	$2	$1	—
R2	$30	$12	—	—	$4	$2	—
R3	$48	$18	—	—	$6	$3	—
R4	$72	$24	—	—	$8	$4	—

*These are the charges for such goods provided by the Operator. Teams may set their prices above or below these.

**Income equals price times number of customers.

Table 2. Association Weights*

From	To	
FI	Term. $4,000	0 $400
PI	Term. $2,000	0 $200
CS and LS	— — —	0 $100
R (per unit)	Emp. $ 300	LS $200
		CS $100

*To determine transportation cost for any land use multiply weight by the appropriate Mode Weight for type of highway and sum over number of unit distances traveled.

Table 3. Probability of Building Loss

Age	Probability	Losing No's.
0	.056	3
1	.111	5
2	.167	7
3	.195	2,7
4	.250	2,7,11
5	.306	2,7,9
6	.362	3,7,8
7	.417	5,7,8
8	.445	6,7,8
9	.500	3,6,7,8
10	.556	5,6,7,8
11–20 See Player's Manual, p. 20		

Steps of Play

1. Purchase Land
2. Provide Utilities
[3. Renovate Buildings]
4. Construct Buildings
5. Designate Employment
6. Sign Trade Agreements
7. Receive Income
8. Pay Employees
9. Pay LS, CS, and 0
10. Pay Transportation
11. Pay Taxes

SHOPPING CONTRACT   Rd. No. ___

Cust. Coord. _____   No. Units _____ Team _____

Supp. Coord. _____   Price _____ Team _____

SHOPPING CONTRACT   Rd. No. ___

Cust. Coord. _____   No. Units _____ Team _____

Supp. Coord. _____   Price _____ Team _____

SHOPPING CONTRACT   Rd. No. ___

Cust. Coord. _____   No. Units _____ Team _____

Supp. Coord. _____   Price _____ Team _____

SHOPPING CONTRACT   Rd. No.___

Cust. Coord. _____   No. Units _____ Team _____

Supp. Coord. _____   Price _____ Team _____

SHOPPING CONTRACT   Rd. No. ___

Cust. Coord. _____   No. Units _____ Team _____

Supp. Coord. _____   Price _____ Team _____

SHOPPING CONTRACT   Rd. No.___

Cust. Coord. _____   No. Units _____ Team _____

Supp. Coord. _____   Price _____ Team _____

LAND PURCHASE OFFER

Coord. _____   Team _____

Price _____   Rd. No. _____

LAND PURCHASE OFFER

Coord. _____   Team _____

Price _____   Rd. No. _____

LAND PURCHASE OFFER

Coord. _____   Team _____

Price _____   Rd. No. _____

LAND PURCHASE OFFER

Coord. _____   Team _____

Price _____   Rd. No. _____

LAND PURCHASE OFFER

Coord. _____   Team _____

Price _____   Rd. No. _____

LAND PURCHASE OFFER

Coord. _____   Team _____

Price _____   Rd. No. _____

LAND PURCHASE OFFER

Coord. _____   Team _____

Price _____   Rd. No. _____

LAND PURCHASE OFFER

Coord. _____   Team _____

Price _____   Rd. No. _____

LAND PURCHASE OFFER

Coord. _____   Team _____

Price _____   Rd. No. _____

LAND PURCHASE OFFER

Coord. _____   Team _____

Price _____   Rd. No. _____

LAND PURCHASE OFFER

Coord. _____   Team _____

Price _____   Rd. No. _____

LAND PURCHASE OFFER

Coord. _____   Team _____

Price _____   Rd. No. _____

LAND PURCHASE OFFER

Coord. _____   Team _____

Price _____   Rd. No. _____

LAND PURCHASE OFFER

Coord. _____   Team _____

Price _____   Rd. No. _____

LAND PURCHASE OFFER

Coord. _____   Team _____

Price _____   Rd. No. _____

LAND PURCHASE OFFER

Coord. _____   Team _____

Price _____   Rd. No. _____

LAND PURCHASE OFFER

Coord. _____   Team _____

Price _____   Rd. No. _____

LAND PURCHASE OFFER

Coord. _____   Team _____

Price _____   Rd. No. _____

LAND PURCHASE OFFER

Coord. _____   Team _____

Price _____   Rd. No. _____

LAND PURCHASE OFFER

Coord. _____   Team _____

Price _____   Rd. No. _____

LAND PURCHASE OFFER

Coord. _____   Team _____

Price _____   Rd. No. _____

SHOPPING CONTRACT Rd. No. ___	SHOPPING CONTRACT Rd. No. ___
Cust. Coord. _____ No. Units _____ Team _____ Supp. Coord. _____ Price _____ Team _____	Cust. Coord. _____ No. Units _____ Team _____ Supp. Coord. _____ Price _____ Team _____
SHOPPING CONTRACT Rd. No. ___	SHOPPING CONTRACT Rd. No. ___
Cust. Coord. _____ No. Units _____ Team _____ Supp. Coord. _____ Price _____ Team _____	Cust. Coord. _____ No. Units _____ Team _____ Supp. Coord. _____ Price _____ Team _____
SHOPPING CONTRACT Rd. No. ___	SHOPPING CONTRACT Rd. No. ___
Cust. Coord. _____ No. Units _____ Team _____ Supp. Coord. _____ Price _____ Team _____	Cust. Coord. _____ No. Units _____ Team _____ Supp. Coord. _____ Price _____ Team _____

LAND PURCHASE OFFER	LAND PURCHASE OFFER	LAND PURCHASE OFFER
Coord. _____ Team _____ Price _____ Rd. No. _____	Coord. _____ Team _____ Price _____ Rd. No. _____	Coord. _____ Team _____ Price _____ Rd. No. _____
LAND PURCHASE OFFER	LAND PURCHASE OFFER	LAND PURCHASE OFFER
Coord. _____ Team _____ Price _____ Rd. No. _____	Coord. _____ Team _____ Price _____ Rd. No. _____	Coord. _____ Team _____ Price _____ Rd. No. _____
LAND PURCHASE OFFER	LAND PURCHASE OFFER	LAND PURCHASE OFFER
Coord. _____ Team _____ Price _____ Rd. No. _____	Coord. _____ Team _____ Price _____ Rd. No. _____	Coord. _____ Team _____ Price _____ Rd. No. _____
LAND PURCHASE OFFER	LAND PURCHASE OFFER	LAND PURCHASE OFFER
Coord. _____ Team _____ Price _____ Rd. No. _____	Coord. _____ Team _____ Price _____ Rd. No. _____	Coord. _____ Team _____ Price _____ Rd. No. _____
LAND PURCHASE OFFER	LAND PURCHASE OFFER	LAND PURCHASE OFFER
Coord. _____ Team _____ Price _____ Rd. No. _____	Coord. _____ Team _____ Price _____ Rd. No. _____	Coord. _____ Team _____ Price _____ Rd. No. _____
LAND PURCHASE OFFER	LAND PURCHASE OFFER	LAND PURCHASE OFFER
Coord. _____ Team _____ Price _____ Rd. No. _____	Coord. _____ Team _____ Price _____ Rd. No. _____	Coord. _____ Team _____ Price _____ Rd. No. _____
LAND PURCHASE OFFER	LAND PURCHASE OFFER	LAND PURCHASE OFFER
Coord. _____ Team _____ Price _____ Rd. No. _____	Coord. _____ Team _____ Price _____ Rd. No. _____	Coord. _____ Team _____ Price _____ Rd. No. _____
LAND PURCHASE OFFER	LAND PURCHASE OFFER	LAND PURCHASE OFFER
Coord. _____ Team _____ Price _____ Rd. No. _____	Coord. _____ Team _____ Price _____ Rd. No. _____	Coord. _____ Team _____ Price _____ Rd. No. _____

SHOPPING CONTRACT	Rd. No. ___		SHOPPING CONTRACT	Rd. No. ___
Cust. Coord. _____	No. Units _____ Team ___		Cust. Coord. _____	No. Units _____ Team ___
Supp. Coord. _____	Price _____ Team ___		Supp. Coord. _____	Price _____ Team ___

SHOPPING CONTRACT	Rd. No. ___		SHOPPING CONTRACT	Rd. No. ___
Cust. Coord. _____	No. Units _____ Team ___		Cust. Coord. _____	No. Units _____ Team ___
Supp. Coord. _____	Price _____ Team ___		Supp. Coord. _____	Price _____ Team ___

SHOPPING CONTRACT	Rd. No. ___		SHOPPING CONTRACT	Rd. No. ___
Cust. Coord. _____	No. Units _____ Team ___		Cust. Coord. _____	No. Units _____ Team ___
Supp. Coord. _____	Price _____ Team ___		Supp. Coord. _____	Price _____ Team ___

LAND PURCHASE OFFER		LAND PURCHASE OFFER		LAND PURCHASE OFFER
Coord. _____ Team _____		Coord. _____ Team _____		Coord. _____ Team _____
Price _____ Rd. No. _____		Price _____ Rd. No. _____		Price _____ Rd. No. _____

LAND PURCHASE OFFER		LAND PURCHASE OFFER		LAND PURCHASE OFFER
Coord. _____ Team _____		Coord. _____ Team _____		Coord. _____ Team _____
Price _____ Rd. No. _____		Price _____ Rd. No. _____		Price _____ Rd. No. _____

LAND PURCHASE OFFER		LAND PURCHASE OFFER		LAND PURCHASE OFFER
Coord. _____ Team _____		Coord. _____ Team _____		Coord. _____ Team _____
Price _____ Rd. No. _____		Price _____ Rd. No. _____		Price _____ Rd. No. _____

LAND PURCHASE OFFER		LAND PURCHASE OFFER		LAND PURCHASE OFFER
Coord. _____ Team _____		Coord. _____ Team _____		Coord. _____ Team _____
Price _____ Rd. No. _____		Price _____ Rd. No. _____		Price _____ Rd. No. _____

LAND PURCHASE OFFER		LAND PURCHASE OFFER		LAND PURCHASE OFFER
Coord. _____ Team _____		Coord. _____ Team _____		Coord. _____ Team _____
Price _____ Rd. No. _____		Price _____ Rd. No. _____		Price _____ Rd. No. _____

LAND PURCHASE OFFER		LAND PURCHASE OFFER		LAND PURCHASE OFFER
Coord. _____ Team _____		Coord. _____ Team _____		Coord. _____ Team _____
Price _____ Rd. No. _____		Price _____ Rd. No. _____		Price _____ Rd. No. _____

LAND PURCHASE OFFER		LAND PURCHASE OFFER		LAND PURCHASE OFFER
Coord. _____ Team _____		Coord. _____ Team _____		Coord. _____ Team _____
Price _____ Rd. No. _____		Price _____ Rd. No. _____		Price _____ Rd. No. _____

LAND PURCHASE OFFER		LAND PURCHASE OFFER		LAND PURCHASE OFFER
Coord. _____ Team _____		Coord. _____ Team _____		Coord. _____ Team _____
Price _____ Rd. No. _____		Price _____ Rd. No. _____		Price _____ Rd. No. _____

SHOPPING CONTRACT   Rd. No. ___

Cust. Coord. _____   No. Units _____ Team _____

Supp. Coord. _____   Price _____ Team _____

SHOPPING CONTRACT   Rd. No. ___

Cust. Coord. _____   No. Units _____ Team _____

Supp. Coord. _____   Price _____ Team _____

SHOPPING CONTRACT   Rd. No. ___

Cust. Coord. _____   No. Units _____ Team _____

Supp. Coord. _____   Price _____ Team _____

SHOPPING CONTRACT   Rd. No. ___

Cust. Coord. _____   No. Units _____ Team _____

Supp. Coord. _____   Price _____ Team _____

SHOPPING CONTRACT   Rd. No. ___

Cust. Coord. _____   No. Units _____ Team _____

Supp. Coord. _____   Price _____ Team _____

SHOPPING CONTRACT   Rd. No. ___

Cust. Coord. _____   No. Units _____ Team _____

Supp. Coord. _____   Price _____ Team _____

LAND PURCHASE OFFER

Coord. _____   Team _____

Price _____   Rd. No. _____

LAND PURCHASE OFFER

Coord. _____   Team _____

Price _____   Rd. No. _____

LAND PURCHASE OFFER

Coord. _____   Team _____

Price _____   Rd. No. _____

LAND PURCHASE OFFER

Coord. _____   Team _____

Price _____   Rd. No. _____

LAND PURCHASE OFFER

Coord. _____   Team _____

Price _____   Rd. No. _____

LAND PURCHASE OFFER

Coord. _____   Team _____

Price _____   Rd. No. _____

LAND PURCHASE OFFER

Coord. _____   Team _____

Price _____   Rd. No. _____

LAND PURCHASE OFFER

Coord. _____   Team _____

Price _____   Rd. No. _____

LAND PURCHASE OFFER

Coord. _____   Team _____

Price _____   Rd. No. _____

LAND PURCHASE OFFER

Coord. _____   Team _____

Price _____   Rd. No. _____

LAND PURCHASE OFFER

Coord. _____   Team _____

Price _____   Rd. No. _____

LAND PURCHASE OFFER

Coord. _____   Team _____

Price _____   Rd. No. _____

LAND PURCHASE OFFER

Coord. _____   Team _____

Price _____   Rd. No. _____

LAND PURCHASE OFFER

Coord. _____   Team _____

Price _____   Rd. No. _____

LAND PURCHASE OFFER

Coord. _____   Team _____

Price _____   Rd. No. _____

LAND PURCHASE OFFER

Coord. _____   Team _____

Price _____   Rd. No. _____

LAND PURCHASE OFFER

Coord. _____   Team _____

Price _____   Rd. No. _____

LAND PURCHASE OFFER

Coord. _____   Team _____

Price _____   Rd. No. _____

LAND PURCHASE OFFER

Coord. _____   Team _____

Price _____   Rd. No. _____

LAND PURCHASE OFFER

Coord. _____   Team _____

Price _____   Rd. No. _____

LAND PURCHASE OFFER

Coord. _____   Team _____

Price _____   Rd. No. _____

SHOPPING CONTRACT   Rd. No. ___

Cust. Coord. _____   No. Units _____ Team _____

Supp. Coord. _____   Price _____ Team _____

SHOPPING CONTRACT   Rd. No. ___

Cust. Coord. _____   No. Units _____ Team _____

Supp. Coord. _____   Price _____ Team _____

SHOPPING CONTRACT   Rd. No. ___

Cust. Coord. _____   No. Units _____ Team _____

Supp. Coord. _____   Price _____ Team _____

SHOPPING CONTRACT   Rd. No. ___

Cust. Coord. _____   No. Units _____ Team _____

Supp. Coord. _____   Price _____ Team _____

SHOPPING CONTRACT   Rd. No. ___

Cust. Coord. _____   No. Units _____ Team _____

Supp. Coord. _____   Price _____ Team _____

SHOPPING CONTRACT   Rd. No. ___

Cust. Coord. _____   No. Units _____ Team _____

Supp. Coord. _____   Price _____ Team _____

LAND PURCHASE OFFER
Coord. _____   Team _____
Price _____   Rd. No. _____

LAND PURCHASE OFFER
Coord. _____   Team _____
Price _____   Rd. No. _____

LAND PURCHASE OFFER
Coord. _____   Team _____
Price _____   Rd. No. _____

LAND PURCHASE OFFER
Coord. _____   Team _____
Price _____   Rd. No. _____

LAND PURCHASE OFFER
Coord. _____   Team _____
Price _____   Rd. No. _____

LAND PURCHASE OFFER
Coord. _____   Team _____
Price _____   Rd. No. _____

LAND PURCHASE OFFER
Coord. _____   Team _____
Price _____   Rd. No. _____

LAND PURCHASE OFFER
Coord. _____   Team _____
Price _____   Rd. No. _____

LAND PURCHASE OFFER
Coord. _____   Team _____
Price _____   Rd. No. _____

LAND PURCHASE OFFER
Coord. _____   Team _____
Price _____   Rd. No. _____

LAND PURCHASE OFFER
Coord. _____   Team _____
Price _____   Rd. No. _____

LAND PURCHASE OFFER
Coord. _____   Team _____
Price _____   Rd. No. _____

LAND PURCHASE OFFER
Coord. _____   Team _____
Price _____   Rd. No. _____

LAND PURCHASE OFFER
Coord. _____   Team _____
Price _____   Rd. No. _____

LAND PURCHASE OFFER
Coord. _____   Team _____
Price _____   Rd. No. _____

LAND PURCHASE OFFER
Coord. _____   Team _____
Price _____   Rd. No. _____

LAND PURCHASE OFFER
Coord. _____   Team _____
Price _____   Rd. No. _____

LAND PURCHASE OFFER
Coord. _____   Team _____
Price _____   Rd. No. _____

LAND PURCHASE OFFER
Coord. _____   Team _____
Price _____   Rd. No. _____

LAND PURCHASE OFFER
Coord. _____   Team _____
Price _____   Rd. No. _____

LAND PURCHASE OFFER
Coord. _____   Team _____
Price _____   Rd. No. _____

LAND PURCHASE OFFER
Coord. _____   Team _____
Price _____   Rd. No. _____

LAND PURCHASE OFFER
Coord. _____   Team _____
Price _____   Rd. No. _____

LAND PURCHASE OFFER
Coord. _____   Team _____
Price _____   Rd. No. _____

Clug Tax Records

Round Number	Total Assessed Value					Tax Rate	Total Taxes Due				
	Red	Yellow	Blue	Green	Brown		Red	Yellow	Blue	Green	Brown
0											
Changes Between Rounds											
1											
Changes Between Rounds											
2											
Changes Between Rounds											
3											
Changes Between Rounds											
4											
Changes Between Rounds											
5											
Changes Between Rounds											
6											
Changes Between Rounds											
7											
Changes Between Rounds											
8											
Changes Between Rounds											
9											
Changes Between Rounds											

Clug Tax Records

Round Number	Total Assessed Value					Tax Rate	Total Taxes Due				
	Red	Yellow	Blue	Green	Brown		Red	Yellow	Blue	Green	Brown
0											
Changes Between Rounds											
1											
Changes Between Rounds											
2											
Changes Between Rounds											
3											
Changes Between Rounds											
4											
Changes Between Rounds											
5											
Changes Between Rounds											
6											
Changes Between Rounds											
7											
Changes Between Rounds											
8											
Changes Between Rounds											
9											
Changes Between Rounds											

Clug Community Financial Status

Round Number	Total Community Assessed Value	Utility Costs @ $2,000/New @ $1,000/Old		Social Service Costs @ $1,000 Per Residential Unit		Debt Service @ 10% Previous Deficit	Total Community Costs	Total Taxes Raised	Round Surplus or Deficit	Cummulative Surplus or Deficit	Debt Limit @ 10% of Total Assessed Value	Debt As % of Debt Limit
		No. New / No. Old	Cost	No. Units	Cost							
1												
2												
3												
4												
5												
6												
7												
8												
9												
0												
1												
2												
3												
4												
5												
6												
7												
8												

Clug Community Financial Status

Round Number	Total Community Assessed Value	Utility Costs @ $2,000/New @ $1,000/Old No. New	Cost	Social Service Costs @ $1,000 Per Residential Unit No. Units	Cost	Debt Service @ 10% Previous Deficit	Total Community Costs	Total Taxes Raised	Round Surplus or Deficit	Cummulative Surplus or Deficit	Debt Limit @ 10% of Total Assessed Value	Debt As % of Debt Limit
		No. Old	Cost									
1												
2												
3												
4												
5												
6												
7												
8												
9												
0												
1												
2												
3												
4												
5												
6												
7												
8												

Summary of Changes for Urban Politics Experiment

Voting Strength

For Each	Number of Votes
R1	2
R2	4
R3	6
R4	8
LS	1
CS	1
O	1
FI	4
PI	2

Standing Agenda for Common Council

1. Provide Utilities.
2. Old Business.
3. New Business.
4. Set Tax Rate for This Round.
5. Elect New Mayor Every Third Round.

Characteristics of Public Facilities

Facility	Cost of Construction	Maintenance Cost per Round	Number of Employee Units	Who Decides on Employee
Parks	Land Cost	$7,000	1	Mayor
Recreation Center	$12,000	7,000	1	Mayor
Public School System	24,000	13,000	2	Council
Medical Services	16,000	8,000	1	Council
City College	16,000	7,000	1	Council
City Hall	12,000	7,000	1	Mayor
Library	10,000	8,000	1	Mayor

Steps of Play

1. Purchase Land	Unchanged.
2. Provide Utilities	Common Council Meeting (see Agenda).
[3. Renovate Buildings]	Unchanged.
4. Construct Buildings	City also builds public facilities. Manager counts and posts new voting strength.
5. Designate Employment	Special pins for city employees.
6. Sign Trade Agreements	Unchanged.
7. Receive Income	Unchanged.
8. Pay Employees	City employees also paid.
9. Pay LS, CS, and O	Unchanged.
10. Pay Transportation	Unchanged.
11. Pay Taxes	According to rate set in Step 2.

Summary of Changes for Rural–Urban Interdependence Experiment — Stage I

Farm Income Levels by Probability and Size of Farm — Stage I Technology

Probability	Winning Numbers	Size of Farm		
		20 to 24 Parcels	25 to 36 Parcels	37 + Parcels
.25	8,9	$ 8,000	$12,000	$18,000
.42	2,3,4,5,6	10,000	14,000	20,000
.33	7,10,11,12	12,000	16,000	22,000

Steps of Play

1.	Purchase Land	Minimum Price per Parcel is $500.
2.	Provide Utilities	FM units can use Private Service Plants. Cost is $1,000 plus maintenance.
[3.	Renovate Buildings]	FM units depreciate at normal rates.
4.	Construct Buildings	FM units cost $20,000 each.
5.	Designate Employment	FM unit is self-employed.
6.	Sign Trade Agreements	Unchanged.
7.	Receive Income	FM income determined by dice roll. Each FM income is determined separately.
8.	Pay Employees	Unchanged.
9.	Pay LS, CS, and O	Unchanged except FM does not pay Office.
10.	Pay Transportation	FM to Terminal Association Weight is $1,000.
11.	Pay Taxes	Maintenance for Private Service Plant is $500. Tax Rate for Round one is 3%.

Summary of Changes for Rural–Urban Interdependence Experiment — Stage II

Farm Income Levels by Probability and Size of Farm — Stage II Technology

Probability	Winning Numbers	Size of Farm		
		25 to 36 Parcels	37 to 49 Parcels	50 + Parcels
.11	9	$10,500	$13,000	$24,000
.39	7,8,11,12	11,500	14,000	25,000
.50	2,3,4,5,6,10	12,500	15,000	26,000

Steps of Play

1.	Purchase Land	No additional changes.
2.	Provide Utilities	R1 units as well as FM units may use Private Service Plants. Maintenance Costs increased.
[3.	Renovate Buildings]	Unchanged. Complete renovation of FM unit required in order to enter Stage II technology.
4.	Construct Buildings	New FM units now cost $40,000. Old units must pay the increase in cost.
5.	Designate Employment	No additional changes.
6.	Sign Trade Agreements	No additional changes.
7.	Receive Income	FM income determined by a single dice roll. Use Stage I tables for non-renovated FM's.
8.	Pay Employees	Unchanged.
9.	Pay LS, CS, and O	FM must pay Office. Instructor's price is $1,000 and Association Weight is same as for LS and CS ($100).
10.	Pay Transportation	Primary and Secondary road weights reduced to ½ : 1.
11.	Pay Taxes	Maintenance for Private Service Plant is $800.

Summary of Changes for Transportation and Technology Experiment — Stage I

Unit Characteristics for Industry — Stage I

	Full Industry	Partial Industry
Construction Cost	$96,000	$48,000
Number of Employees	4	2
Payroll	$24,000	$12,000
Maximum Office Cost	$ 4,000	$ 2,000
Energy Cost	$10,000	$ 5,000
Gross Income	$65,000	$32,000

Transportation Costs for Industry to Market — Stage I

	Port Fee*	Location of Market		
		Near	Intermediate	Far
Die Number		1	2,3	4,5,6
Full Industry	$5,000	$5,600	$5,800	$6,000
Partial Industry	3,000	2,800	2,900	3,000

*Port Fee plus Cost of Shipment equals Transportation Cost from Port to Market.

Steps of Play

1. Purchase Land	Unchanged.
2. Provide Utilities	Unchanged.
[3. Renovate Buildings]	Unchanged.
4. Construct Buildings	Industries must touch Energy Source.
5. Designate Employment	Unchanged.
6. Sign Trade Agreements	Unchanged.
7. Receive Income	FI = $65,000; PI = $32,000.
8. Pay Employees	Unchanged.
9. Pay LS, CS, and O	Instructor also collects Energy costs: FI = $10,000; PI = $5,000.
10. Pay Transportation	All within city travel computed as in Basic CLUG with a Mode Weight of 3. Industries must also pay shipping costs to market according to die roll plus Port Fee of $5,000 for FI and $3,000 for PI.
11. Pay Taxes	Unchanged.

Summary of Changes for Transportation and Technology Experiment — Stage II

Unit Characteristics for Industry — Stage II

	Full Industry	Partial Industry
Construction Cost	$96,000	$48,000
Number of Employees	4	2
Payroll	$24,000	$12,000
Maximum Office Cost	$ 4,000	$ 2,000
Energy Cost	$ 6,000	$ 3,000
Gross Income	$65,000	$32,000

Association Weights for Industry — Stage II

Purpose of Trip	Full Industry	Partial Industry
Goods to Siding or Port	$1,000	$500
Energy Transportation	400	200

Transportation Costs for Industry to Market — Stage II

	Siding Fee*	Location of Market		
		Near	Intermediate	Far
Die Number		1	2,3,4	5,6
Full Industry	$1,500	$4,400	$5,000	$5,600
Partial Industry	800	2,200	2,500	2,800

*Siding Fee plus Cost of Shipment equals Transportation Cost from Rail Siding to Market.

Steps of Play

1.	Purchase Land	Unchanged.
2.	Provide Utilities.	Unchanged.
[3.	Renovate Buildings]	State of renovation determines level of technology.
4.	Construct Buildings	Industry may now locate anywhere.
5.	Designate Employment	Unchanged.
6.	Sign Trade Agreements	Unchanged.
7.	Receive Income	Same as in Stage I.
8.	Pay Employees	Unchanged.
9.	Pay LS, CS, and O	Collect energy costs also. Lower for Stage II.
10.	Pay Transportation	Four components to industrial costs. Rest unchanged. Mode Weights still 3.
11.	Pay Taxes	Unchanged.

Summary of Changes for Transportation and Technology Experiment — Stage III

Unit Characteristics for Industry — Stage III

	Full Industry	Partial Industry
Construction Cost	$96,000	$48,000
Number of Employees	4	2
Payroll	$24,000	$12,000
Maximum Office Cost	$ 4,000	$ 2,000
Energy Cost	$ 2,000	$ 1,000
Gross Income	$65,000	$32,000

Association Weights for Industry — Stage III

Purpose of Trip	Full Industry	Partial Industry
Goods to Siding, Port or Interchange	$1,000	$500
Energy Transportation	0	0

Transportation Cost for Industry to Market — Stage III

Die Number	Loading Fee*	Location of Market		
		Near	Intermediate	Far
		1,2,3	4,5	6
Full Industry	$200	$1,600	$3,000	$4,400
Partial Industry	100	800	1,500	2,200

*Loading Fee plus Cost of Shipment equals Transportation Cost from Interchange to Market.

Steps of Play

1. Purchase Land — Unchanged.

2. Provide Utilities — Unchanged.

[3. Renovate Buildings] — State of renovation determines level of technology of industries.

4. Construct Buildings — Now the same as in Basic CLUG.

5. Designate Employment — Unchanged.

6. Sign Trade Agreements — Unchanged.

7. Receive Income — Same as in Stages I and II.

8. Pay Employees — Unchanged.

9. Pay LS, CS, and O — Collect energy costs also. Lower for Stage III.

10. Pay Transportation — Three components to industrial costs. Rest unchanged. Mode Weights are ½ and 2.

11. Pay Taxes — Unchanged.

Summary of Changes for Municipal Finance Experiment

Reduced Construction Costs Due to Specialization*

Unit To Be Built				Type of Unit					
	FI	PI	O	CS	LS	R4	R3	R2	R1
1st	$96	$48	$36	$24	$24	$48	$36	$24	$12
2nd	90	48	36	24	20	48	36	24	12
3rd	85	48	36	20	18	48	36	24	12
4th	80	48	36	18	18	44	33	22	11
5th	80	48	36	18	18	44	33	22	11
6th	80	48	36	16	16	44	33	22	11
7th	75	48	36	16	16	40	30	20	10
8th	75	48	36	15	15	40	30	20	10
9th	75	48	36	15	15	40	30	20	10
10th or more	75	48	36	15	15	36	27	18	9

*In thousands of dollars.

Federal–State Tax Schedule

FI	$1200 per round
PI	500 per round
R1	200 per round
R2	400 per round
R3	600 per round
R4	800 per round
LS, CS, and O	formula below

$$\frac{Price \times No.\ Customers}{10} - \$1,000$$

Residential Service Charges

R1	$1,000 per round
R2	2,300 per round
R3	3,600 per round
R4	5,200 per round

Steps of Play

1. Purchase Land	Unchanged.
2. Provide Utilities	Unchanged except separate votes and payments by city and suburbs.
[3. Renovate Buildings]	Unchanged except that the community is charged double the service charge for buildings over six rounds old.
4. Construct Buildings	Reduced costs for specialization. Higher density residences are changed in cost. Instructor codes any buildings over six rounds old.
5. Designate Employment	Unchanged.
6. Sign Trade Agreements	Unchanged.
7. Receive Income	Unchanged.
8. Pay Employees	Unchanged.
9. Pay LS, CS, and O	Unchanged.
10. Pay Transportation	Unchanged. Mode Weights are ½ and 1 for Major Highways and Primary Roads.
11. Pay Taxes	Unchanged except separate accounts are kept for city and suburbs.

Summary of Changes for Environmental Pollution Experiment

Instructor's Retail and Wholesale Prices for LS Goods

Total Net Pollution Level	LS Retail Price to Residence from Instructor	LS Wholesale Price per Customer from Instructor to LS Store
0 to 5	$3,000	$1,000
6 or 7	3,200	1,200
8 or 9	3,400	1,400
10 or 11	3,800	1,800
12 or 13	4,200	2,200
14 or 15	4,600	2,600
16 or 17	5,000	3,000
18 or 19	5,500	3,500
20 or more	6,500	4,500

Steps of Play

1. Purchase Land	Unchanged.
2. Provide Utilities	Maximum Utility Plant capacity is ten lines. River can be substituted for one or two Utility Lines. Industries require two Utility Lines, Private Waste Facility or river.
[3. Renovate Buildings]	Unchanged except Residences may increase probability of loss due to pollution.
4. Construct Buildings	Unchanged except care must be taken to insure some form of waste disposal is available, possibly including river.
5. Designate Employment	
6. Sign Trade Agreements	Both steps played simultaneously with all wages, prices, employment and agreements renegotiable on rounds divisible by two. Instructor announces new LS retail and wholesale prices each round.
7. Receive Income	FI = $52,000; PI = $24,000.
8. Pay Employees	Unchanged except for variable wages.
9. Pay LS, CS, and O	Unchanged. LS pays Instructor for wholesale prices according to number of customers.
10. Pay Transportation	Mode Weights are ½ and 2 on Major Highways and Secondary Roads, respectively. Industry to Terminal Association Weights are: FI = $8,000; PI = $4,000.
11. Pay Taxes	Unchanged. Instructor also collects $2,000 per round for each Private Waste Facility.